Religion and Career

A Study of College Graduates

Religion and Career

A Study of College Graduates

by Andrew M. Greeley
with a Foreword by Peter H. Rossi

A PUBLICATION OF
THE NATIONAL OPINION RESEARCH CENTER

SHEED AND WARD – NEW YORK

Manufactured in the United States of America

To His Eminence Albert Cardinal Meyer

Foreword

IT IS ALTOGETHER too rare that social science can make direct and immediate contributions to the large-scale issues that arise so often in our quickly changing society. Father Greeley's book is therefore a rather unusual monograph, being at the same time an excellent example of the exercise of social science skills and a contribution to the important question as to whether American Catholics are contributing enough to the intellectual life of our society.

This book will be easily misunderstood. The roots of the misunderstanding lie both in the nature of his findings and in the method he has employed to reach them. There are many who will find his data disturbing to their fondly held opinions and many of these will find fault with his procedures in order to bolster the integrity of their opinions.

The data reported in this monograph arise from a large scale study of the post-graduate career plans and aspirations of the June 1961 graduating classes of American universities and colleges. The National Opinion Research Center drew a sample of 40,000 seniors graduating in June 1961 from a sample of 135 institutions of higher learning. In May and June 1961, seniors throughout the country diligently and seriously answered a lengthy and complicated questionnaire (appended to this volume) which probed into their plans and hopes for the future.

The major concern of this study was with the numbers and qualities of college graduates going into the critical occupations of our complex society. For better or for worse, a bachelor's degreee nowadays is only another hurdle in the progress toward entering upon a career in science, letters, and the major professions. Hence, the focus of our study on post-graduate education which, even when not formally required, is virtually a necessity if a young man or woman is to perform successfully at the highest levels in these fields.

Our study produced many surprises. We learned, for example, that our college graduates are eager to go on to careers in these critical fields. There is no dearth of motivation for careers in science, letters, and the major professions. Despite deeply felt feelings about being rejected by American society, we found that college graduates thought that being a college professor was an interesting career, more so than being a business executive.

Father Greeley's findings were among the more startling of our major surprises. American Catholics have reached intellectual parity, at least as far as averages are concerned. Catholics, whether from secular or parochial schools, are going on to graduate study in about the same proportions as are non-Catholics. Whether there will be Catholic Einsteins (or Protestant ones, for that matter) coming out of this new breed of Americans remains for the future to reveal. Averages conceal a range of differences: When we concern ourselves with the very topmost levels of creative talent, we deal with matters which averages do not reveal, or with matters which the techniques employed in our study are not designed to measure.

It is important for the reader to understand that this book is not a study of American intellectuals. Rather, it is a study of a typical group of recent college graduates from among whom some of our intellectual leaders will be drawn. Father Greeley shows that American Catholics are not avoiding the career paths which are taken frequently by those who rise to intellectual prominence. He understands, as should the reader, that starting out on a path which has so many side roads and winds about so tortuously does not mean that you will arrive by necessity at some particular destination. It only means that you are headed in the right direction. American Catholic college graduates are headed in the right direction finally. We can only hope that some will get there. Only the future can tell whether few or many of these Catholics will find their way into the first ranks of America's intellectual elites.

Father Greeley also finds that Catholic colleges on the average are doing as well as non-Catholic colleges as far as producing graduates eager to pursue advanced studies in the arts and sciences. I am sure that some readers will construe this finding to mean that the critical comments which have been made concerning Catholic colleges and universities are not justified. Such an interpretation cannot be sustained by Father Greeley's findings. They should be interpreted to mean that Catholic schools are just as good (or as bad) as other schools *on the average*. But it is perfectly obvious that first-rank Catholic universities with faculties and facilities to match have yet to appear on the American scene. There are few major Catholic figures in science and letters, and there are no Catholic universities which can come near to the best in non-Catholic schools. Indeed, it almost looks as if the Catholic college graduate is a step ahead of the system that produced him.

The modern reader, so often called the intelligent layman, has not yet had educational experiences which have left him with the ability to read easily statistical tables. The author has made concessions to this unfortunate state of affairs by confining the tables which support his text to the back of the book. I would like to draw the reader's attention to them. In a very real sense, these columns and rows of figures are the substance of Father Greeley's thesis. The tables are dramatic, contain very striking findings, and although Father Greeley's prose provides an excellent guide to their meaning, the reader will be well rewarded to read them for himself.

A final comment: The newer and more empirical branches of social science, among which sociology is one of the newest, arose out of an intellectual tradition which in its origins was alien and even antithetical to the major intellectual traditions of Roman Catholicism. Sociology is changing, maturing, becoming less a polemical weapon and more a useful tool for understanding ours and other societies. Catholicism is also changing, absorbing new intellectual emphases and assimilating the newer social sciences. Father Greeley represents in his work one of the best demonstrations that to be a sociologist and a man of God is not a necessary contradiction. I hope that his present and future work will put to rest the idea prevalent among social scientists as well as among Roman Catholics that a man cannot commit himself both to empirical social science and to God and serve both with excellence.

Peter H. Rossi
Chicago

Contents

Introduction

THE PURPOSE of this book is to examine certain commonly held theories concerning American Catholicism against a large amount of information gathered about June 1961 college graduates. The ingenuity of man has yet to devise a way in which survey research material can be presented in exciting fashion. The rhythm of fact, fact, interpretation, fact, fact, interpretation and summary seems to be unbreakable. To make matters worse, in this particular report the facts that are being reported usually concern the absence of difference. Hence there is little consolation that can be offered to the brave reader. Even though this volume has been written so that he will not *have* to look at tables, there is no way he can escape plodding through a long catalogue of facts, facts that often may seem rather dull. However, when all the facts are assembled, the result is anything but dull; American Catholics emerge looking rather different from what most people would have thought. In one sense, there is nothing more exciting than dramatic social change and it is with one such change that this book is concerned.

It is possible, of course, to indulge in all kinds of speculations about what the ultimate meaning of this change might be, about where it started and where it is going. I have no aversion to such speculation, but I thought it best in a volume such as this to keep the speculation at a minimum so that the broad factual outline will not be obscured. The speculations can be postponed till another day.

Even though I have tried to make all the proper qualifications as to what this book proves and does not prove, I should think that it will be obvious that I feel that it proves that many common assumptions about American Catholics are at least open to grave doubt. However, I am compelled to say that the case is by no means closed and that much further careful study is needed before the picture is completely clear.

Many people must be thanked for their cooperation in various stages of the volume: His Eminence Albert Cardinal Meyer who made possible the years of study at the University of Chicago; Professors Peter Rossi and James Davis of the staff of the National Opinion Research Center who were the principal directors of NORC Survey 431 on which this work is based; Richard Jaffe, Norman Bradburn, Jacob Feldman, Norman Miller, Joseph Zelan and Richard McKinlay of the NORC Staff; James Vanecko and James Squires who acted as research assistants at various times. Thanks must also be expressed to Professors John Donovan of Boston College and Gerhard Lenski of the University of Michigan for their critical comments. Since I do not propose that any of the aforementioned assume responsibility for the book, it is only fair to absolve them from all blame.

Andrew M. Greeley

Religion and Career
A Study of College Graduates

CHAPTER *1*

The Great Debate

FOR A DECADE OR SO there has raged a "great debate" on the intellectual qualities of American Catholicism. Ranged on one side have been a group of outstanding scholars—historians, theologians, sociologists, a large number of journalists, lay and clerical, and some Catholic educators. On the other side were to be found many Catholic educators and school administrators and a good-sized segment of the clergy and hierarchy. The first group argued that, in effect, Denis Brogan was right when he said, "In no Western Society is the intellectual prestige of Catholicism lower than in the country where, in such respects as wealth, numbers and strength of organization, it is so powerful." [1] The second group responded by maintaining that the self-critics were wrong or were exaggerating or that even if they were right they were doing more harm than good by their criticism.

The argument has been obscured because it has become one of the issues around which many of the newly emerging lay elite in the United States have tended to rally. Self-criticism has been mixed up with the inevitable frictions that are part of the readjustment in clergy-lay relations now taking place in this country as the social and economic condition of the Catholic population undergoes dramatic change. Thus if a layman feels frustrated be-

3

cause of the slowness of his pastor's implementing the 1958 decree on participation in the liturgy (or his slowness in building a new parking lot), he can find therapeutic release in attacking the Catholic schools or proclaiming that the clergy are anti-intellectual. Indeed, in some quarters one is hardly permitted to be a Catholic intellectual if he is suspected of having kind thoughts about Catholic schools.

On the other hand, it must not be denied that a good many Catholic scholars have not been given much in the way of opportunities to do their work at Catholic universities, that many thoroughly competent Catholics have been treated like children on the parish level, and that some of the self-critics have occasionally been the object of rather shabby treatment. None of these faults and mistakes on both sides should confuse the factual question as to the scholarly level of American Catholicism, but of course such confusion is inevitable. The question is thus one with a tremendously high level of emotional charge. One can be sure that even the most moderate reference to it will fray tempers.

For all the ink that has been spilled on the subject in the last decade there has been very little in the way of concrete empirical data to substantiate either side of the argument. A handful of studies made many years ago have been the main weapons of the self-critics, who normally do not permit themselves to be notably encumbered by empirical evidence. The other side has tended to be suspicious of data collection, partly out of fear of what the behavioral sciences are up to, partly because so many behavioral scientists are self-critics; thus certain elements of the "anti-self-critics" have contented themselves with denouncing the self-critics and trying to prevent them from speaking in certain parts of the country.

Thus there has been very little in the way of empirical study of American Catholicism. Those that are able to do it, usually lack the money; and many of those who have the money, have been, at least until recently, reluctant to take the chance that empirical study might discover embarrassing information. Yet it ought to be perfectly clear that the argument about the intellectual level of American Catholicism cannot be settled, indeed cannot be moved off dead center, until someone begins to find out what the *facts* really are.

I was pondering this need for facts in the spring of 1961 during my doctoral studies at the University of Chicago, when I heard that the University's National Opinion Research Center (NORC) was engaged in a massive study of American college graduates. It occurred to me that such a study might be a gold mine of data against which the theories of the self-critics and the fears of the anti-self-critics might be examined. It would also furnish a vast amount of other information about American Catholicism. So I descended upon Professors Peter H. Rossi and James A. Davis of NORC and pointed out that they unquestionably needed someone to analyze the influence of religion on the career plans and occupational values of the some 33,000 June 1961 graduates they proposed to study. As a matter of fact, they *did* have such a need; and this particular investigation began.

The present volume is a report on part of the NORC study. It is essentially an analysis of the influence of religion and religious education on occupational orientations. If one is to study Catholic graduates, one must also study Protestants and Jews to be able to make comparisons. However, the scope and the content of this book indicate that its main concern is with Catholic graduates. There are two main reasons for this emphasis, besides the author's personal and professional interest in Catholicism. First of all, the origins of the investigation were concerned with the intellectuality of American Catholics. Secondly, it seems that a review of certain generally held opinions concerning American Catholicism ought to be of considerable sociological interest.

Although the main concerns of the book will have to do with the intellectual state of American Catholicism, we will also ask other questions. We will see whether the "Protestant Ethic" hypothesis applies to the American situation, whether, as Gerhard Lenski has suggested recently,[2] American Catholics are less inclined to value economic achievement than Protestants or Jews. We will also investigate apostasy and conversion in college and try to ascertain whether there is still a considerable difference among the Catholic ethnic groups within the larger society. In the remaining part of this chapter, we will describe the various theories that went into our investigation and the hypotheses which were to be tested.

Theoretical Background

There were three main sources for the hypotheses we intended to investigate: the recent findings of Gerhard Lenski, the work on productivity of scholars done by R. H. Knapp and his associates, and the self-criticism of American Catholics.

The Lenski study is based on interviews with 658 respondents in the Detroit Metropolitan area in 1958. The major theoretical concern of this work was an attempt to determine whether the Protestant Ethic theory of Max Weber still had relevance in explaining the differences which exist among the four [3] religious groups investigated. Lenski found a considerable number of differences in economic values, educational attitudes, family values, and political orientations in the various groups. He discovered that the Catholics in his study were less upwardiy mobile and less influenced by considerations of economic rationality than were either Protestants or Jews; and, therefcre, he argued that the influence of the "Protestant Ethic" was still at work. He also found evidence that the anti-scientism of Catholics—which he had predicted on the basis of the Knapp studies—was substantial.

On the basis of the findings of this study it appears that overt conflict between the churches and the modern scientific movement is only one of the factors accounting for the disinclination of Catholics to enter scientific careers. In our opinion other less visible factors are equally important. Especially influential is the basic intellectual orientation which Catholicism develops, an orientation which values obedience above intellectual autonomy. Also influential is the Catholic tendency to value family and kin group above other relationships. In brief at both the conscious and subconscious levels of thought and action, membership in the Catholic group is more likely to inhibit the development of scientific careers than is membership in either Protestant or Jewish groups. The implications of this for the future of American society are not difficult to discover.[4]

(Lest the anxious reader lose too much sleep worrying about the dire future Lenski seems to imply for the Republic, we might be permitted to anticipate the findings of this study and suggest that things are not all that bad.)

The two Knapp volumes are devoted essentially to the compilation of indices of the productivity of scientists and scholars by various colleges and universities. In both studies the index of productivity from Catholic colleges was quite low. Catholic liberal arts colleges achieved 2.8 "scientists" per thousand graduates while Catholic universities had an index of 1.7.[5] In the study of "younger scholars" sixteen Catholic men's colleges had an index of 1.96 as opposed to 10.85 for twenty-three non-Catholic men's colleges.[6]

Two quotations from Knapp summarize his explanation of this phenomenon:

The conspicuously inferior position of virtually all Catholic institutions in the production of scientists apparently requires . . . explanation. . . . Without wishing to pose any final interpretation of the low production of Catholic institutions, we may at least present the following considerations which have been advanced in partial explanation. First, Catholic institutions are in good part concentrated in the eastern sections of the United States, a region not noted for the high production of scientists. Second, the Catholic population of America, from which these institutions have largely drawn their students, has come from parent European cultures not conspicuous in recent times for scientific accomplishments. Third, Catholicism has permitted comparatively little secularization of outlook among its constituents and has maintained a firm authoritarian structure. Fourth, Catholicism has been a consistent opponent of physical monism, that philosophic tradition under which science has for the most part advanced. However, though this class of institutions has made small contributions to the ranks of American scientists it is noteworthy and probably significant that its contributions to the legal profession . . . have been exceptional.[7]

We expected that Catholic institutions would be marked by relatively large contributions to the field of humanities. In this speculation, however, we were again mistaken. Catholic institutions, although exceptionally unproductive in all areas of scholarship, achieve their best record in the sciences.[8]

Perhaps the most interesting body of comment on the anti-intellectualism of American Catholics is the theory or demi-theory which has been evolved in the last decade and a half by Catholic self-critics. Some of the more famous works—those by Ellis,[9] O'Dea,[10] and Weigel[11]—have been part of a program of the Catholic Commission on Intellectual and Cultural Affairs. Other writers —the Callahans,[12] Herzfeld,[13] Cunneen,[14] McCluskey,[15] McKernan,[16] and the editorial writers of *America*[17]—have joined in the chorus. In addition, the presidents of the University of Notre Dame have periodically commented on the poor state of the Catholic college system (presumably they would except their own university from the charges); one even asked where the Catholic Salks and Einsteins were.[18] Finally Christ and Sherry[19] have gathered the entire discussion into a single volume of excerpts which runs well over three hundred pages. So great has been the intensity of the self-criticism that one commentator has referred to it as "mass masochism."[20]

O'Dea sums up the position of the self-critics: "The fact is that though American Catholics have the largest and the most expensive educational system of any Catholic group in the world, a genuine Catholic intellectual life is still dependent upon the translation of European works."[21] And Weigel puts the matter even more succinctly, "The general Catholic community in America does not know what scholarship is."[22]

There seem to be at least eight elements in the theory which the self-critics have evolved to explain the intellectual weakness of American Catholicism. The first point made is that the generally authoritarian approach of American Catholicism inhibits the development of scientific curiosity. In Herzfeld's words, "There is no conflict between the results of science and the doctrines of the Church, but there is in my opinion a conflict due to training method." [23]

A second aspect of the explanatory theory is the clerical domination of American Catholic life. Weigel says,

Another common persuasion among our people is that smart boys should go into the priesthood. Those students who distinguish themselves in high school are always asked if they intend to study for the priesthood. Actually the seminaries get a good percentage of them. What is not recognized, often not even by priests, is that priestly formation need not be scholarly nor is scholarship its true aim . . . (there) is a vague, widespread persuasion that young people with manifest capacity for scholarship should be directed to the priestly or religious life. This persuasion does not favor the swelling of Catholic scholarly ranks because it is not in general the function of priestly and religious training to produce scholars. Secondly, it overlooks the secular dimension of current scholarship, distracting the attention of youngsters away from the appeal of secular disciplines. [24]

And O'Dea adds even more forcefully,

The intellectual life is not likely to grow up in a situation where community is transformed into bureaucracy and where a clerical monopoly tends to damage the quality of clerical leadership itself. If the laity remain the feet and the clergy the head in terms of constructive thinking, then we shall perpetuate a situation that inhibits the development of intellectual responsibility and creativity on the part of all. Such a condition not only inhibits the development of intellectuals but drives potential intellectuals away from and often into antagonism to the church. [25]

A third explanation would suggest that the concern of the

Church with the next world leads it to place little value on the present life and to have little concern for the temporal order which is the object of scientific research. It is assumed that the piety of the largely Irish-dominated American Catholicism is not especially interested in the transitory events of this vale of tears.

A fourth explanation suspects that there is actually a fear of scientific knowledge within the Catholic community. In O'Dea's words,

The American Catholic community not only fails to produce an intellectual elite, but even tends to suspect intellectuals because American Catholics sense the relation of the intellectual to these two partially repressed American problems. The intellectual symbolizes in some way the facing of crises and the challenges of uncertainty, as well as a critical attitude toward the accepted values of middle-class life, especially those which are most crassly materialistic. Catholics, who pride themselves on their spirituality, are more prone to support anti-intellectualism than are many other of their countrymen. They see the intellectuals as those who seek to reveal the basic existential ambiguities that they themselves wish to evade. They often project this dilemma onto current politics and see such intellectuals—who are in our culture . . . often liberals—as "disloyal." One sometimes feels that for some Catholics "loyalty" is so supreme a virtue that it would be disloyal to ask, "loyalty to what?" [26]

And the Callahans comment,

Surely the Catholic college which says, in effect: you are intellectually mediocre, you need our strict control to mature and to keep your faith, and it might be harmful if you were left to your own devices in your newspapers and student groups, cannot be said to foster a spirit of engagement and responsibility. . . . One might well ask if the general run of Catholic education when not inspired by a desire to develop personal insight and integrity, does not in fact simply indoctrinate in the bad sense of the word.[27]

And Cuneen concludes that

both training in the techniques of learning as well as disinterested top level scholarship suffer from understandable but misguided desire to have the educational content itself provide the direct motives of piety.[28]

Perhaps the most obvious element in the explanation is the immigrant status of the American Catholic group. Some of the bolder of the self-critics have felt that this condition was probably at the root of most of the other problems and that when and if American Catholics left their immigrant mentality behind, there would be the beginnings of an intellectual development. It was, in fact, with a notion something like this one that the writer began the present study.

Monsignor Ellis [29] in a careful historical study suggests that part of the explanation must be the absence of a tradition of scholarship among American Catholics due at least in part to the socio-economic difficulties of the immigrant groups. Ellis's work is probably the most influential of all the comments made on American Catholic intellectualism.

Closely related to the immigrant origins of American Catholicism is the presumed materialism of the descendants of the immigrants who are attempting to "succeed" in American life. Says Herzfeld,[30] "It seems, therefore, that a much higher percentage of Catholic than of non-Catholic students stop their studies after college to go into business." In this view Catholics are too busy trying to make money to be concerned about being scholars.

Finally, it is often suggested that one of the causes of American Catholic anti-intellectualism is the ghetto attitude of defensiveness which is taken to mar American Catholics. Weigel argues,

American Catholicism until very recently has always had the feeling of being a beleaguered community. An ubiquitous, formidable enemy was threatening its very existence. Loyal defense was needed, not a divisive effort of criticism. Everything that was, took on a holy aspect; to be loved and died for. Such an atmosphere was not propitious to American Catholic intellectualism.[31]

The self-critics have not had much concrete data to back up their position. Ellis cites a considerable number of studies, although most of them date to the Pre-World War II era. Herzfeld mentions the Catholic percentage at Johns Hopkins and the fact that there are no American Catholics who have won Nobel prizes in physics. McKernon, McClusky, and the editors of *America* discuss the paucity of National Science Foundation, Rhodes, and Fulbright scholarships for American Catholics. References are also made on occasion to the Knapp data (which would again apply to a generation coming out of college before the War).

One can only marvel at the vigor of the self-criticism and wonder what would happen to the poor Protestant who dared to say such things about American Catholics.

Background of the Present Study—and Its Problems

It is our intention to form a group of hypotheses from the three sources of theory discussed above and test them against a body of data compiled on the plans, performances, and values of June 1961 college graduates. The techniques of survey analysis will be used on data collected in a recent study of the National Opinion Research Center.[32] Under a grant from various agencies of the Federal Government (The National Institutes of Health, The National Science Foundation, and the Office of Education), NORC administered precoded questionnaires to some 33,000 June 1961 college graduates. These graduates represented a sample of all the June graduates from 135 colleges and universities. The schools in turn were selected by a stratified sampling process. For further details about the methods of sampling, the percentage of non-respondents and the design of the study the reader is referred to the various reports on NORC Survey 431 prepared by Davis and his associates.[33] The main focus of interest of the survey (whose questionnaire is appended) was the career and graduate school plans of the June 1961 class. However, three religious questions—family religion, current religious preference, and degree of religiosity—make secondary analysis possible.

Such analysis labors under the advantages and disadvantages of all similar efforts. Broad, general outlines of the wording of the religious factor can be obtained with some ease; Lenski's major conclusions, for example, can be tested to see if they apply to the current crop of college seniors. On the other hand, when one attempts any kind of sophisticated analysis of processes and mechanisms underlying the operation of the religious factor, one is in a position to twist the data to suit purposes for which they were not originally designed. One may be forced, moreover, to make assumptions one would rather not have to make. The theories that are tested and the hypotheses that are developed are, therefore, on somewhat shaky ground. Secondary analysis is almost always bound to raise more questions than it answers; however, it may still be defended on the grounds that it at least offers a convenient way of providing suggestive theoretical hunches and reveals areas which must be subjected to more precise probing that is specifically designed for the problem at hand.

An added difficulty for the present analysis is that the measures used for religiosity in Survey 431 are considerably less sophisticated than those designed by Lenski, who had indicators for associational and communal participation as well as for devotional activity and orthodoxy in belief. Other questions had been planned for Survey 431, but were not included in the final draft of the questionnaire. This liability is somewhat offset by the fact that data of Survey 431 are from a national sample and represent a considerably larger number of respondents than do Lenski's data. Even though the complete file of some 35,000 cards was not available for most of the questions covered in this analysis, the 10 per cent representative sample (N = 3397) is still some six times larger than the sample in the Detroit study. Hence much more safety is to be found in cross-tabulations.

There is the further problem that the division of the American population into five religious categories ("Protestant," "Catholic," "Jew," "Other," and "None") is a highly abstract codification. Not only may "Protestant" cover everything from High Episcopalian to Southern Baptist, and "Catholic" everything from a daily church-goer to those who are in Church only three times in their life, but each category also conveys both more and less than the other categories. Each term implies not only religious beliefs, but hundreds of years of history and culture tangled together in an intricate web. To be Jewish implies far more than a connection with a group which has certain religious dogmas and certain moral practices; it also implies a long history of opposition from other groups. One remains a Jew even if one no longer practices Judaism. To say that a man is "Jewish" is to say something more about him than if one were to say that he were "Protestant." On the other hand, while "Jewish" gives us hints about certain aspects of a man that "Protestant" does not, it is equally true that "Protestant" subsumes certain kinds of information that "Jewish" does not; "Protestant" connotes a certain attitude towards the American Establishment, for example, that is not involved in Judaism or Catholicism.

To look at the matter from another viewpoint, to be a "Catholic," even in the minimal sense of the word, requires more "church-going" than to be a "Protestant" and to be a "Protestant" requires somewhat more church connection than to be a "Jew." Each of the terms contains many comparable elements, but each one also connotes a number of non-comparable factors.

Similar cautions must be made concerning the various ethnic groups, especially within Catholicism. To be a member of an ethnic group means various things at various stages of the acculturation process. Indeed, as Nathan Glazer has pointed out,[34] many of the ethnic groups became ethnic only upon arrival in America. The Norse and the Italians, for example, only thought of themselves as Norse or Italians after leaving their native lands; in the Old Country they are from Throndheim or Bari rather than from Norway or Italy. Thus the connection between ethnicity and religion is complex and probably varies with different groups at different times. At one time it could be argued that many Irish were Catholic because they were Irish. On the other hand, it seems possible that the emerging Irish [35] aristocracy in this country may well think of themselves as Irish because they are Catholic. How much of a given supposedly religious phenomenon can really be attributed to some stage of ethnicity is not easily determined. Herzberg's suggestion that religion is fast becoming some kind of super ethnic group complicates the picture even more.

The qualifications we have mentioned are intended only partly as a protection before embarking on a dangerous mission. It is the writer's conviction that any generalizations about religion as a predictor variable must—in the present stage of our understanding about the effect of religion on social structure—be highly tentative.

Hypotheses

From the various theoretical sources described earlier in the chapter the following hypotheses were formed:

1. There exist a considerable number of differences in the American population which correlate with religion.

2. These differences are connected with the "belief system" of the various religious groups.

3. Protestants and Jews will score high on items indicating "economic rationality" (the Protestant Ethic), such as an inclination to small business or self-employment, an emphasis on "drive" and the making of money. Jews will score higher than Protestants.

4. Catholics will show less inclination to economic rationality and more to the quest for security as an employment value.

5. Protestants and Jews will score high on items indicating an interest in intellectual pursuits such as academic performance, graduate school intentions, inclination to academic careers, interest in ideas and creativity on the job. Jews will score higher on these items than Protestants.

6. Because of the anti-intellectualism and anti-scientism of Catholicism

   a. Catholics will be less likely to go to college.

   b. Catholics from the working class will be less likely to go to college than Protestants from the working class.

   c. Catholic family ties will interfere with college education.

    d. Catholics will be less likely to go to graduate school.

    e. Among those Catholics going to graduate school, there will be a smaller proportion going into the academic fields than for the other religious groups.

    f. Catholics will not be inclined to go into the physical sciences.

    g. Those Catholics who go into academic pursuits will show a tendency to drift away from the Church.

    7. Catholics from Catholic schools will be even more Catholic than the general Catholic population and hence will score higher on Catholic items than Catholics in other schools. It seems fairly obvious that this hypothesis is strongly held by many of those Catholics who argue for a separate Catholic school system. A contrary hypothesis could be developed from certain elements in the studies of Fichter,[36] Schuyler,[37] and the Rossis.[38]

    8. Catholics will be more likely to think of themselves as religious than Protestants and Jews, while Jews will think of themselves as more liberal politically than Protestants or Catholics.

    Even though the hypotheses represented the theoretical orientation with which the study began, confirmation was obtained only for two of them—the first ("There exist a considerable number of differences in the American population which correlate with religion") and the eighth ("Catholics will be more likely to think of themselves as religious than Protestants and Jews, while Jews will think of themselves as more liberal politically than Protestants or Catholics"). Partial confirmation was obtained for the Jewish-Gentile comparison implied in several others.[39] However, the fact that this study turned out to be in part a work of demolition does not seem to make its contribution merely negative. The fact that Protestants and Catholics have similar scores on many items on which similar scores were not expected is a positive finding and one which, since it runs against past theory, requires explanation.

A Word about Personal Bias

    It should be obvious that the writer is hardly unbiased about

Catholicism; hence the Lenski findings of anti-intellectualism and lack of economic rationality among Catholics would certainly be embarrassing to him. It would be hard for me to accept the accusation of anti-intellectualism without making a distinction: for while the Church of Copernicus is also the Church of Galileo, so also is the Church of Torquemada the Church of Pierre Teilhard de Chardin. It would also be hard for me to accept the charge of a lack of economic drive, partly because as an American I cannot help but believe that a bit of the Protestant Ethic is a good thing and partly because from history and personal experience I know all too well that Catholics are just as eager as the next man to pile up treasures in this world, despite the proven rate of consumption of these treasures by rust and moth.

However, the hypotheses set up in this chapter were not intended to be straw men to be knocked down. One need only glance through the self-criticism in which American Catholics have engaged in the last decade to realize that Lenski's comments are mild indeed by comparison. Since I am rather close both ideologically and personally to many of these critics, I had imagined that this study would produce more grist for their mill, although I had hoped that control for economic and social variables would go far towards explaining the apparent intellectual deficiencies of American Catholicism. I am still far from convinced that the American Church has made use of the best in the Catholic intellectual tradition.

An investigation such as this can never really disprove a theory. All it can establish is that propositions which seem to flow logically from the theory are not supported. This is the only claim that we are making at the present time. There is virtually no evidence to be found in the present investigation to support the notion that American Catholics or American Catholic schools are anti-intellectual or anti-scientific. This does not mean that American Catholics are becoming intellectuals or scientists, but it means that there is no evidence that they are not. Our evidence does not necessarily prove that a Catholic intellectual life or a tradition of scholarship has begun to emerge. Many things can intervene between enrollment in graduate school and a Ph.D., many more things can intervene between the doctorate and competent scholarship, and many, many things between competence and preeminence. However, one might at least advance the suggestion that without a large group of beginners it would be unrealistic to expect a given social group to produce a handful of great men of science. The June 1961 graduates may not represent a fully developed Catholic intellectual tradition in this country; but it is at least possible that they may represent the beginning of such a tradition.

I do not think I am showing signs of paranoia when I express the fear that a book such as this one is going to be misunderstood. Some of the articles which have already appeared have been hailed by people with whom I could not possibly ally myself as proving at last that the self-critics are wrong. Some of the self-critics have accused me of being a conservative, of defending the status quo, and, even worse, of being an optimist.

I should like to think that I have been misunderstood by both sides. I would like to feel that all the following chapters prove is that at the present time there is no statistical evidence of gross intellectual inferiority among Catholics coming out of college. A good number of people have no patience with statistical arguments. They will claim that the percentages through which the readers of this volume will have to struggle do not disprove the "well established" fact of the anti-intellectualism of Catholics and of Catholic colleges.[40] Perhaps no statistical argument ever proves anything with certainty; however, it seems to me that it is very clear what the NORC study does not prove. It offers no evidence for the alleged intellectual inferiority of Catholics or of Catholic schools at the present time. Those within the Church who feel that such inferiority does in fact still exist are now in a position where they must bring up new evidence or at least retreat in silence. No claim is made that Catholic colleges are the best in the country;

probably not one would rank in the top ten or even perhaps in the top twenty; but neither would one rank in the last ten or the last twenty. As far as scholarship goes the evidence in this volume suggests that Catholics are much like other Americans. Whatever anti-intellectualism still exists, is probably more American in origin than specifically Catholic.[41]

I have no basic quarrel with the self-critics. I would like to think that I am still one of their number. Indeed, any thinking Catholic must be a self-critic since it is quite clear that we have a long way to go before the ideals of the Gospel are realized in our lives. There is a considerable amount of evidence in this investigation that in fact the pressure of the self-criticism is partly responsible for the somewhat surprising findings we are going to report. We can never be satisfied with the quality of Catholic intellectual life, nor can we be satisfied with the quality of our college system. There is always room for considerable improvement. I do not intend this volume to be consoling or soothing, but only factual. Self-criticism, if it is to be realistic and useful, must take account of the facts as they are today and not twenty or thirty years ago.

NOTES

1. Denis W. Brogan, *U.S.A. An Outline of the Country, Its People and Institutions* (London: Oxford University Press, 1941).

2. Gerhard Lenski, *The Religious Factor* (New York: Doubleday, 1961).

3. Lenski considers white Protestant, Negro Protestant, Catholic, and Jew. One might well wonder why he did not divide the Catholic group into its ethnic components as he divided the Protestant group into its racial components. As Rosen says in his review of the Lenski volume, "I wonder why Lenski did not seriously follow up the possibility that what appears to be a religious factor is in fact a more inclusive ethnic one. The failure to control for ethnicity is in my opinion the most serious flaw of this study. Surely it is time for the sociologist to stop lumping all Roman Catholics in one category without first looking for significant inter-ethnic differences. To group Irish, German, Polish, Italian, and Middle European Catholics into one Catholic category, ignoring their historical and cultural differences,

may be unfortunate to say the least. There is a growing body of data to suggest that the differences between various Catholic groups are often greater than those between Catholics and Protestants." Bernard C. Rosen, *American Sociological Review*, XXVII, No. 1 (February, 1962), 112. We will return to these themes in the course of the present work.

4. Lenski, *op. cit.*, p. 255.

5. R. H. Knapp and H. B. Goodrich, *Origins of American Scientists* (Chicago: University of Chicago Press, 1952).

6. R. H. Knapp and J. J. Greenbaum, *The Younger American Scholar* (Chicago: University of Chicago Press, 1953), p. 46.

7. Knapp and Goodrich, *op. cit.*, p. 29.

8. Knapp and Greenbaum, *op. cit.*, p. 48.

9. John Tracy Ellis, "American Catholics and the Intellectual Life," *Thought* (Autumn, 1955).

10. Thomas F. O'Dea, *American Catholic Dilemma: An Inquiry into the Intellectual Life* (New York: Sheed and Ward, 1958).

11. Gustave Weigel, "American Catholic Intellectualism: A Theologian's Reflections," *The Review of Politics*, Vol. XIX (July, 1957).

12. Daniel and Sidney Callahan, "Do Catholic Colleges Develop Initiative?" *The Catholic World*, Vol. CLXXXVI (December, 1957).

13. Charles Herzfeld, "Scientific Research and Religion," *The Commonweal*, March 20, 1929.

14. Joseph Cunneen, "Catholics and Education," *The Commonweal*, August 7, 1953.

15. Neil G. McCluskey, S.J., "Too Few Catholic Rhodes Scholars," *America*, April 7, 1956.

16. Louis McKernan, C.S.P., "The New Religion of Science," *The Catholic World*, Vol. CLXXXVI (January, 1958).

17. "Where Are the Catholic Scientists," *America*, April 10, 1954.

18. To which humorist Dan Herr added a plaint over the absence of a Catholic Mort Sahl. (This was before the appearance of Bob Newhart.)

19. Frank L. Christ and Gerard E. Sherry, *American Catholicism and the Intellectual Ideal* (New York: Appleton-Century-Crofts, 1959).

20. Edward Duff, S.J., in a conversation with the author.

21. O'Dea, *op. cit.*

22. Weigel, *op. cit.*

23. Herzfeld, *op. cit.*

24. *Weigel, op. cit.*

25. *O'Dea, op cit.*
26. *Ibid.*
27. Daniel and Sydney Callahan, *op. cit.*
28. Cuneen, *op. cit.*
29. Ellis, *op. cit.*
30. *Herzfeld, op. cit.*
31. Weigel, *op. cit.*
32. J. A. Davis, *et al.*, *Great Aspirations: Career Plans of America's June 1961 College Graduates* (Chicago: National Opinion Research Center, 1961).
33. *Great Aspirations* was a preliminary report. A final report and several more detailed analyses are in process at present.
34. Nathan Glazer, *American Judaism* (Chicago: University of Chicago Press, 1955).
35. Andrew M. Greeley, "Religious Segregation in a Suburb," *Social Compass* (in press).
36. Joseph Fichter, S.J., *Parochial School* (Notre Dame: University of Notre Dame Press, 1958).
37. Joseph B. Schuyler, S.J., *Northern Parish* (Chicago: Loyola University Press, 1960), p. 271.
38. Peter H. Rossi and Alice R. Rossi, "Some Effects of Parochial School Education in America," *Daedalus,* Spring, 1961.
39. One or two critics have suggested that the hypotheses were altered after the data were examined. However, a copy of my original hypotheses was given to Professor Davis before the data collection began; this copy is still in his files, should anyone wish to see it.
40. Two colleagues from NORC and I journeyed to a Catholic educational meeting to make a preliminary report on our study. My friends expected that our report would be very well received since its main burden was that Catholic colleges were not inferior in the production of arts and science graduate students. They were quite surprised to be attacked from the floor for saying things that were in opposition to "obvious" facts. One objector said that we had obviously forgotten about all the anti-intellectual students and deans at Catholic colleges. One of my colleagues, not realizing that self-criticism of this kind has taken on almost biblical importance in Catholic circles, commented, "What makes you think *you* have a monopoly on anti-intellectualism?" What indeed?
41. In a footnote to the paperback edition of *The Religious Factor,* Doctor Lenski graciously summarizes the findings of an earlier report on the present study and adds the following qualifying comments:

1. He is disturbed by my frequent references to his thesis of Catholic anti-intellectualism since he does not hold that Catholics are anti-intellectual but that they have adopted a variant form of intellectualism which lays heavy emphasis on revealed truth and the importance of individual assent to this truth.
2. The theories of O'Dea and others point out the problems of this kind of intellectual variant.
3. The key "to the explanation" of my "unique and intriguing findings" is that they deal with the intentions and aspirations of young people.

To reply to these comments (it is apparently our fate to conduct this controversy in footnotes) may I say:

1. In deference to Doctor Lenski's insistence I have dropped the term "anti-intellectual" from references to his thinking about Catholics. However, I am not so sure that what he accuses Catholics of is not in reality anti-intellectualism in any normal use of the word. The very sentence he footnotes says that Catholicism develops an orientation which values obedience above intellectual autonomy. If Catholicism does in fact do this, then I should think it could deservedly be called anti-intellectual. So does Lenski, it seems to me, when he concludes the paragraph in question by noting that membership in the Catholic group is more likely to inhibit the development of scientific careers and that the implications of this for the future of American society are not difficult to discover. I should think that some Catholics might be tempted to reply to Lenski that heavy emphasis on revealed truth in one branch of human knowledge (theology) does not necessarily hinder the development of the empirical spirit in all other pursuits. Indeed all basic ontological assumptions (including those of positive science) are beyond the powers of empirical analysis and demonstration. These Catholics would further argue that if indeed, as Doctor Lenski suggests they do, many Catholics turn away from scientific careers, because of a misunderstanding of the relationship between theology and empirical science, then they are anti-intellectual. If on the other hand it should develop that Catholics, despite their adherence to revealed truth in theology, develop scientific careers as much as anyone else, then the thesis of anti- or variant intellectualism is either mythical or an historical accident.
2. There are two major weaknesses in the O'Dea kind of study. First of all, such studies show no historical perspective. One often gets the impression that a group which is only recently emerging from

its European peasant origins is asked to produce as many scholars as groups which either had been in America a long time or came from a much more sophisticated European background. One looks in vain in these works for any sense of a dynamic process of social change accompanying the assimilation of the immigrant groups into the main stream of American academic life. Secondly, these studies contain dreadfully little in the way of empirical data about the recent situation among American Catholics.

3. Lenski is clearly implying that while their theological predispositions may not keep Catholics from beginning scholarly or scientific careers, they will keep them from persevering in such careers. There is no evidence in the NORC findings reported in this volume of any inclination for Catholics to change their plans more than anyone else. Indeed after the first year of graduate school Catholics were persevering in their studies as much as anyone else. I wonder if Doctor Lenski would care to predict at what point the defections will begin. NORC is going to follow these students for four more years, so it will be possible to see if and when they start to leave during this period. I suppose that the differences between the present writer on the one hand and Doctor Lenski and the O'Dea group on the other can only be resolved by the kind of performance as men of science and letters the current crop of graduates will display in their careers. For this we must wait and see. However, at present it is difficult to see how Catholic graduates are different from the vast majority of other Americans, while the performance of their ancestors can readily be explained by the immigration factor. If these are "sweeping conclusions" as Doctor Lenski says they are, then I must plead guilty to the charge. However, at least I am not suggesting that the Catholic disinclination to scientific careers will furnish serious problems for "the future of American society" on the basis of 230 Catholics in one not necessarily typical Mid-western city.

CHAPTER 2

Profile of the
Catholic College Graduate

MANY A PROUD PARENT, many an anxious professor, and perhaps a few cynical parish clergy must have listened to the graduation addresses of June 1961 with a fair amount of curiosity. Who indeed were these graduates? What did they think of their education? What did they want out of life? What did they think of themselves? What did they plan for the future? These are the kind of questions that no survey can answer completely. Yet the IBM cards representing the college graduates of 1961 can tell us a great deal about them; they can confirm some of our impressions and rather disconcertingly upset some others.

Who were the Catholics [1] who graduated from college in 1961? They were in their early twenties, more likely male than female, white, native-born Americans, unmarried (though if they were married, they very likely had children) and hailed from cities of over 100,000 in population and located in the northeastern part of the country. Their mothers and fathers had graduated from high school; their fathers were in managerial or professional positions; their family income was over $7,500. They went to church every week, thought of themselves as liberal, and described themselves

25

as conventional and religious. They liked their colleges, liked their professors, viewed education as essentially "intellectual," planned to go to graduate school, wanted a "professional" career, expected their major satisfactions in life to come from family relationships, looked for service and intellectual values from their occupation, and worried about their career plans and life goals. In most of these matters, they were not very different from their Protestant or Jewish fellow graduates.

Such is a *modal* profile of the Catholics in the June 1961 senior class and it is based on the most frequent responses to our questions. However, there is more to the picture than just the profile outline. In the rest of this chapter we will try to fill in the details by reporting on the demographic and social background of the Catholic graduates, their self-description and life goals and worries, on their educational experiences, their church attendance, and their career plans and values.

Demographic Background

Table 2.1 in the back of the book summarizes the differences among the three religious groups.[2] Protestants are the oldest and Jews are the youngest among the graduates. The Protestants have a higher proportion of girls; Protestants have a higher proportion of non-whites; Catholics and Jews are concentrated in the northeastern part of the country and in larger cities; Jews lived closest to their schools, Protestants were farthest away. Protestants were more likely to be married than the other two groups. Catholics came from larger families, and if they were married were more likely to have children. Such is the general picture of the demographic differences among the three religious groups. Now let us look at some of the details.

In each religious group, the majority of the graduates are 21 or 22 as we would expect (Table 2.2). However 18 per cent of the Jews had graduated by the time they were 20 and a third of the Protestants were 23 or over. Catholics were in between with very few of them graduating at 20, and slightly more than one-quarter of them graduating after 22. There are several possible explanations for this age difference. The fact that most of those from rural regions are Protestant and that early beginning of school work and acceleration are not common in rural or small-town schools, might explain the older age of the Protestant graduate. On the other hand, the tradition of learning among the Jews and their presence in large cities where acceleration is common would explain the younger age of the Jews. Another explanation would be that the Jews coming from a higher income group were less likely to have to work their way through college. In any event, it is quite clear that for Protestants and Catholics, delayed education is by no means uncommon, with about one-sixth of each graduating after they are 25.

Protestant girls (Table 2.3) are more likely to go to college than Catholic or Jewish girls though the difference between the Protestants and the Jews is not "significant." [3] Fifty-seven per cent of the Protestant graduates are male while 61 per cent of the Jewish graduates are male and 64 per cent of the Catholic. One might explain the fact that only one-third of the Catholic graduates are girls by appealing to a Catholic tendency to underplay the importance of educating a woman whose place is traditionally taken to be in the home, or one might see the difference as a function of the greater inclination to getting ahead in the world on the part of a more recent immigrant group whose sons, after all, will be the wage earners that *need* a college degree. The similarity between the Catholic and the Jewish sex ratio tends to confirm such a suspicion.

As we might expect, the Protestants (Table 2.4) are the only group with a sizeable proportion of non-whites with 6 per cent of the graduates of Protestant faith being non-white, 4 per cent being Negro. (Father Anthony Vader of the Archdiocese of Chicago is preparing an analysis of the Negro college graduates in the NORC sample.)

Our question (Table 2.5) about the home town of the graduate was arranged to measure two dimensions—the size of the city or town of origin and the fact of residence in city, suburb, or rural area. Jews and Catholics tend to be from big cities with four-fifths of the Jews and two-fifths of the Catholics concentrated in metropolitan regions with over a half-million population. On the other hand only one-fourth of the Protestants are from these large urban areas. The Catholics are the most suburban (42 per cent) and the Jews the most urban, with 60 per cent of Jews in large cities (and 45 per cent in cities over two million). We might remark parenthetically that the fact that almost half of the Catholic graduates are from suburban areas says a great deal about the changes which have taken place in the American Church in the last generation.

While we might be a little surprised at the suburbanization of the Catholic graduate, there is little in the way of surprise about the regions of the country from which Catholic graduates come (Table 2.6). Fifty-six per cent of the Catholics and 76 per cent of the Jews are concentrated in the New England and Middle Atlantic states, while the Protestants are much more evenly distributed with one-fifth in the Middle Atlantic, one-third in the North Central regions, and one-fourth in the South. Thirty per cent of the Catholics are in the North Central regions and there are very few Catholics or Jews in the South and West.

There has been considerable anxiety in some recent writings about the increase in early marriages among the college population. It is clear, however, from our study of June 1961 graduates that almost three-fourths of the graduates were unmarried at the time of graduation and about two-thirds did not think they would be married by the following autumn. There are some differences among the religious groups however (Table 2.7A). Almost a third of the Protestant graduates are married, about a fifth of the Jews and fourteen per cent of the Catholics. If they are married, Catholics are more likely to have children (70 per cent of the married Catholic graduates either had or were expecting children), though the difference between Catholics and Protestants on this matter is not "significant." It is also worth noting in Table 2.7B that Catholics are more likely to come from families with three or more children (37 per cent) but that the difference between Catholics and Protestants (31 per cent) is not as great as we might have expected. According to the same table, 62 per cent of the Catholics came from families with at least two children, as did 55 per cent of the Protestants and 37 per cent of the Jews. The over-all and very indirect picture we get of the fertility practices of both the graduates and their parents would suggest that Catholics have slightly more children than Protestants and that both have more than Jews. (It should be noted that Protestants are more likely to live in rural areas where the birth rates are higher than in the urban areas where Catholics are concentrated.)

We might remark here that if, as La Pierre contends, the tendency to early marriage is a sign of the decline of the Protestant Ethic, then the Protestants in our sample were the least "Protestant" in their tendency to get married. The postponement of the pleasures of family life until education is completed seems to be more prevalent among Catholics and Jews.

Before we turn away from matters of demography, we must consider one more extremely important question: Are Catholics graduating from college in their proportion in the total population? The following table suggests that they are.

RELIGION IN WHICH JUNE 1961 GRADUATES WERE RAISED
COMPARED WITH 1957 CENSUS ESTIMATES

	Graduates	1957 Census
Protestant	61%	66.2%
Catholic	25%	25.7%
Jew	8%	3.2%
Other	3%	1.3%
None	3%	2.7%

Jews and "Other" seem to be over-represented among the graduates, Protestants are under-represented, and Catholics and "Nones" are present in the graduate group in about the same proportion as in the national population. However, to some extent the figures in the table might be misleading since the Protestant percentage will be pulled down by the fact that most Negroes are Protestants and Negroes are decidedly under-represented among the college graduates (3 per cent as opposed to 10 per cent of the national population). Nevertheless a comparison of just the white populations does not change the picture too much; Catholics are 26 per cent of the white college graduates and 28 per cent [4] of the white national population. Thus Catholics are not appreciably less likely to graduate from college than Protestants. This represents a dramatic change since in the adult population Catholics are only slightly better than half as likely to have graduated from college as Protestants. The theme of change will be one which will recur constantly in this book; even though there is a general awareness that the Catholic population is changing, it often seems that the nature and extent of this change is not appreciated either inside or outside the sociological profession, inside or outside the Church. One of our major themes will be that generalizations made about the Catholic population of twenty years ago are no longer valid and that the generalizations made about the intellectual accomplishments of the preceding generation are therefore suspect.

We can therefore say that the hypothesis that Catholics are less likely to go to college than others has not been supported. In the next section, we will turn to the suggestion of Gerhard Lenski that Catholics of the working class are less likely to desire college for their sons and are therefore less inclined to the upward mobility which comes from the "Protestant Ethic." We should also note that the suggestion of Doctor Lenski, that the Catholic attachment to family life will interfere with their economic or scholarly progress, does not seem to be borne out, at least by the marriage data we have reported in this section.

The repetition of demographic data can be tedious. However if

we are to compare different population groups, we must know
how different they are in matters such as sex, age, home town,
marital status, and family size. In summarizing this section, we
may say that Jews and Catholics are likely to be younger than
Protestants at the time of graduation, to be from large cities, to
come from the northeastern part of the country, and to be unmarried. Catholics are more likely to come from large families and
both Protestants and Catholics are more likely to have children
if they are married at the time of graduation. There is no evidence
for a Catholic tendency either not to go to college in their population proportion or to enter marriage at an earlier age than
Protestants.

Social Class

This is neither the time nor the place to enter a long discussion
on the nature of social class. It suffices to say that, whatever social
class may be, it is somehow connected with occupation, income
and education. In this section, we are going to compare the three
religious groups on these various dimensions of social class and
then see how they rank on a combined index of "social-economic
status" (SES).

The first generalization we can make (Table 2.8) is that there
is little over-all difference between Protestants and Catholics in
parental occupation or income if the categories are broad enough
and that the major differences are between Jews and Gentiles and
between Protestants and Catholics in education. Forty-five per cent
of the Protestants, 46 per cent of the Catholics and 57 per cent of
the Jews report their family's income to have been over $7,500 a
year. Forty-six per cent of the Protestants and 47 per cent of the
Catholics were from families whose occupational background was
professional or managerial, while 67 per cent of the Jews were
from similar backgrounds. On the other hand, there is not much
difference between Protestants and Jews with regard to father's
education, with slightly more than two-fifths of their fathers having

gone to college, while the Catholic proportion is about one-third. Parenthetically we note once again the suggestion of rapid social change for Catholics.

Let us now examine in some detail the generalizations we have made in the preceding paragraph (Table 2.9). One-quarter of the Catholic fathers and one-fifth of the Catholic mothers had not gone beyond grammar school, and 45 per cent of the Catholic fathers and 39 per cent of the mothers had not graduated from high school. On the other hand, 64 per cent of the Protestant and Jewish fathers and 72 per cent of the Jewish and Protestant mothers had graduated from high school. The disadvantage in educational background of the Catholic students was therefore notable though not overwhelming.

However, there was little in the way of comparable disadvantage in family income—at least in relation to the Protestant graduates (Table 2.10). Nineteen per cent of the Protestants and 16 per cent of the Catholics were from families with less than $5,000 income, and 14 per cent of the Protestants and 15 per cent of the Catholics came from families in the over $15,000 bracket. One must remember, of course, that the curve of Protestant income must be revised slightly upward because of the 4 per cent of the Protestants who are Negro. Nevertheless, this change does not substantially alter the picture of comparative equality except at the very top (over $20,000) of the income span which Protestants are almost twice as likely to be enjoying as Catholics (9 per cent as opposed to 5 per cent). The Jewish income profile is radically different with only 10 per cent coming from families with less than a $5,000 annual income and 24 per cent in the over $15,000 bracket.

The similarity in income between Protestants and Catholics would lead us to suspect a similarity in occupation. If we divide (Table 2.11) the occupational scale into four classes—Upper (managers and proprietors), Middle (clerical, sales, craftsman), Lower (semi-skilled, unskilled, and service), and Farm, we find that the only difference between the Protestant and Catholic graduates is that there are more Catholics in the Lower group and more Protestants who are farmers. In the Upper and Middle groups, there is very little difference (both having a little less than half in the Upper and a little less than a third in the Middle). The Jews again are radically different with two-thirds in the Upper group and another one-fourth in the Middle.

With this information in mind, we are able to examine more closely the suggestion of Doctor Lenski that Catholics from the lower classes are less likely to send their children to college. We do not wish to go into great detail on this question since the comparison of percentages from two different studies is tricky. However, the reader who wishes to examine Table 2.11 more closely will see that the contrary to Doctor Lenski's suggestion seems to be true. Since Catholics are present in the college graduation group in about their proportion in the population and since somewhat more of these graduates come from working-class families, it seems improbable that Catholic members of the working class are failing to send their children to college, especially since the 1957 occupational figures would suggest that there is not much difference in the distribution of the two religious groups across the occupational hierarchy (with the exception of the farm-working class groups). The difference between our findings and Lenski's requires greater consideration; in another chapter, we will suggest that the key to this difference (as well as to many others) is that Lenski's Detroit sample was made up of precisely those Catholic nationality elements least likely to strive for upward mobility and for college education.

Since there is obviously a close connection between income, occupation, and education, a scale was put together which would enable us to combine these three factors and get some vague single measure of social class.

An SES scale was prepared for the project based on father's occupation, father's income and father's education. The following eight categories were used:

Occupation	Education	Income
Blue collar	No college	Less than $7,500
Blue collar	No college	More than $7,500
Blue collar	College	Less than $7,500
White collar	No college	Less than $7,500
Blue collar	College	More than $7,500
White collar	No college	More than $7,500
White collar	College	Less than $7,500
White collar	College	More than $7,500

Obviously, such a scale leaves much to be desired from the point of view of stratification theory. However, it is of some use in breaking down a population into broad categories. In most of the analysis used in this book, the first four groups were combined into the "lower" half and the last four into the "upper" half. There is little difference between the Protestant and Catholic distribution on the scale with 47 per cent of the males of each group being in the upper half and the slight Catholic deficiency in education being made up for by a slight Catholic superiority in income (Table 2.12). The distribution of the Jewish graduates is much different with 67 per cent in the upper half. There is a slight difference among the girls with 57 per cent of the Protestants and 53 per cent of the Catholics being in the upper stratum (and 74 per cent of the Jews).

To sum up our information on social class, we can say that Jewish graduates are more likely to come from families of higher income and occupation than the other groups and hence have the highest social status. Graduates of Protestant families are more likely to have college-educated parents than Jews or Catholics (though the basic difference between Protestants and Jews is that the Protestant mothers are more likely to have gone to college; there is little difference among the fathers). There is practically no difference between Protestants and Catholics as far as income and occupation go, but Protestants rank somewhat higher on the status scale because of the superior educational attainments of their parents. There is no evidence however that members of the Catholic working class are less likely to send their children to college than Protestants from the same level. College education means upward mobility for all three groups, but the most upward mobility seems to be found in the Catholic group, which is improving its educational standards considerably. One might suggest that it is reasonable to argue that the previous generation of Catholics improved the economic level of the Catholic group to a rough parity with Protestants, while the present generation of young people is bringing the educational level to parity. This is a theme to which we will return.

Interaction of Demography and Social Class

Just as we combined the three elements of class into one index, it is possible to combine some of the demographic elements and social class to get an over-all picture of the relationship between religion, social class, sex, and home town (Table 2.13). We must ask even the most dedicated foe of statistical tables to look at Table 2.13.

The two largest Catholic categories are the big-city males from both halves of the SES measure; these two groups account for some two-fifths of the Catholic population. The two biggest Protestant groups on the other hand are the small-hometown males from upper and lower SES brackets, with these groups accounting for almost two-fifths of the Protestant group. Practically the same proportion of Jews are big-city males. The key comparisons that will be made with this scale in the next chapter will be among big-city, high SES males—in which group are to be found 18 per cent of the Catholic population, 13 per cent of the Protestant population, and 39 per cent of the Jewish population. Differences —or similarities—among these groups will be taken to be of great importance.

Self-Description and Personality

We have some idea now of the social and demographic background of the three religious groups among our college graduates;

now we turn to the question of what they think of themselves. The last question in the survey presented the respondents with a list of adjectives which they might check as a self-description. The most frequently checked adjectives by the whole sample were "cooperative" (62 per cent), "ambitious" (56 per cent), "happy" (49 per cent), "fun-loving" (46 per cent), "easy-going" (36 per cent), "idealistic" (33 per cent), "athletic" (32 per cent), "cautious" (31 per cent). However, some adjectives seemed especially popular with the respective religious groups. The following list presents the adjectives which were over-chosen by each group:

Protestant	*Catholic*	*Jew*
	Good-Looking	Ambitious
	Idealistic	Cultured
	Witty	Dominant
		Moody
		Outgoing
		Good-Looking
		Hard-Driving
		Idealistic
		Intellectual
		Talkative
		Witty

The following were those which were under-chosen:

Good-Looking		Reserved
Idealistic		Quiet
Witty		Low Brow

Once again we note that there are striking differences between the Jews and the Gentiles but not much in the way of difference between Protestants and Catholics. We will leave it to personality analysts more expert in that field than the present writer to divine why Jews would be more inclined to think of themselves as witty and good-looking than Catholics, and why Catholics are more inclined to so describe themselves than Protestants.

Certain of the adjectives seem to fit into patterns; thus if one checked ambitious, one was also likely to check energetic and hard-driving, and unlikely to check lazy and easy-going. Professor

Norman Bradburn of the NORC staff found five such clusters of correlated adjectives and fashioned five scales from them. On four of the five scales—Sophistication, Emotionality, Intellectual-Idealism, and Extroversion—(Table 2.14), Jews scored higher than Gentiles in all but one category—as one would expect from the fact that Jews seemed to have checked more adjectives; but on only two scales were there differences between Protestants and Catholics (Catholics scoring higher on Intellectual-Idealism and Protestants higher on Drive).

On the Drive scale ("energetic," "hard-driving" and "ambitious"), the Protestants scored seven percentage points higher than Catholics and Jews (54 per cent ranking high as opposed to 47). On the Sophistication scale ("poised," "good-looking," and "sophisticated"), the differences were not "significant" though Jews scored higher than Gentiles (a quarter for Jews opposed to about a fifth for Protestants and Catholics). On the Emotionality scale ("high-strung," "impetuous," "moody," "rebellious"), one-fifth of the Jews scored high, significantly above the Protestants and Catholics. On the Intellectual-Idealism scale ("cultured," "idealistic," intellectual"), about one-quarter of the Catholics and Jews rated high as opposed to 17 per cent of the Protestants. Finally, on the Extroversion scale ("outgoing," "talkative," "witty," "fun-loving"), Jews had an eight to nine point lead over Gentiles.

Thus Jews are more inclined than Gentiles to think of themselves as sophisticated, extroverted, intellectual, and emotional, while Protestants think of themselves as possessing more drive and Catholics think of themselves as more intellectual than Protestants, though not as intellectual as Jews.

What is one to make of these different patterns of self-description? Some patterns seem to make intuitive sense. The history and experience of the Jewish people has been so different from that of the Gentiles that we would expect them to think of themselves in quite different fashions—and indeed the words "intellectual," "sophisticated," "extroverted," and "emotional" are not bad words to describe the self-perception we would expect of people who had undergone the "Jewish experience." Further, we can understand why, in the finest traditions of the Protestant Ethic, Protestants would think of themselves as possessing more drive, though why the Jews—surely a hard-working people—would not think of themselves as possessing as much drive is hard to understand. Nor do we find any easy explanation as to why Catholics would score higher on a scale of intellectual-idealism than Protestants.

Furthermore, even though these scales are interesting and obviously correspond to some kind of personality dimensions which exist in reality, they apparently do not have much predictive power in the determination of career choice—not nearly as much as occupational values do (to which we turn in the next chapter). About all we can say of the adjective scales is that they suggest basic personality differences between Jews and Gentiles which could not be explored with better instruments and that they do not suggest too much in the way of personality differences between Protestant and Catholic college graduates.

Another approach to self-description was used when the respondents were asked to rate themselves on scales describing their attitude toward modern art, conventionality, political stance, and religiosity (Table 2.15). Jews were more favorable to modern art than Catholics, and Catholics were more conventional than Jews. Catholics were the most religious, Jews the least religious; Protestants the most conservative, Jews the most liberal.

On the matter of modern art (Table 2.16A), there was once again not much difference between Protestants and Catholics with 26 per cent of the former and 29 per cent of the latter being unfavorably disposed to it; the Jews were more sympathetic with only 19 per cent in opposition. The same pattern held for conventionality (Table 2.16B); 28 per cent of the Gentiles thought of themselves as unconventionals as opposed to 37 per cent of the Jews. The Jews (Table 2.17) were the least conservative with only 17 per cent willing to admit that they were conservative as opposed .to 42 per cent of the Protestants and 33 per cent of the Catholics.

With only 8 per cent of the Protestants and 6 percent of the Catholics describing themselves as "very conservative," there did not seem much evidence of the alleged "New Conservatism" on the campus in June 1961. The vast majority of each group were "moderates"—approximately 85 per cent from each religion—and would not admit to being either very conservative or very liberal.

We will defer to the next section our comments on the religiosity scale. To conclude this section, the major differences in self-description are between Jew and Gentile, with Jews scoring higher on liberalism, unconventionality, sophistication, extroversion, emotionality, and intellectualism. The differences between Protestants and Catholics are relatively minor with Catholics tending to think of themselves as more liberal politically and more intellectual and Protestants tending to think of themselves as possessing more drive.

Church Attendance

There is a notable difference in the church attendance that the graduates reported a year after they left college. Four-fifths of the Catholics are going every week, approximately two-thirds of the Protestants are going at least once a month, and the same proportion of the Jews are going at least two or three times a year. The high proportion of frequent church-goers among Catholic graduates will come as an unpleasant shock to certain European sociologists who refuse to accept the fact of church-going among American Catholics, but will be no surprise to those who have read other national surveys of Church attendance—especially Lazarewitz's report. In fact, the percentages in Table 2.19 tend to underestimate the actual percentage of those claiming to go to church every Sunday since the table is concerned with those who were Catholics in their original religion. Some 90 per cent of those who are still Catholic claim weekly church attendance.

Life Satisfactions

There are some rather interesting differences among the three religious groups in their answer to the question about where they expect to find the most life satisfactions. All three look to the family as the most important source of such happiness, but the Jews are more likely to choose the family (70 per cent) and leisure (7 per cent) than the Gentiles. The major difference between Protestants and Catholics is that the latter are more likely to mention religion (15 per cent as opposed to 7 per cent), while the former over-choose family (63 per cent to 59 per cent). The Catholic emphasis on religion would suggest that there might be some kind of personality orientation at the root of the difference in church attendance and self-description as religious.

Worries

The major differences (Table 2.20B) in the kind of worries the June 1961 graduates had are between Jews and Gentiles with the Jews worrying more about school studies (perhaps because more of them are going to graduate school), dating, relations with parents, world conditions and less about physical health, finances, and their jobs. Catholics worry more than Protestants about life goals and career plans. As we shall see in a later chapter, extremely interesting differences on worries are to be found among the various Catholic ethnic groups. There appears some tendency in the present material for Jews to worry more about human relations problems and less about physical or material subjects than Gentiles, and for Catholics to worry more about future plans than Protestants. Neither tendency would be opposed to what we know of the history of the two groups.

The most important single finding of this chapter is that the Catholics who have graduated in June of 1961 were somewhat more likely to be from the big cities than Protestants, somewhat less likely than Jews, a little bit more male than the Protestants but about the same as the Jews. Their SES rating was less than that of the Jews but little different from that of the Protestants.

Their self-description was about the same as that of the Protestants, though different from that of the Jews. There were major differences in church attendance between Catholics and other groups and some interesting and suggestive differences in expectations of life satisfaction and in worries. Thus it could be said in summary that Catholics were different from their fellow graduates only in their church attendance and their evaluation of religion as a source of life satisfaction. In the next chapter we will attempt to discover whether this basic similarity in background can coexist with vastly different career plans and with an undervaluation of the intellectual life.

NOTES

1. Unless otherwise stated in the text, "religion" always refers to the religion in which the graduates were raised and not current religious preference. In most of this book the analysis will be based on a representative subsample of 3,397 students (coded in the tables as RSS). In some sections, however, the Total Weighted Sample (TWS) or the Total Sample (TS) will be used.

Since the materials are actually based on two series of questionnaires, one administered to the graduates in June of 1961 and one administered a year later (with an 85 per cent response rate), all tables based on the second questionnaire will have 1962 after the code letters. It should be noted that questions about ethnicity, church attendance, life goals, and worries were part of the 1962 questionnaire and not of the 1961 questionnaire.

2. Summarizing statistical data for a general readership can be a difficult task, since only the addicted sociologist finds tables easier to read than prose. On the other hand, when prose attempts to substitute for tables, it runs the risk of becoming insufferably dull. Our compromise solution will probably satisfy no one: the tables will be in the back of the volume for those who wish to consult them; the text will be written in such a way that it will normally be unnecessary to consult tables. However, in some instances, we will abandon our principles and put a table in the text.

3. The word "significant" will be used fairly frequently in this book, almost always in the technical sense of "statistically significant." A word ought to be said about what this means. Since our information

is based on data gathered from only a sample of the June 1961 graduates, it might be wondered what the chances are that a difference in percentage between two subgroups within our sample does not reflect a difference that actually exists in the whole population. When one says that a difference is significant at the .05 level, he means that according to the laws of probability there is one chance in twenty of the difference not existing in reality. Statistical significance does not necessarily mean that a difference is socially significant. If a sample is big enough a difference of one or two percentage points between two groups would be statistically significant, but the two groups would not be very different. However, if a difference is not statistically significant it is not likely to be socially significant. Thus, we will use significance tests in this volume to establish what differences are certainly not important. However, we will not necessarily argue that a statistically significant difference means that two groups are very different. As we shall see, Catholics are "significantly" more likely to go to graduate school than Protestants, but the difference is still relatively small and it seems safe to argue that American Catholics and Protestants are very similar in their graduate school plans. On the other hand, Jews are not only "significantly" more likely to go to graduate school, but the difference is so great as to suggest that the Jews are *not* similar to Gentiles in this matter. Most of the findings of the book, however, are based on the absence of even statistically significant differences. The following table presents the percentage differences needed for .05 significance in comparisons among Protestants, Catholics, and Jews (the differences are somewhat higher than in ordinary probability sampling because a special kind of sampling was used in this study—cluster sampling): Between Protestants and Catholics 5 per cent, between Catholics and Jews 8 per cent, between Protestants and Jews 7 per cent.

4. These figures are based on a recomputation of the data in Donald Bogue's *The Population of the United States* (Glencoe: The Free Press, 1959) and Bernard Lazarewitz's "A Comparison of Major United States Religious Groups," in *Journal of the American Statistical Association* (September, 1961), pp. 568-579.

CHAPTER 3

School and After

THE MAIN PURPOSE of the last chapter was to describe the background of the Catholic college graduate in comparison with his Jewish and Protestant classmates. In the process of this description, we were able to examine some of the hypotheses about Catholics not going to college. In this chapter we turn to the actual college experiences and the career plans and values which the graduates had in June of 1961. By so doing, we will be able to test more of the major hypotheses with which we started.

School Experiences

The first question we might ask about the educational experiences of our college graduates is "what kind of school did they go to?" An index of school quality was prepared, based on the average score of entering freshmen at the school on the National Merit Scholarship examination. There were 11 schools in the A (top) category on the index, 12 schools in the B category, 71 in the C category and 41 in the D category. There was little difference (Table 3.1) between Protestants and Catholics in the upper categories with 12 per cent of each in A and B, although two-fifths of the Protestants and one-fifth of the Catholics were in the lowest category (D). As we have come to expect by now, the main difference was between Jews and Gentiles with one-fourth of the Jews in A or B schools and only one-sixth in the D schools. At least part of the explanation for the differences is to be found in the area of the country in which a population is concentrated (since the quality schools are in the North East where the Jewish population is and the D schools tend to be in the South which is mostly Protestant).

If we try to discover the physical location of the school from which the students graduated we see that this explanation is reasonable (Table 3.2). Two-thirds of the Jews, better than half the Catholics, and only one-fourth of the Protestants attended school in the North East part of the country—where most of the better schools are located. Only 13 per cent of the Catholics and 18 per cent of the Jews went to schools in the South or the West, while 45 per cent of the Protestants attended schools in these regions. The Protestant college population as well as the Protestant population in general is much more evenly distributed throughout the country than the Catholic and Jewish populations. This difference in distribution is bound to have an effect on many other aspects of life.

One of the effects is that Jewish and Catholic graduates were able to go to school much nearer to home (Table 3.3). Two-fifths of the Catholics and three-fifths of the Jews were within commuting distance of their schools. However, approximately three-fourths of each group were within four hours drive of school and only a fifth had to leave the state. Schools were not completely inaccessible to the Protestants, but they had to go farther to them than did the other two groups.

Hence (Table 3.4) Jews and Catholics were much more likely to live with their parents (41 per cent of the Jews and 36 per cent of the Catholics lived at home as opposed to 14 per cent of the Protestants). Jews and Catholics who lived at school were not very likely to be found in fraternity or sorority houses (9 per cent for

Jews, 5 per cent for Catholics), but fraternity houses were not particularly popular for Protestants either (13 per cent). Surprisingly enough, off-campus housing provided approximately a third of the residences for graduates of all groups.

At least one of the effects of differential residence patterns seems to have been a different pattern of meeting friends (Table 3.5). Even though members of all three religions were most likely to meet their friends in class in their field of study, residence and campus activity were more important for Protestants and Catholics than for Jews (40 per cent of whom had met their closest friends before they came to college). The reason seems to be that the Jews are likely to live at home and go to college with friends from the same neighborhood. There is not as much need for them to make friends on campus.

As they look back on their four years of higher education, what did they think it was all about? The answers are somewhat surprising and hold no comfort for the proponents of Catholic anti-intellectualism (Table 3.6A). About two-thirds of each group think that the basic purpose of college has something to do with the appreciation of ideas, and another one-third think it is connected with career training. There is no indication that Catholics are more inclined to vocationalism than Protestants or Jews—at least in their stated judgments of what college is for. Interestingly enough, students of all three religious groups are not inclined to view the "typical" student at their college as "liberal," a view which they in fact hold of themselves. Even though two-thirds of each group think that the "appreciation of ideas" is the main purpose of college, only 35 per cent of the Protestants, 44 per cent of the Catholics, and 27 per cent of the Jews (Table 3.6B) think that the "typical" student thinks this way. And 26 per cent of the Protestants, 18 per cent of the Catholics and 29 per cent of the Jews think that the purpose of college for the "typical" student is having a good time(though practically no one will admit that this is his own view of things). There are two very curious elements in this picture of graduate cynicism. First, the "typical" student is in reality the one who is answering the question, since the questionnaire was given to all graduating seniors at the colleges. Thus the graduates are badly misjudging what their fellows think (or say they think). This may be a realistic appraisal of the situation or it may be a misperception based on the curious phenomenon that graduates do think that "appreciation of ideas" is the purpose of college; but since they do not believe that this is a "typical" purpose, they must act as though they had other purposes and by so doing deceive each other.

Secondly, for reasons by no means clear, the Catholic graduate is much more willing to concede "liberal" educational intentions to his fellows than other graduates. One could attribute this either to Catholic naiveté about the goals of others or to a more acute perception on the part of Catholics as to what others really want out of college or finally to some kind of combination of naiveté and perception which could hide under the name of charity. At the present state of our knowledge of religious differences, there is no clear answer to this puzzle.

Did they like their schools? Anyone who must deal with college age young people is aware that griping is mammoth. However, when the chips are down (which is to say, when an NORC questionnaire is shoved in front of you), the graduate tends to have kind thoughts for his alma mater (Table 3.7). Seventy-seven per cent of the Protestants, 71 per cent of the Catholics, and 71 per cent of the Jews had positive feelings towards their schools. Less than 10 per cent of each group were willing to say that they did not like their schools.

There were practically no differences in the rating of schools between Catholics and Protestants for the males (Table 3.8). "Excellent" ratings were given to classroom teaching by one quarter, to curriculum by 29 per cent, to research facilities by 27 per cent, to student housing by one quarter, to the caliber of students by about one fifth, and to the caliber of faculty by 43 per cent. Jewish males, however, were considerably more likely to give excellent

ratings to the curriculum, research facilities and caliber of faculty
than Gentiles. This is not surprising since the Jews were more
likely to go to high quality schools, and presumably those who go
to better schools will be more satisfied with these schools. The
Jewish girls likewise rated curriculum and research facilities higher
than did the Gentiles and also were more pleased with the quality
of student housing. Catholic girls were more satisfied with the
teaching, student housing, caliber of students, and caliber of faculties than were Protestants. As we will note in a later chapter, this
is almost entirely a result of the votes of Catholic girls in Catholic
colleges.

What kind of marks did our June 1961 graduates get in college?
There are three different answers we can give to this question. We
can look at the grade point average the student reported, his own
estimate of his position in class, and finally a weighted scale based
on his reported average and the quality of the school he went to.

There is little difference among the males in raw grades; the
somewhat smaller percentage of Jews getting "A's" (4 per cent
as opposed to 5 per cent for the Catholics and 7 per cent for the
Protestants) is probably the result of the Jews being concentrated
in the better schools where an A average is hard to come by. The
Protestant girls out-perform both the Catholics and the Jews with
10 per cent getting an A average (as opposed to 5 per cent and
6 per cent for the other groups). About three-fourths of all groups
are concentrated in the C+ to B+ bracket.

Since it is harder to get an A in a difficult school than in an
easier school, a scale (called the Academic Performance Index or
API) was prepared based on grade point average weighted by the
quality of school (as judged by the School Quality Index). The index is divided into three parts—the top fifth of the sample, the
remaining fraction of the top half, and the bottom half. Such an
index is a tricky measure since, as we saw, Jews were more likely
to go to high quality schools and thus to some extent the scale is
weighted in their favor. However, this weight must not be exag-
gerated since the quality index is based in its turn on the abilities

of the students. There is no significant difference between Protestants and Catholics (Table 3.10B) with 19 per cent of the former being in the top fifth of the sample and 15 per cent of the latter (although the difference is close to "significant"). The difference between Jews and Gentiles is quite clear, however, with one-fourth of the Jews in the top one-fifth.

Do members of one religious group tend to find certain kinds of courses more congenial than others? Are Catholics, for example, less interested in physical sciences than other students as some of the past theory would lead us to believe? As a matter of fact, the differences in interests are relatively small (Table 3.11). Protestants found biology more interesting than did either Catholics or Jews (44 per cent to 37 per cent); Catholics found English more interesting than did Protestants and Protestants found it more interesting than did Jews (54 per cent to 49 per cent to 37 per cent). There were no differences in social sciences, physical sciences or mathematics. As we shall see in the next section and in a later chapter, this pattern of interests carries over into career choice.

Was there much in the way of research experience during the college years (Table 3.12)? Not as much as might have been desirable with three-fifths of each religious group reporting no research experience and about one-sixth of each group having had their own research project. There were no major differences among the religious groups.

To sum up this section, Catholics were less likely to go to top quality schools than Jews and less likely to go to "low" quality schools than Protestants. Catholics were somewhat less likely than Jews to go to the schools in the North East and less likely than Protestants to go to schools in the South and West. Catholics lived nearer to their schools than Protestants and farther than Jews, and hence were more likely to commute than Protestants and less likely to commute than Jews. Catholics were less likely to live in fraternity and sorority houses than members of the other religions and more likely to live in dorms and off-campus housing than Jews, more likely to live at home than Protestants. Finally,

Catholics were less likely than Protestants to have made their closest friends on campus, but more likely than Jews. Practically all of these differences are closely related to the geographical distribution of the Catholic population.

Catholics liked their schools in overwhelming numbers but no more than did Protestants and Jews. They also saw the purpose of education as "liberal" in about the same proportion as Protestants and Jews. However, they detected more "liberalism" in their classmates than did members of the other faiths. They got poorer marks than Jews and about the same marks as Protestants. They liked biology less than the Protestants (but about as much as Jews), and they liked English more than either of the other groups. There was no evidence of difference either in research experience or in liking for the physical sciences, mathematics, or the social sciences.

Career Plans

It is probably clear by this time that with the exception of some demographic and geographical differences there is not much to mark off the Catholic graduate from the Protestant (with the exception of religious practice). Hence we might be inclined to suspect that the past theories about lack of intellectualism or economic ambition might be brought into question. In the present section we get to a crucial question: Do Catholics have different career plans than the majority of other Americans? To give a brief answer, we might say "not very different."

Catholics (Table 3.13) are somewhat more likely than Protestants both to go to graduate school and to go to schools in the arts and sciences (the traditional "intellectual" fields) than Protestants.[1] Catholics are more likely to plan business careers and work for large companies than either Protestants or Jews, less likely to plan work in education than Protestants, less likely to envision careers in the traditional professions (law and medicine) than Jews, and not a bit different from Protestants or Jews in planning careers in the academic professions (Physical Sciences, Social Sciences and Humanities).

The following table is so important that we put it in the text:

PER CENT GOING TO GRADUATE SCHOOL IN THE FALL OF 1962 BY RELIGION

	Protestant	Catholic	Jew
Professional School	12	16	18
Arts and Sciences	16	18	29
Total	28	34	47

If failure to go to graduate school, especially in the arts and sciences, is a sign of anti-intellectualism, then there is no evidence in the June 1961 class for Catholic anti-intellectualism. Catholics are, in fact, more likely to go to graduate school and to go in the arts and sciences than Protestants are. (One humorist on the NORC staff commented when this first raw cross-tabulation of religion and graduate school plans emerged from the IBM machine, "It looks like Notre Dame beats Southern Methodist this year."[2] Catholics are less likely to go to graduate school than Jews, though most of the difference is in professional school plans and not in academic graduate school plans. [3] It ought to be made quite clear that the important fact is not that Catholics are slightly ahead of Protestants in plans for graduate school; the differences are so small as to be relatively unimportant. The significant phenomenon is that Catholics are not far inferior in graduate school plans, and especially academic graduate school plans.

Nor can we explain the relative parity merely in terms of the Protestants planning to go at some later date. Some three-fourths of the sample plan to go to graduate school eventually (an astonishing finding in itself), but there is no difference between Protestants and Catholics (Table 3.14), though only 17 per cent of the Jews do not have eventual graduate school plans.

It is not too much of an exaggeration to say that the basic finding of this volume is contained in the rather simple table above; the supposedly unintellectual Catholics are not at all disinclined to go to graduate school, even to arts and science graduate schools. There have been three preliminary reactions to this finding in certain Catholic circles. The first is to say, "well, they are going to graduate school all right, but they are going for different reasons than the non-Catholics." The second objection argues, "yes, they're going to graduate school, but they're not going to stay." And the third maintains, "you haven't proven anything; just because people are going to graduate school, doesn't mean they're intellectual."

The answer to the first objection is simple enough: as we will show in the next section of this chapter, the occupational values of the Catholic graduate are not different from those of the Protestant graduate. If there are some other hidden motivations explaining their inclination to graduate school, it is up to the objectors to uncover these motivations.

The reply to the second objection is equally simple: at least a year after graduation there is no sign of Catholics dropping out of graduate school (Table 3.15) in numbers very different from Protestants, though the Jewish survival rate is better than that of the other two groups. A year after graduation the rate of those actually going to graduate school among those who had planned to go was 81 per cent for Protestants, 80 per cent for Catholics and 87 per cent for Jews. The differences between Protestants and Catholics are minor. Three per cent more of the high API Protestant males who had planned to go to graduate school actually went than did Catholics in the comparable group (93 per cent to 90 per cent). Protestants also had a lead in middle API for females (65 per cent to 59 per cent). However, Catholics were ahead in recruiting to graduate school high API males and females who had not planned to go in the fall of 1961 (24 per cent to 18 per cent for the males, and 22 per cent to 16 per cent for females). The over-all Catholic recruitment rate is 18 per cent and the Protestant is 15 per cent. The differences virtually cancel each other out.

The Jews lead the Gentiles in almost all categories of both recruitment and retention.

We should also note that a year after graduation about the same proportion of each religious group planned to continue studies until the doctorate, 24 per cent of the Jews, 22 per cent of the Protestants, and 21 per cent of the Catholics. [4] Thus there is no evidence to support the objection brought against the findings of this study that Catholics indeed are going to graduate school but will not stay or are not planning to get the coveted Ph.D. Actually they are staying (at least for the first year) and are planning on the doctorate.

The third objection is a little more tricky because it tries to force me to prove something I have no intention of proving. We are defining intellectualism in this volume as an inclination to devote one's life to scholarly pursuits. Now this is not the only possible definition of intellectualism nor necessarily the best; however, it is a valid one and one that can be tested against the currently available data. It is reasonably safe to argue, I think, that if a substantial portion of a given population is willing to devote its lives to scholarship, then it follows that the population in question is not grossly anti-intellectual. However, our present argument does not in fact go quite that far. All we are claiming is that the large proportion of Catholic graduates going on for higher studies is a "non-proof" of anti-intellectualism. Surely, if we had found (as we had expected to find) that Catholics were not going to graduate school in their proper proportion, such a finding would have been taken as proof of what the self-critics have been saying and this volume would have been hailed as a damning indictment of American Catholicism. A final judgment on the June 1961 class will, of course, take several decades. However, at this point, it would seem to me that the burden of proof is on the self-critics. There is no evidence that the Catholics in the June 1961 class are more anti-intellectual than anyone else.

If we turn to the specific careers [5] that the graduates have in mind, we see that there is practically no difference (Table 3.13) in the proportion of each group going into the academic professions (17 per cent for Protestants, 16 per cent for Catholics, 18 per cent for Jews), though the Jews substantially over-chose the traditional professions of law and medicine (16 per cent as opposed to 6 per cent for Catholics and 4 per cent for Protestants). Catholics over-chose business (23 per cent to 17 per cent for Jews and 15 per cent for Protestants) and this is, of course, in direct conflict with the expectations of the "Protestant Ethic" hypothesis. However, the Catholic over-choice of business is not at the expense of the academic life but at the expense of primary and secondary education where Protestants have a one-third to one-fourth lead over the other two groups. Finally, Protestants lead both Catholics and Jews in the "Other Professional" group (a category standing for all kinds of fields from dentistry and nursing to agricultural science and forestry).

Even though there is similarity in the general kind of occupational choice among the three religious groups, certain interesting differences appear when occupational choice is described in terms of more specific occupations. Table 3.16 is based on the long range career plans of all the respondents in the 1962 follow-up questionnaire. If we consider a five per cent variation from the proportion of a group in the total population, we observe that Protestant males are over-represented in civil and mechanical engineering, zoology, all the education fields, the farming fields, social work, and the military, and are under-represented in chemistry, medicine, pharmacology, biochemistry, non-clinical psychology, political science, English, history, philosophy, journalism, accounting, advertising, public administration and law. Catholic men are over-represented in political science, business, accounting, advertising, public administration and law and under-represented in geophysical sciences, mathematics, civil engineering, dentistry, zoology, "other" biosciences, the farming fields, elementary and scientific secondary education, clinical psychology, economics, sociology, the fine arts, philosophy and theology. Jewish males are over-represented in medicine, dentistry, pharmacology, biochemistry, microbiology, psychology, philosophy and law and under-represented in biology, zoology, the farming fields, secondary education, educational administration, "other" humanities, theology, and the military. The inclination of Catholics to business, Protestants to education, and Jews to the free professions seem to be consistent within the components of these fields.

For girls the picture is somewhat different. Protestant girls are under-represented in chemistry, medicine, the social sciences, languages, and law and over-represented in the fine arts, library science, and home economics. Catholic girls are under-represented in clinical psychology, library science, the fine arts, home economics, and elementary education. The last item is especially interesting since elementary education is the largest single field for girls and since the Catholic shortage can not be explained in terms of geography or city size because Jews are not under-represented. This under-choice ought to be of particular interest to Catholic school administrators who must recruit an ever increasing number of lay teachers each year. Instead of being school teachers, the Catholic girls over-choose chemistry, physics, engineering, medicine, bio-chemistry, the social sciences, the languages, law and housewifery. Clearly there seems to be some kind of professional orientation among Catholic girl graduates that is not to be found in the other groups. Jewish women over-choose clinical psychology and law and under-choose nursing, medical technology and library science.

The differences in career plans are manifested in the differences in future employer anticipations (Table 3.17). Catholics expect to work for large companies (one-third as opposed to one-fourth for the other groups). Jews expect to work for small firms and partnerships or for themselves more than do the other two groups and 36 per cent of the Protestants as opposed to 27 per cent of the other two groups plan to be involved in primary or secondary educational systems. About the same percentage in each group (12 per cent) see themselves involved in college work, though Jews are somewhat more likely to check research organizations (10 per cent) than the other two faiths (7 per cent). The pattern that emerges from the question of careers is very clear. Protestants over-choose education, Catholics over-choose business, Jews over-choose the independent professions. All three groups are going into the academic life in about equal proportions. In the face of these data, both the anti-intellectualism and Protestant Ethic theories apparently collapse.

Occupational Image

The graduates were asked to rate six different occupations on a variety of measures (Table 3.18). Jews were more likely than Protestants or Catholics to think that the research chemist did work which was interesting and to feel qualified for such work, but they were dissatisfied with the financial rewards of the field. The college professor was the most attractive field for all three groups, though the Jews and to some extent the Catholics were not happy over the income possibilities. Jews did not think that high school teaching was as interesting as did Protestants or Catholics and thought it offered no challenge. Jews and to some extent Catholics were not impressed with the financial possibilities of teaching. Very few members of either group doubted their abilities in this field.

Jews were more likely to see medicine as interesting and less likely to think that they lacked the necessary ability than Gentiles. Very few were dissatisfied with the financial rewards of medicine. Jews further did not find engineering interesting and doubted their ability in the field. Catholics were the most interested in the work of the business executive. In summary, Jews were well disposed to business and medicine but were not inclined to chemistry, teaching, and engineering, apparently because of the poor incomes in these fields. They found the college professor's job interesting but once again were dissatisfied with the money. There was not too much difference between Catholics and Protestants, though the former were more favorably disposed to business and the latter took a somewhat more sympathetic view of the work of a high school teacher. Catholics were somewhat more concerned than Protestants with the poor income possibilities of chemistry and college and high school teaching.

Occupational Values

One last set of data must be examined before we can bring this chapter to a close. Is there any connection between religion and the occupational values—the things a graduate deems important about a job—of the graduates?

Eleven possible occupational values were listed for the graduates' consideration (the number being dictated by the size of an IBM card). The Protestant Ethic theory would hypothesize that Protestants should score higher than Catholics on making money, freedom from supervision and leadership as occupational values and lower than Catholics on being helpful to others, avoiding high pressure, and slow and sure progress. It would also be expected that Jews would be very much like Protestants on these scores. The anti-intellectualism hypothesis would suggest that Catholics would score lower than others on chance to be creative, work in a world of ideas, and work with people, not things. Virtually none (Table 3.19) of these canons of the conventional wisdom find any support in the data. Indeed, there are only three "significant" differences between Protestants and Catholics and two of them are in the "wrong" direction. Catholics are more interested in making money than Protestants (27 per cent to 21 per cent) and less interested in being helpful to others (61 per cent to 68 per cent). The main differences once again are between Jews and Gentiles, with Jews more interested in money, a chance to be creative, and an opportunity to work in a world of ideas than Protestants and Catholics. It is worth noting, incidentally, that if making a lot of money is taken to be a fair indicator of the Protestant Ethic, then the Protestants in the group are the least "Protestant" of the lot; and if helping others is taken to be a sign of the Catholic "faith and good works" doctrine, then the Protestants are the most "Catholic" in the group. At this point it would perhaps not be out of place to propose a permanent moratorium on the use of the term "Protestant Ethic."

We cannot close this chapter without commenting that the occupational values reported by the June 1961 graduates would make them, regardless of religion, some of the most idealistic young people in history. Despite the fears of *The Organization Man-Lonely Crowd* brand of sociology, there is no sign that money and security and the avoidance of pressure have become the most important values in the lives of the college graduates. Rather, helping others and a chance to be creative seem to be the most important things to be sought in a job, while working with people and in a world of ideas comes next. The problem facing society may not be so much the lack of idealism as the lack of concrete outlets for idealism.

To sum up this section, we note that the Catholic graduate is no less inclined to the academic life than the Protestant or Jewish graduate, that he is somewhat less interested in the independent professions than the Jew and less interested in education than the Protestant, and more interested in business than either. He is as inclined to go to graduate school as the Protestant is (a bit more, in fact), and as much interested in arts and science graduate schools as any one. He is more interested in making money than Protestants and less interested in it than Jews. He is somewhat less interested in being helpful than Protestants and less interested in creativity and working with ideas than Jews.

Very little in the way of confirmation was found for the following propositions in this chapter or the preceding one:

1. Catholics are less likely to go to college.

2. Catholics from the working class are less likely to go to college than Protestants from the working class.

3. Catholic family ties will interfere with college education.

4. Catholics will be less likely to go to graduate school.

5. Among those Catholics going to graduate school, there will

be a smaller proportion going into the academic fields than for the other two religious groups.

6. Catholics will not be inclined to go into the physical sciences.

7. Catholics will not be as interested in economic activity as Protestants but will be more concerned with security.

Although the predicted differences between Catholics and Protestants did not occur, most of the expected differences between Jews and Gentiles did occur. These can be summed up by saying that Jews are more inclined to both intellectual and economic pursuits than either Catholics or Protestants and are more likely to engage in these pursuits as self-employed professionals than members of the other religions. In short, in terms of the Protestant Ethic theory, the Jews are the most "Protestant" of the three religions and the Protestants—at least in many instances—the least "Protestant." In the following chapter we will try to see if the predicted differences between Jews and Gentiles can be explained away and if the unpredicted similarity between Protestants and Catholics can likewise be interpreted.

NOTES

1. It should be noted that the Negro group within the Protestant population does not decrease the Protestant proportion going to graduate school, since 28 per cent of the Negroes in the June 1961 class have graduate school plans.

2. No actual comparisons were made of course between these schools.

3. The Jewish over-choice of graduate school is the result of the Jewish inclination to the professions of law and medicine, rather than to any specific Jewish tradition of learning. Of course, the Jewish scholarly tradition (which is unquestioned) is probably working in the choice of these two professions. One does not wish to get into an extended discussion of the point; but rabbinic learning, like law and medicine, was an eminently practical science. Perhaps a more potent reason for the Jewish choice of the independent professions is that these professions have been associated with occupations where prejudice was less an obstacle to success than in other occupations. There

is no evidence in Table 3.13 that a much greater proportion of Jews are planning academic careers than Protestants or Catholics.

4. There was no difference in plans for the Ph.D between Catholics who had graduated from Catholic colleges and Catholics who had graduated from other colleges.

5. The major categories used in the tabulations were made up in the following fashion:

Physical Sciences: Astronomy, Astrophysics, Chemistry, Geography, Geology, Geophysics, Mathematics, Metallurgy, Meteorology, Oceanography, Physics, Physical Science, General and Other.

Biological Sciences: Anatomy, Biology, Biochemistry, Botany, Biophysics, Entomology, Genetics, Microbiology, Pathology, Pharmacology, Physiology, Zoology, Other Biological Science Fields.

Social Sciences: Clinical Psychology, Social Psychology, Experimental and General Psychology, Other Psychological Fields, Anthropology, Archeology, Economics, Area and Regional Studies, Political Science, International Relations, Sociology, Social Science General and Other.

Humanities and Fine Arts: Fine and Applied Arts, English, Creative Writing, Classical Languages and Literatures, History, Modern Foreign Languages and Literatures, Philosophy, Humanities General and Other.

Education (excluding junior college, college and university): Elementary Secondary English, Modern Foreign Languages, Latin, Greek, History, Social Studies, Natural Science, Mathematics (all secondary), Physical Education, Music Education, Art Education, Education of Exceptional Children including Speech Correction, Agricultural Education, Home Economics Education, Business Education, Trade and Industrial, Industrial Arts Education (non-vocational), Counseling and Guidance, Educational Psychology, Administration and Supervision, Education General and Other Specialties.

Engineering: Aeronautical, Civil, Chemical including Ceramic, Electrical, Engineering Science, Engineering Physics, Engineering Mechanics, Industrial, Mechanical, Metallurgical, Mining, Engineering General and Other.

Medicine

Law

Other Professional Fields: Dentistry, Nursing, Optometry, Pharmacy, Physical Therapy, Occupational Therapy, Veterinary Medicine, Medical Technology, Dental Hygiene. Other Health Fields, Agricultural Sciences, Forestry, Fish and Wild Life Management, Farming,

Architecture, City Planning, Journalism, Radio-Television, Communications, Library Science, Theology and Religion, Public Administration, Foreign Service, Social Work, Home Economics, Military Service.

Business: Industrial and Personnel Psychology, Advertising, Public Relations, Accounting, Secretarial, All Other Business and Commercial Fields.

CHAPTER 4

Controls and Denominations

THE BRAVE READER who has plowed through the last three chapters may have two serious objections to our conclusions. The first objection would go something like this: your conclusions leave out the fact that the demographic, socio-economic, and geographic differences among the three religious groups, while they may be relatively minor, could nevertheless change the picture considerably. What you ought to do is to compare upper class Protestants, Catholics, and Jews from big cities in the North and see what similarities and differences exist there.

The second objection would point out that it is grossly unfair to lump all Protestants in one group, since everyone knows that there are many differences among the Protestant denominations. If, as has been hinted in the previous chapter, the ethnic background of Catholics may play an important part in shaping their career plans and occupational values, it would follow that the denominational background of the Protestants might play an equally important part. Indeed a fairly good case can be made that the various "national" churches within American Catholicism are not so different from the denominations among American Protestants—at least in a good many respects.

This chapter will be an attempt to reply to these two objections. In answering the first we will use "controls" and in answering the second we will present data on the members of the various Protestant denominations on certain key matters.

A "control" is a background factor which may explain away the differences between two groups. Thus it is possible that the reasons more Jews go to graduate school than Gentiles is that Jews live in big cities and people from big cities are more likely to go to graduate school than those who are from smaller cities or towns. Therefore we ought to compare Jews and Gentiles who live in big cities.

Normally controls are used to explain away, or to attempt to explain away, differences which have occurred between groups. Part of our analysis had this goal in mind: we wondered if there were any explanations for the consistent—and expected—differences between Jews and Gentiles. There were no such explanations. Under all the controls, the Jewish difference from Gentiles on the three measures remained substantially unchanged. The other part of our analysis represents something rather unusual in sociological analysis: we tried to make differences appear where there were not any—mainly because the differences which failed to appear had been expected on the basis of previous theories. This attempt was not particularly successful. Even though there were eight instances where the controls did make some change in the Protestant-Catholic comparisons presented in the last chapter, in none of these instances was there a substantial change in the basic conclusion: the differences between Catholics and Protestants on these measures are relatively minor, despite the predictions of the anti-intellectualism and Protestant Ethic hypotheses.

Controls

As a first step in the control process twelve different variables were examined to see if any one of them would modify the picture presented in the last chapter—sex, hometown size, social-economic rank (on the SES scale), region, income, father's education, mother's education, and the five personality dimensions, viz., drive, sophistication, emotionality, intellectual-idealism, and extroversion. Only the first three variables seemed to produce much in the way of a change, so these three were combined into a new index—the Index of Background Characteristics (IBC). Each religious group was subdivided into eight subgroups based on sex, hometown size (over 100,000 or under 100,000), and SES rank (upper half or lower half). Even though the numbers in some of these subgroups are rather small and comparisons must be made with some care, there are enough respondents in the important groups (for example, big-city, high SES males) for each of the three religions to enable us to judge to what extent background characteristics are responsible for the similarities and differences reported in the last chapter.

Graduate School Plans

It will be remembered from the previous chapter that Catholics were six percentage points ahead of Protestants in plans for graduate school the autumn after graduation. This lead continues (by 4 points) in the key group of high SES, large hometown males and also is unaffected in all female groups (Table 4.1). Only among small-city, low SES males do Catholics fall behind Protestants (5 per cent) in graduate school plans; among large-city, low SES males there is exact parity. In general, we can say that the surprising showing of Catholics in the matter of graduate school plans cannot be explained away by background characteristics. In all but one of the eight comparison groups, Catholics are either ahead of Protestants in graduate school plans or even with them. In the four groups where there are enough cases to make a comparison, the Jewish lead over the other two groups continues, although it seems that among high SES males from large hometowns, the Jewish lead is substantially reduced (from 13 to 7 points ahead of Catholics).

Career Plans

In the last chapter we saw that there was virtually no difference among the three religions in those planning arts and science careers, despite the prediction that Jews would be more likely than Gentiles to plan such careers and Protestants more likely than Catholics. Table 4.2 shows a very interesting phenomenon for Jews. More than twice as large a proportion of low SES Jewish males choose the academic professions as do high SES males (although the reverse is true for Jewish girls). Indeed, high SES Jewish males are much less likely to choose the academic life than either Protestants or Catholics. There is little difference between Protestants and Catholics in the large hometowns, whether they be male or female, in their plans for academic careers, though the small hometown Protestant males are ahead of the Catholics and the small hometown Catholic females are ahead of the Protestants. We note once again no evidence for a disinclination of Catholics to go into the academic life and a somewhat surprising under-choice of academic careers by well-to-do Jewish sons.

The reason for the under-choice of academic careers by this group becomes clear in Table 4.3; almost two-fifths of the high SES Jewish males from big cities are choosing the traditional professions of law and medicine while only one-tenth of the low SES Jewish males are making the same choice. Thus well-to-do Jewish sons choose the traditional professions and "lower" class sons choose the academic professions. Even though the numbers on which this last statement is based are somewhat small, it should be noted that the differences are statistically significant. The Catholic over-choice of the professions in comparison with Protestants holds up in all male categories.

Table 4.4 supports the finding that primary and secondary education is in high favor among the Protestants. The Protestant lead over Catholics in this career is to be found in all groups with the exception of the low SES, small hometown females (where there are so few Catholics that the finding is dubious). It is worth noting that Jewish girls are the ones most likely to choose education while Jewish males are the least likely. It is also worth noting that while Protestant males are ahead of Catholic males in all categories in the choice of education, the lead is especially pronounced among the low SES groups. Apparently education is the popular means of upward mobility for "poor" Protestant males just as the academic life is for "poor" Jewish males.

Something of the same phenomenon is to be observed among Catholics in the choice of business careers (Table 4.5). Catholics are ahead of Protestants in choosing business in all categories (except the troublesome low SES, small hometown females), but the biggest over-choice is among low SES males. Each religious group apparently has its own favorite path of upward mobility—the Protestants choosing education, the Catholics choosing business, and the Jews choosing academia. For the first two groups the choice is merely an exaggeration of what the upper SES groups are choosing, but for the Jews the choice is totally different from the upper SES choice of the traditional professions. However interesting these trends are, none of them give the slightest backing for any theory of Catholic anti-intellectualism or economic indifferentism.

Future Employers

A similar pattern emerges, as we might expect, in the expectation of future employers (Table 4.6). Catholics are more likely to expect to work for a large corporation (except for the high SES, big-city group which ties with the Protestants in this expectation) but the big and indeed striking lead is among low SES groups. Exactly the same may be said of the Protestant expectation of working for a school system; it is the low SES Protestants who are drawn to such employers. Although the figures are not given in the table, we might add that 23 per cent of the high SES Jewish males from large hometowns expect to be self-employed as befits members of the traditional professions, while 17 per cent of the Jewish boys who are low in SES expect to work for research institutes—twice as many as any of the other twenty-three categories into which the respondents have been placed. Thus it would appear the lower SES groups from all three religions expect to achieve upward mobility through working for an organization; the difference is in the kind of organization they choose, Protestants opting for school systems, Jews for research centers, and Catholics for corporations.

Occupational Values

The IBC has no effect on the ordering of the three religions as to the importance of money as an occupational value (Table 4.7). It is more important to Jews than to Catholics in all categories and to Catholics than to Protestants. The slight Catholic deficiency in the desire to be "original and creative," which we noted in the last chapter, seems to result primarily from the performance on this item of low SES Catholics in large hometowns, regardless of sex, and of Catholic girls from large hometowns. The Jewish lead in "people, not things" (Table 4.9) on the other hand is a high SES phenomenon, probably not unrelated to the interest of this group in the professions of law and medicine. We find no evidence in these values of any anti-intellectualism or anti-economic achievement in Catholics.

In general we may say that even under a wide variety of controls, Catholics are more likely to choose business, Jews more likely to choose law and medicine, and Protestants more likely to choose education. All three groups are about equally represented in the arts and sciences. There seem to be different paths of upward mobility for the lower SES members of each religion. One need not look too far for an historical explanation of the differences we have reported: the American public school system, whatever its present orientations, was surely Protestant in its origins and early history; the Jews, traditionally victims of prejudice, would be inclined to look to the professions as the best way to get ahead despite prejudice, and the Catholics, as latecomers to the economic battles, would find that the business corporation was best suited to their needs. Whether there is anything in each religion which would predispose its members in these directions remains to be seen. It could be argued that the practical bent of rabbinic scholarship would incline the Jews to the professions and the large organizational apparatus of the Catholic Church would orient its members towards the large corporation. Perhaps even the "service" tradition of much of American Protestantism could be linked with primary and secondary education. But such propositions require much more careful investigation.

Protestant Denominations

We now turn to a subject of considerable interest—Protestant denominationalism—to see whether the over-all similarity between Catholics and Protestants is the result of lumping all Protestant denominations together. On the face of it, it should be quite clear that the Protestant denominations have different kinds of membership—even in their college-attending members—and that therefore Catholics will resemble some Protestants more than others.

Our first step (Table 4.10) is to investigate the different social and economic background of the various denominations by use of the SES scale. Catholics and Methodists have about half their members in the upper part of the scale, while Baptists and Lutherans are behind them (36 per cent and 42 per cent respectively) and Episcopalians (81 per cent), Presbyterians (69 per cent) and Congregationalists (67 per cent) are ahead. Thus as far as social class goes, the Catholic graduates are about in the middle.

Despite this socio-economic handicap, Catholics are the most likely of all to go to graduate school and the most likely to choose the arts and science graduate school (Table 4.11). The order of graduate school choice is as follows: Catholics (34 per cent), Episcopalians (31 per cent), Methodists and Presbyterians (29 per cent), Congregationalists (27 per cent), Baptists (26 per cent), and Lutherans (22 per cent). The differences, of course, are not very great, but significantly for our discussion, the Catholics are not inferior.

There are not very many surprises in career choices (Table 4.12). The order for the academic professions is Episcopalians (20 per cent), Congregationalists (19 per cent), Catholics (16 per cent), Methodists (16 per cent), Presbyterians (15 per cent), Lutherans (15 per cent) and Baptists (12 per cent). For the traditional professions the order is Episcopalians (7 per cent), Catholics (6 per cent), Methodists (5 per cent), Baptists and Presbyterians (4 per cent) and Lutherans and Congregationalists (3 per cent). There is no difference in engineering with each group having about 8 per cent in this field. In education, the order is Lutherans (42 per cent), Baptists (37 per cent), Methodists (36 per cent), Presbyterians (33 per cent), Catholics (26 per cent), Episcopalians (24 per cent), and Congregationalists (23 per cent). On the other hand, despite the Protestant Ethic theory, Catholics are far and away the most likely to pick business (23 per cent), followed by Congregationalists (19 per cent), Presbyterians (17 per cent), Baptists (16 per cent), Methodists (14 per cent), Episcopalians (13 per cent), and Lutherans (12 per cent). The control for denomination does not really change the picture very much—Catholics hold their own in the academic professions and the traditional professions, have a strong lead in business and are near the bottom in primary and secondary education.

Nor are there any very unexpected changes in occupational values (Table 4.13). Catholics lead in having the making of money as a value (27 per cent), followed by the Congregationalists (24 per cent), Presbyterians (23 per cent), Episcopalians (21 per cent), Lutherans (20 per cent), Methodists (19 per cent), and Baptists (18 per cent). The Episcopalians take the lead in rating creativity important (64 per cent), the Lutherans and the Congregationalists are next (55 per cent), then the Catholics, Methodists and Presbyterians are bunched around 50 per cent, and finally come the Baptists with 40 per cent. Working with people instead of things is most important to the Lutherans (64 per cent), followed by the Methodists (60 per cent), Presbyterians (58 per cent), Catholics (57 per cent), Congregationalists (55 per cent), Baptists (55 per cent), and Episcopalians (51 per cent). It is clear that Protestant graduates from the various denominations often differ more with each other than they do with Catholics.

By now we should be able to predict the differences that will occur in academic performance (Table 4.14). The Episcopalians, Congregationalists, and Presbyterians will have about three-fifths of their graduates in the upper academic category. The Catholics, Lutherans, and Methodists will be in about the middle (with one-half in the upper group); and the Baptists will be at the bottom with about two-fifths in the upper reaches of the API scale. As in most other measures, Catholics are in the middle when compared with other Protestant groups.

Thus we can summarize our investigation of the various Christian denominations up to this point by saying that even though they are at the middle in socio-economic status and academic performance, Catholics are at the top in graduate school plans and near the top in academic inclinations. They lead in plans for business careers and are near the bottom in plans for careers in primary and secondary education.

However, this conclusion is not yet safe since several Protestant groups have a higher proportion of girls among the graduating seniors and we know that sex can have some effect on the proportion of a group making graduate school and academic career choices. In Table 4.15 we note that while Baptists, Lutherans and Methodists have about the same sex ratio as Catholics (3 to 2), the ratios for Presbyterians, Congregationalists and Episcopalians are somewhat less. Therefore we must determine what happens when graduate school plans, career choice, API, and occupational values for the various religious denominations are controlled for sex.

A control for sex changes the picture of graduate school plans only slightly (Table 4.16). Among the males, the Episcopalians lead (40 per cent), while the Catholics, Presbyterians and Methodists are bunched some 3 per cent behind them. The Baptists, Lutherans, and Congregationalists bring up the rear. The Protestant denominations all send about one-fifth of their girl graduates to graduate school, but the Catholic girls (29 per cent) are actually substantially ahead of most Protestant groups.

Nor does a comparison allowing for different proportions of sexes in the various denominations notably change the picture as far as career plans are concerned. Catholics—male and female—continue to be high on business, low on education, high on the traditional professions and about equal on the academic professions. On the subject of greatest concern in this study—the choice of the academic profession—Catholic males are tied with Episcopalians, Congregationalists, and Lutherans (at 16 per cent), ahead of Baptists, and behind Methodists and Presbyterians. Once again we find no evidence of a Catholic aversion to the academic life.

Only the Presbyterians catch up with the Catholics among the men in their evaluation of the importance of money (Table 4.18), while Catholic girls are more interested in money than are members of other denominations. Catholic males are behind the Episcopalian and Lutheran males in importance placed on creativity but tied with the Methodists and Presbyterians. The same can be said of the girls with the exception of the Congregationalists who take second place among the girls, perhaps because of the small number of cases. Similarly in their valuation of "people, not things," Catholic males and females form a middle group between the Lutherans and Methodists on the one hand and the Baptists, Episcopalians, and Congregationalists on the other.

The comparison of the various denominations is obviously an interesting subject and one to which much more space could be devoted than the present sketchy chapter. However, we must not depart from our central concern of investigating the alleged intellectual deficiencies of the Catholic graduate and his alleged lack of inclination to engage in economic competition. In this chapter, we have established that controls for background characteristics and for religious denomination do not confirm either of these allegations. On most measures, Catholics are more or less in the middle of the Christian denominations, a middle that could easily have been predicted on the basis of what we know of the social and economic history of these denominations.

CHAPTER 5

The Catholic Colleges

IN THE LAST TWO CHAPTERS we established that between Catholics and Protestants and between Jews and Gentiles there were certain differences which survived the battery of controls that the survey questionnaire provided. We also demonstrated that while the differences between Jew and Gentile followed the predictions of previous theory, the differences between Catholic and Protestant —where they existed—tended to run against previous theory. An argument might be advanced against this latter proposition that the influence of Catholic education had not been taken into account. It might be maintained that the effect of secular college education on a good part of the Catholic group had watered down the influence of Catholicism on its members, but that the graduates of Catholic denominational colleges would be different from other Catholics and would respond to the questions of this survey according to theory-based predictions. In this chapter we will examine such an argument and conclude that while there are some social and demographic differences between Catholics in Catholic colleges and Catholics in other colleges, there are very few differences in career plans, occupational values, or intellectual orientations. The hypothesis that Catholics in Catholic colleges will be appreciably different on these items from Catholics graduating from other private or public colleges will be rejected. We will then conclude this chapter by asking whether Catholic high school education has any appreciable effect on the total picture.

Catholic Colleges

Some 53 per cent of those who were raised Catholics graduated from the sixteen Catholic colleges of the sample (Fordham, Boston College, Holy Cross, Xavier of Cincinnati, Merrimac, St. Bonaventure, Detroit, Marquette, De Paul, Notre Dame of Maryland, St. Scholastica, St. Benedict, Briar Cliff, Manhattanville College of the Sacred Heart, Notre Dame, Le Moyne).[1] The proportion is somewhat higher than we might expect, since, according to the best available estimates, only some 45 per cent of the Catholics of elementary and secondary age are in Catholic schools.[2] The reason for the high proportion may well be that it is the more well-to-do Catholics who send their children to Catholic schools, and it is also the more well-to-do Catholics who send their children to college. Those people who are inclined to send their children to non-Catholic schools are simply less inclined to send them to college.

In Table 5.1 we note some confirmation for this possible explanation. There are major and "significant" differences between the Catholics in Catholic colleges and the Catholics who did not go to such schools. The former group is more female (43 per cent as opposed to 31 per cent), more likely to be from a city over 500,000 (48 per cent as opposed to 35 per cent), to be unmarried (81 per cent as opposed to 68 per cent), to have a college-educated father (40 per cent to 26 per cent) and a college-educated mother (37 per cent to 21 per cent), to have a family income over $7,500 (50 per cent as opposed to 42 per cent), and to be in the upper half of the SES measure (57 per cent as opposed to 41 per cent). It is quite clear that economically and demographically those in Catholic colleges are very different from those not in Catholic colleges. It would seem reasonable to conclude that the choice of a non-Catholic college is largely a matter of the class position and quite possibly of the financial resources of the family.

Attitudinal Differences

There are some interesting attitudinal differences. In Table 5.2 we see that Catholics in non-Catholic schools judge themselves to be more liberal (53 per cent to 45 per cent) and less religious (76 per cent to 92 per cent), but no different in their attitudes towards modern art and conventionality. It is worth noting, however, that Catholics in Catholic schools are still more "liberal" than Protestants and Catholics in non-Catholic schools are still more religious than Protestants.

Plans, Performance and Values

There are no "significant" differences (Table 5.3) between Catholics in the two kinds of schools in their academic performance or career plans. Catholics in Catholic schools are slightly more likely to plan graduate school (3 per cent), slightly less likely to plan an academic occupation (15 per cent to 17 per cent), more likely to plan a traditional profession (10 per cent to 6 per cent), less likely to plan engineering (6 per cent to 11 per cent), less likely to plan education (25 per cent to 28 per cent) and more likely to plan business (24 per cent to 23 per cent). However, almost all these differences are so small as to be practically irrelevant. It is quite clear that as far as future career plans go, it does not make much difference whether a Catholic went to a Catholic college or not. Past theory, however, would argue that it should make a difference, since those who went to Catholic colleges were presumably in a less intellectual atmosphere. Perhaps, as we will suggest in the next chapter, there have been some changes in this area.

Comparisons with Other Schools

It might well be wondered where this level of production of potential scholars would place the Catholic college "system" with regard to other schools. Table 5.4 offers some indication as to where the Catholic "system" stands.

There were seven "Ivy" schools, eight other high quality private schools, twelve Midwestern liberal arts colleges and eight Big Ten schools in the survey. In the production of total graduate students and of those specializing in the academic subjects, the Catholic schools were behind the high quality schools (10 per cent for arts and science graduates), behind the Ivy League (6 per cent for arts and science), ahead of the Big Ten (6 per cent for arts and sciences) and ahead of the Mid-western liberal arts schools in total graduate students (4 per cent), but equal to the Midwest in arts and science students.

Father Weigel may well be correct when he says that the American Catholic community does not know what scholarship is, but there does not seem to be any evidence that the graduates of Catholic colleges are any less informed on what scholarship is than anyone else—at least if a tendency to choose a scholarly life is a sign of knowing what scholarship is.

Occupational Values

There are more points in the way of interesting differences in occupational values (Table 5.5) between the two kinds of graduates, though only two of them make it to the level of significance. Those in Catholic colleges are more interested in being helpful to others (5 per cent) and more interested in working with people instead of things, but less interested in being creative (3 per cent), in avoiding high pressure (5 per cent), in working in a world of ideas (5 per cent), in freedom from supervision (9 per cent—a "significant" difference), in slow sure progress (12 per cent and "significant"), and in getting to a new area (6 per cent). On the other values, there are no appreciable differences. One of the significant differences runs against the Protestant Ethic hypotheses and the other is irrelevant to it. The difference on high pressure also runs against this hypothesis. The other differences would suggest that those who went to Catholic colleges are slightly more service-oriented and slightly less intellectually-oriented than those who did not, but these differences are so marginal as to be unimportant in the face of the overwhelming similarity on occupational choice.

School Evaluation

How did the graduates of Catholic colleges rate their schools one year after graduation (Table 5.6)? Catholic males from Catholic colleges were less pleased with the curriculum and the research facilities (20 per cent saying excellent as opposed to 36 per cent with regard to courses and 14 per cent to 37 per cent on research facilities). However, they also were more pleased with the caliber of their fellow students (26 per cent saying excellent as opposed to 16 per cent). There was little difference on classroom teaching, student housing, and caliber of the faculty. Catholic girls in Catholic colleges, on the other hand, were much more satisfied with everything save research facilities at their schools than were the Catholic girl graduates of non-Catholic colleges. The differences in percentage ranking their school as excellent are impressive: 5 per cent on curriculum, 16 per cent on teaching, 9 per cent on student housing, 15 per cent on caliber of fellow students, and a whopping 19 per cent on caliber of faculty. There can be no question about the fact that the girl graduates of Catholic colleges were still very much in love with their schools a year after graduation. My assistant on this part of the analysis, Mr. James Squires, is preparing a paper on this love affair which he somewhat ungraciously refers to as the "Pollyanna Syndrome."

Church Attendance and Apostasy

Certainly one of the major reasons for the founding of a separate

Catholic school system was the fear that the faith of the children of the immigrants would be lost in a non-Catholic educational environment. In the ecumenic age this "ghetto" approach may not be altogether as popular as it once was. Indeed, much better arguments can be advanced for having Catholic schools than the protection of the faith. So the data reported in this section are not to be taken as indicating that there is no point in having Catholic colleges. However, they do suggest that loss of faith or decline in religious practice are not too common among Catholics who did not go to Catholic colleges.

Some 12 per cent of those who were born Catholic and went to non-Catholic colleges were not Catholic at graduation (Table 5.7). We do not know, of course, whether the apostasy was the cause or the effect of the kind of college to which they went, though as we will suggest in a later chapter it would seem that the apostasy syndrome was present before college began. Some 88 per cent of those who went to non-Catholic colleges still considered themselves to be Catholics at the time of graduation.

Now was their church attendance appreciably affected by the experience of going to a non-Catholic college? Of those who were still Catholic at the time of graduation 83 per cent were going to Mass every week or several times a month a year after their graduation (as opposed to a very impressive 96 per cent for the graduates of Catholic colleges). Now this percentage is not all that might be desired, but it is still substantially ahead of the national church attendance figures for Catholics which indicate that about 70 per cent go to Mass weekly or several times a month.[3]

It seems therefore that we can conclude that the axiom of Newman Club chaplains which affirms that the faith of the well-instructed Catholic is not in serious peril on the secular campus is supported by the data discovered in this study. It is obvious that further research into the religious effects of Catholic education is needed.

Life Satisfactions and Worries

In a previous chapter we noted that Catholics were more likely than others to report that religion was a main source of life satisfaction to them. In Table 5.8 we see that this is a Catholic College phenomenon with some one-fifth of the graduates of these colleges listing religion (22 per cent as opposed to 8 per cent at other colleges). All other sources of satisfaction suffer, with even the family being checked by only 57 per cent of the respondents. Indeed, for the Catholic college graduate religion is as important as a career as a source of life satisfaction.

This somewhat unusual finding is tantalizing, but we are unable to say very clearly what it means. It may well represent an effect of Catholic education which is more important than the mere protection of faith. It is possible, though we do not have the data to prove it, that Catholic higher education does make religion more important in the life of those who have received such education (or perhaps they go to Catholic schools because religion is more important to them to begin with). One young lady who was in the June 1961 sample had this comment to make, "That question about life satisfactions really put a lot of us on the spot. How can you expect us to pass over religion? Yet how can we compare religious satisfactions with family satisfactions?" Judging by the response of her fellow Catholic college graduates to this question, many others had the same problem.

There are only a few differences in worries. The graduates of Catholic colleges were less worried about money (though the present financial condition of both groups was about the same), more worried about life goals and less worried about career plans. Once again, these are thin differences (about 10 per cent in each case) on which to build a theory, but one wonders if those who are responsible for Catholic education would be unhappy to realize that their students were less concerned about money and their career plans and more concerned about ultimate problems such as life goals. Would it be too much to suggest that these might be the sort of effects one should expect from religious education?

In this section, we have asked whether Catholics in Catholic colleges are different from Catholics in other colleges. We have found that they are less likely to be male, more likely to be from large cities, more likely to be from a higher social class, less likely to think of themselves as politically liberal, more likely to think of themselves as religious, and less likely to be interested in slow sure progress. There is a slight suggestion that they may be more service-oriented and less intellectually-oriented in their occupational values, but there is no difference in occupational choice or academic performance. They are less likely to leave the Church (though 88 per cent of those in non-Catholic colleges are still Catholics at graduation) and somewhat more likely to go to church every Sunday.

In short, there is no evidence for anti-scientism or anti-intellectualism or anti-economic rationality among the graduates of Catholic colleges.

The Effect of Catholic High Schools

One can push the question of the effect of religious education back one step further and ask whether the kind of high school a graduate went to had any effect on his career plans or occupational values. Some 13 per cent of the Catholics in our subsample went to Catholic high schools but not Catholic colleges (to be called CHO); another 18 per cent went to Catholic colleges only (CCO); 34 per cent went to Catholic high schools and colleges (AC), and 35 per cent went to all non-Catholic schools (ANC). Perhaps we should note that our only indication of the kind of school they attended is their graduation. It is possible that there were some changes before graduation.

Demographic and Social Differences

According to the findings of Table 5.9, of those who went all the way through the Catholic system, less are male than those who went to non-Catholic schools or at least to non-Catholic colleges; they are more urban than those who merely went to Catholic colleges or did not attend Catholic schools (a fact probably related to the availability of Catholic schools). They are also the youngest and the highest on SES, the latter perhaps being explained by the high cost of Catholic education.

Of those who did not attend Catholic schools, more are from small hometowns, older, and lower in SES than the other three, none of which are particularly surprising findings.

Of those who went only to Catholic colleges, less are male, are second youngest, second highest on SES, and tend to be from small hometowns. They probably tend to be the offspring of relatively well-to-do Catholics in areas of the country where there is not any elaborate Catholic school system, and have gone away to a Catholic college in another part of the country.

Of those who went only to Catholic high schools, most are male, tend to be urban, over twenty-three and low on SES. They would seem to fit a pattern of delayed education among upwardly mobile city dwellers.

Four different modal portraits emerge from these data:

All Catholic: Well-to-do, young, big-city boys and girls.

All non-Catholic: Upwardly mobile, older males from smaller hometowns.

Catholic College only: Well-to-do young boys and girls from smaller hometowns.

Catholic High School only: Upwardly mobile older males from big cities.

Clearly not all people in any group fit the profile, but the profile represents the tendency within the group.

Attitudes

The AC group (Table 5.10) is the second most conventional, the least liberal, and the second most loyal to their schools. The ANC group is the most unconventional, second most liberal and the second least loyal to the school. The CCO group are the most conventional, the second least liberal and the most loyal to the school. The CHO group are the second most unconventional, the most liberal and the least loyal to their schools. The Catholic colleges apparently produce a more conservative and conventional Catholic than do the other colleges. Graduates of Catholic colleges also display more loyalty to their schools. The lesser loyalty of Catholics from other colleges may have to do with their being in an unfavorable environment and possibly with their older age.

Course Reactions

In Table 5.11, we have listed two items out of the "course" reaction question to determine whether Catholic high schools, as is often reported, give poor preparation for college in the sciences. There seems to be little evidence for this. Even though, as we will note in the next chapter, Catholics from Catholic colleges are not under-represented in the physical sciences, graduates of Catholic colleges took fewer courses in the physical sciences, mathematics and biology, and were less interested in these fields. There is no evidence of a failure of Catholic high schools to prepare their students for physics, chemistry or mathematics, since graduates of these schools who did not go to Catholic colleges were not at all averse to taking these subjects or in showing interest in them. Only those who went all the way through non-Catholic schools are up to the sample norm in biology. The lower scores of the other groups may be in part attributable to the lack of courses and in part to urban origins. The humanities (as represented by English) apparently receive considerable stress in Catholic colleges.

Graduate School Plans and Future Careers

Those who went to Catholic colleges (Table 5.12) are more inclined to go to graduate school than those who did not, but high school had little influence on their inclinations. Actually there is practically no difference in graduate plans for any of the groups and all are ahead of the Protestant average. Future career choices (Table 5.13) show little variation, with the AC group under-choosing education and over-choosing business, and those who did not go to Catholic colleges over-choosing engineering—probably because there are few Catholic engineering schools. In the matter of occupational values (Table 5.14), slow and sure progress is more important for the upwardly mobile students who did not go to Catholic colleges, as are creativity and ideas. Those who went to Catholic colleges are less concerned over freedom and more concerned over being helpful and working with people. The high schools attended apparently have little impact on this finding which is the same as reported in the last section.

Church Attendance

There is some difference in church attendance for Catholics who (Table 5.15) have had different educational patterns, with 95 per cent of those who went to Catholic high schools and colleges, 93 per cent of those who just went to Catholic colleges, 85 per cent of those who went to Catholic high schools only, and 72 per cent of those who did not go to Catholic schools, going to Mass weekly or several times a month. However, the differences among the four groups are mainly in the per cent who have left the Church with only 1 per cent and 3 per cent having left from the all Catholic or Catholic college groups, and 9 per cent and 18 per cent having left respectively from the Catholic high school only and all non-Catholic categories. Among those who did not go to Catholic schools and are still Catholics, the per cent of those who do not go to Mass regularly is not very different from the other groups. Approximately seven-eights of the all non-Catholic education group who are still Catholics are regular church-goers as are more than nine-tenths of those who went to Catholic high schools only but were still Catholics at graduation from college. The risk of apostasy increases somewhat with secular education but for those who do not apostasize there seems to be little diminution of church attendance. Thus one can say that those who have not gone to Catholic schools are more likely to apostasize and less likely to go to church regularly than those who have had Catholic education, but that the differences in church attendance are not especially impressive. Over 70 per cent of those who were born Catholic and attended neither Catholic high school nor Catholic colleges are still Catholics and going to weekly Mass. It should be noted that this is higher than the national average of mass attendance for Catholics. One would be hard put to argue on the basis of these data that secular education is causing serious harm to the religious practice of Catholics, especially since some of those who did not attend Catholic schools probably were not seriously practicing Catholics before their secondary and higher education began.

However, there still seems to be one notable effect of Catholic education that deserves more investigation. We noted in a preceding section that the graduates of Catholic colleges were much more likely to see religion as a source of life satisfaction and to be more concerned about life goals than about a career and finances. In Tables 5.16 and 5.17 we can see that this is a Catholic college phenomenon. It does not seem to make any difference what kind of high school the student went to. Catholics who went to Catholic high schools and not Catholic colleges are indistinguishable from Catholics who did not go to Catholic schools. One is tempted to suggest that if this very indirect indicator of religious concern and interest does measure an important dimension, then Catholic colleges would seem to be more effective than Catholic high schools. However, such a suggestion must be very tentative indeed until much further research is done.

The pattern of secondary and higher education which Catholics follow seems to be connected with their socio-economic position, their age, their sex, and the size of their hometown. Youth and high SES, female sex, and large hometown make for Catholic education. Older age, low SES, male sex and small home-town make for non-Catholic education. Catholic education tends to make for loyalty, conservatism, and religiosity in self-description. There are few differences in career or graduate plans. Catholic colleges make for service orientations and less intellectual orientations (though to a small extent). There are apparently fewer science courses taken in Catholic colleges, but no evidence of faulty science preparation in Catholic high schools (though obviously the data on this are very indirect).

Even though there are some striking social and demographic differences between Catholics who went to Catholic schools and Catholics who did not, there is little evidence of major difference in career plans or occupational values. Apostasy is somewhat higher in non-Catholic schools, though apparently the kind of college attended is not of decisive importance in religious practice.

There is little evidence in this chapter to indicate that Catholic colleges are any more anti-intellectual than other American colleges which Catholics attend. In the next chapter, we will examine the Catholic graduate student in greater detail to see if any evidence has been missed.

NOTES

1. Whenever this list of Catholic colleges is presented, someone is sure to cry out, "but those aren't typical Catholic schools." Well, it is hard to say what the typical schools would be. However, these are the schools which were selected according to the design of the probability sample. The larger schools had a better chance of being selected since the purpose of the design was to select a sample of students and not of schools and there are more students in larger schools. For further details of the sample design the reader is referred to the appendix describing it.

2. This estimate is based on preliminary data from a study being done by NORC for the University of Notre Dame Catholic School Study Project.

3. For a discussion of Church attendance figures, see A. M. Greeley,

"Some Data on the Present Condition of American Catholics," *Social Order* (April, 1963), and Bernard Lazarewitz, "Some Factors Associated with Variations in Church Attendance," *Social Forces* (May, 1961). Lazarewitz concludes that about 89 per cent of Catholics with college education go to weekly mass, a figure which is in substantial agreement with those reported here.

CHAPTER 6

The Catholic "Scholar"

PERHAPS the most startling finding yet given in this report is the apparent interest of Catholic college graduates of June 1961 in scholarly pursuits, contrary to all expectations of previous theory. In this chapter we will study this finding in greater detail. We will propose that our findings represent a social change which has occurred since the findings on which past theory has been based. To defend this hypothesis we will consider four counter hypotheses:

1. Catholics were interested in scholarship in years gone by, but past studies did not recognize this interest.

2. The Catholic interest in scholarship is limited to the humanities and perhaps the social sciences, but does not represent a new interest on the part of Catholics in the most scientific of sciences —the physical sciences.

3. Catholics are definitely going to graduate school, but will not use their graduate training for scientific or scholarly purposes.

4. Catholics, indeed, are becoming scholars, but to the extent they are becoming scholars they are also becoming "less Catholic."

In a concluding section of this chapter we will describe an in-

teresting process which seems to be going on at Catholic colleges
(and indeed all denominational colleges) and which affords a
partial explanation of the method of the social change we have apparently uncovered.

The Hypothesis of Social Change

Thus far we have found that Catholics are more likely to go
to graduate school than Protestants; and of those going to graduate school, a higher proportion of Catholics are going into the
"arts and sciences" than of the other religious groups. Nor are
Catholic colleges inferior in either of these respects. What explanations are available for this dramatic difference? The most
likely one, it seems to the present writer, is social change. The
Knapp studies, as well as earlier ones which are quoted in much
of the current literature, are anywhere from one to four decades
old; they reflect a situation which once existed but does not
any longer. At one time in their history in this country Catholics
were not interested in scholarship; that time is past. Young Catholics are going into the scholarly life in great numbers; they have
not yet reached the pinnacles of fame and success in their fields
because the change is recent; but in a few more decades a rep-
lication of the Knapp studies or the examination of the catalogues of scientists and scholars will find Catholics (including
those from Catholic colleges) in their proper proportion.

If this hypothesis is valid, it is perhaps the most important
finding of our study because it represents a dramatic reversal of
long-standing social trends. However, before we can assume that
the hypothesis is sound, we must consider several possible counter
hypotheses.

The Counter Hypotheses

The first such hypothesis would be that our findings do not
represent a dramatic social change but rather a long-standing con-

dition which simply has not been recognized before. Such an explanation is more than just a logical possibility since we have no earlier study of a comparable group of college graduates. All the evidence on which the present state of the discussion rests comes from studies of people who are already scientists or scholars. It might be argued that large numbers of Catholics always went into the scholary fields in the past but never became great in their work and hence did not find their way into the lists of the famous. At best, such an explanation seems highly improbable although our evidence against it is more impressionistic than anything else. One might merely ask what happened to all these Catholic scientists and scholars? Where did they vanish to? Certainly the Catholic educational system would not have been able to absorb them all. Nor does it seem very likely that the business world is peopled by Catholics who were frustrated in the academic occupations. While it is highly likely that the great scholars and scientists emerge only from a climate created by large numbers of journeymen in the academic trade, there is no evidence which indicates that these large numbers of Catholic journeymen have been laboring invisible to all around for the last quarter of a century. If there was an earlier generation of Catholic scholars, one might ask, where are they now? Where have they been hiding?

Unless strong evidence to the contrary is adduced, there seems to be no way to demolish the word of researchers like Knapp.

Confirmation for the idea that few Catholics went to graduate school in past decades can be found in a study done by Defferari in 1931.[1] In a study of 25,719 graduate students at fourteen universities, Defferari found that only 7.2 per cent were Catholic. This compares with 25 per cent in the 1957 study of Davis.[2]

To say that the interest of Catholics in the life of academia is new is not to imply that it is brand-new. We have no idea of exactly when this trend might have started. My own hunch, which must be investigated further in other research, is that the trend did not exist in the thirties and probably was well under way in the early fifties. With this view, we might assume that the Second World War and the G.I. Bill represent the turning of the tide.

Another possible explanation is that while Catholics are indeed going into the arts and sciences in larger numbers than before, most of the interest is in the humanities, where there is a strong Catholic tradition, and not in the physical sciences. Even though a table in an earlier chapter demonstrated that Catholics were more likely to go into the physical sciences than Protestants, the numbers were small enough to leave room for doubt. Therefore, a special deck of IBM cards was prepared to test this finding further; the deck represented all those in the total sample who planned to go to graduate school in the fall of 1961 in the arts and sciences. Table 6.1 shows the distribution of the religious groups in this deck. The only significant difference is between Protestants and Jews in the biological sciences.

There is virtually no difference between Protestants, Catholics and Jews in their choice of the physical sciences. Catholics are a bit behind Protestants and a bit ahead of Jews in the choice of biology. Jews are slightly ahead of both groups in the choice of social sciences, and Catholics ahead of the others in the choice of humanities. However, and this finding is extremely important, there is not a great deal of difference in the distribution of any religious group in the broad graduate field categories. There is surely no indication that Catholics are inclined to reject the physical sciences.

In Table 6.2, we present a breakdown of all the graduate fields taken from the final report of the NORC survey. The fields that Catholics over-chose are Chemistry, Biochemistry, Economics, Political Science, English, Languages, Business, and Law, while they under-chose the "other" Physical Sciences, Geology, Geography, Biology, Botany, Zoology, the Fine Arts, and the "other" Social Sciences. In crucial fields (for the purposes of this study) Catholics are represented in their proper portion (25 per cent) in Physics, Mathematics, Physiology, Sociology and History. Perhaps the restless spirit of Galileo will be at last put to rest in all sociology text books.

Nor is there any sign that interest in physical sciences is weak in the Catholic colleges (Table 6.3). The basic differences are that Catholics in Catholic colleges over-chose humanities and under-chose the biological sciences (about 9 per cent each way). Thus if there is a deficiency in the Catholic colleges, it is in training graduates who will go into the biological sciences. (Though one might argue that there is a superiority in training in the humanities.) In any case, the difference in these two fields among Catholic graduate students is almost entirely a Catholic college phenomenon, the only distinctive such phenomenon (besides the low apostasy rate) to be discovered in this study.

The next question to ask is whether the Catholics who are going to graduate school are really interested in scholarly careers, or whether they are more interested in teaching, or other kinds of work. The graduates were asked what kind of activities would constitute major concerns for their career. In Table 6.4 we note that there is no difference in the choice of activities between Protestants and Catholics. Catholics are just as likely to plan research careers as Protestants, though neither is as likely to as are Jews. However, it should be noted that Jews tended to check more activities than did the other groups. In any case some three-fifths of the Catholics going to academic graduate schools plan careers which will involve research as a major activity.

There is a slight decline from the 60 per cent (3 points) for those in Catholic colleges, but this change is so small as to be "insignificant" and not especially important. Almost three-fifths of those going to graduate school from the Catholic colleges plan research careers.

We might wonder whether this production of potential Ph.D.'s represents a change from the situation reported by Knapp and his associates a decade ago. Some of the schools in the Knapp sample were also in the NORC sample; a comparison between the two revealed that there were seven Catholic schools which were in both samples (and 67 other schools). Table 6.6 shows the relative change in position for Catholic schools from the earlier study to the present one.

We can see that in this very crude rank order of students going into the academic life, five Catholic schools improved their position in the last decade—one held the same position and one slipped. Obviously, the two lists are not strictly comparable because the Knapp rank order is based on productivity of Ph.D.'s while the NORC order is based on productivity of students planning careers in the arts and sciences. The NORC students have a long way to go before they get their Ph.D.'s. However, the two orders tend to confirm our suggestion of a definite change within the Catholic college system.

In view of the almost universal assumption that there is a conflict between Catholicism in America and intellectual pursuits, another objection might be raised. It might be argued that there is indeed a new interest in science and scholarship among Catholics, but it exists precisely insofar as the people involved drift away from the Church. They can be good scientists, it is alleged, only to the degree that they are not attached to the Church. Thus what may be going on is not an intellectual awakening but the beginning of a massive apostasy. However, there is no sign of this happening among the June 1961 graduates (Table 6.7). The Catholic apostasy rate does increase among scholars but by a meagre 2 per cent, while it increases 16 per cent among Protestants and 11 per cent among Jews. News about the conflict between science and religion has apparently not gotten through to the Catholic graduates. There is an increase in irregular Church attendance among Catholic "scholars" (about 10 per cent). However, more than four-fifths of the Catholics who were planning arts and science graduate school and who had not left the Church were going to Mass regularly the year after their graduation from college.

In short, there is not much evidence that the large number

of Catholics going into academic graduate schools represents a long-standing situation, nor that it represents a notable over-choice of the humanities at the expense of the physical and social sciences, nor that it has led to a substantial apostasy from the faith. Thus we can argue that our hypothesis of social change receives a fair amount of support, though we are still too much in the middle of things to make definite conclusions. It is beyond question that Catholics are going into the academic areas and into scholarship (research) in much larger numbers than previous writing or data would lead us to believe. But neither the *terminus a quo* nor the *terminus ad quem* of the presumed change are clearly established. We do not know for certain that large numbers of Catholics did not plan to go to graduate school in the arts and sciences a generation ago, although such a possibility does not seem too probable. Nor do we know how many of the young 1961 graduate students will become competent scholars, much less great scholars. Many an event can intervene between the first year of graduate school and the Ph.D., and many more can intervene between the Ph. D. and scholarly competence, and yet many, many more can intervene between competence and greatness. Investigation of the *terminus a quo* would require a careful historical study of whatever data are available on the graduate school plans of Catholics during the last half century. Proof for the *terminus ad quem* still lies in the dim mists of the future. Follow-up studies on the 431 survey may provide some hints. In any case, the data provided in this chapter do not offer any support to the hypotheses that (1) Catholics are not going into the academic fields, (2) they are not going because of the influence of their religion, and (3) those deviants who do go are likely to drift away from the Church.

Scholarship and Social Mobility

Who are these potential Catholic scholars? Do they represent a social class different from the main body of the Catholic population? Catholic scholars are somewhat more likely to come from the upper occupational brackets than are other Catholic graduates. However, the difference is not great and the fact that there is a greater upward change for Protestant scholars and an actual decline for Jewish scholars from the upper class score of the total graduate population would apparently indicate that the increase of Catholic interest in scholarship, if indeed there is one, does not flow merely from the fact that Catholics are more successful in the business and professional world than they were generations ago. It is true that the greatest number of Catholic scholars come from the upper class occupations, but then so do the greatest number of college graduates of any religion. If a group does not have a large number of professionals and proprietors, it will not have a large number of college graduates and if it does not have a large number of graduates, it will not have a large number of graduate students. Thus Catholic upward mobility is certainly one of the remote reasons for the presumed change. However, middle and lower class Catholic graduates are also going into scholarly pursuits in almost their proportion in the graduate population, so that something else besides upward mobility must be at work. (Our own highly speculative hypothesis is that two factors are at work—the fury of internal self-criticism and the waning of the immigrant-minority group trauma. Only when a group feels secure in a country can it turn its interests to scholarship. Or perhaps more accurately we might guess that after a group has proven itself financially and politically, it must then turn to proving itself intellectually.)

Factulty Pressure at Denominational Colleges:
  A Partial Explanation

In view of the general impression that the gifted Catholic college graduate is oriented towards the professions rather than the arts and sciences, we begin to wonder if, in response to the self-criticism and in a quest for "excellence," faculties at Catholic colleges were beginning to put pressure on their more gifted students to begin graduate studies in the arts and sciences. One would expect that these colleges, spurred on by the taunts of the self-critics, would be eager to acquire some of the status symbols which are reckoned to be important in the influential sections of the academic groves. Hence it might be argued that there would be special efforts within the Catholic colleges to turn out as many Ph.D.'s as possible and that therefore faculties would encourage their students to consider the advantages of an academic career. Since there was a question in the survey about faculty influence on the respondent's career plans, it is possible to make some tentative probings to learn whether such mechanisms are really at work. Our first probe turned up no evidence; Catholic graduate students reported no more faculty influence than graduate students from other colleges. However, on second thought it occurred to us that the faculties would be interested not in sending just anybody to graduate school but rather in sending their more promising students into the academic life. The students were therefore divided academically into the upper fifth and the lower four-fifths. When faculty influence was investigated along these lines, a very surprising phenomenon emerged (Table 6.9). The gifted students from the Catholic colleges who were going to arts and science graduate school reported more faculty influence than the less gifted students who had chosen the same career, while the exact opposite was true of the students from other colleges. The influence "weight" among graduate study planners in the Catholic schools is with the higher achievers and in the other schools the "weight" is with the lower achievers.

Professor James A. Davis has suggested an interesting explanation for this phenomenon: In schools unworried by the status problems of the transition process, the faculty is more concerned with giving advice to the less gifted students on the premise that these are the ones who are in most need of assistance and that the gifted students can take care of themselves. On the other hand, in the schools in the transition process towards full-fledged acceptance in the American academic system, the desire for prestige will lead the faculty to send its most promising protégés into the "big leagues" of graduate school training (Table 6.10).

It should be noted that this is *not* a private school phenomenon. Indeed, if the respondents who are not in Catholic colleges are divided into private and public college categories, the influence pattern at the public schools is more likely to resemble that of the Catholic colleges than is the pattern of the non-Catholic private schools. Furthermore, the pattern existing at Catholic colleges also seems to be present at the small Protestant denominational colleges in the survey (Table 6.11). One might argue that the influence pattern is a function of the religious atmosphere of a college, although such an explanation does not exclude the "transition status search" explanation, since virtually all the small Protestant denominational colleges in the study might be assumed to be as eager for the status conferred by Ph.D. alumni as the Catholic colleges are.

There is a considerable amount of discussion today as to whether colleges really recruit for graduate school or merely channel people who had graduate school inclinations before they came to college. It is beyond the purpose of the present study to engage in discussion of this general question. However, a series of fairly complex probings (Tables 6.12 and 6.13) into the NORC materials strongly suggests that faculty influence at the Catholic colleges is indeed recruiting for the academic life gifted students who did not come to college with such an orientation and that this recruiting effort is more successful than in the "average" college (as determined by the sample mean).

Little evidence was found in the NORC survey of 1961 college graduates to support the notion that the graduates of Catholic colleges are less "intellectual" than the average college graduate (and we should note here that the Catholic graduates of non-Catholic colleges were not very different from their co-religionists in Catholic colleges on the indicators we have discussed). Graduates of the Catholic schools were no less likely to go to graduate school, to choose the arts and sciences for their careers, to specialize in physical sciences or to plan a career of research. They were more inclined to be loyal to their schools and to see the purpose of education as "intellectual." There was no evidence that the apparently new-found interest in scholarship was creating any religious problems; whether this absence of conflict between science and religion was the result of the problem having been resolved in the minds of the potential scholars or the compartmentalization of their lives is a question beyond the scope of the present work.

In this chapter we have advanced two theories, neither of which have been completely confirmed, but both of which find some support in the data at hand. (1) The large number of Catholics going to graduate school in the arts and sciences represent a dramatic social change which in its turn represents a milestone in the acculturation of a minority group. (2) One of the mechanisms that has produced this change is the pressure on brighter Catholic students in Catholic colleges to go to graduate school in the arts and sciences, a pressure which also exists at other religious colleges for reasons that are parallel but not the same. In defending the first theory, we established that in all likelihood the studies on which previous theory was based were accurate, that there are no significant differences in scholarly fields chosen by Catholics and by members of the other two religions, that there is no significant disinclination of Catholics to use their graduate training for scholarly purposes—at least when compared with Protestants—and that there is little tendency for the Catholic potential scholar to drift away from his religion. We admitted that the mere quantity of graduate students did not indicate the quality of future scholarship, but affirmed that in the absence of quantity, quality seemed improbable and that in any event time alone would tell whether the Catholic graduate students would produce some outstanding scholars. We could find no social or economic explanation for the presumed social change and were forced to hypothesize a "turning point" in the acculturation process at which an immigrant group began to desire to "prove itself" in intellectual matters.

We discovered a mechanism which might be part of that desire for intellectual respectability. Faculties at Catholic colleges apparently put more pressure on their bright students to go to graduate school, while exactly the reverse was true of other colleges. However, we also found the same mechanism at work at other denominational colleges and suggested that, for somewhat different reasons, a desire for intellectual respectability—as represented by a high productivity of graduate students—was also at work at these schools.

Alumni with Ph.D.'s are important status symbols for a school system in transition as it tries to move into the restricted central precincts of the Groves of Academe. One suspects that competition for future Nobel Prize winners will grow more acute and that the Catholic colleges are in the game to stay.

NOTES

1. Roy J. Defferari, "Catholics and Scholarship," *The Commonweal,* June 4, 1931, quoted in Christ and Sherry, *op. cit.,* p. 95.

2. James A. Davis, *Stipends and Spouses* (Chicago: University of Chicago Press, 1962).

CHAPTER 7

Ethnicity, Social Class
and Career Plans

THE MAJOR DISCOVERY of this volume is that American Catholics are much more likely to be going to graduate school and planning arts and science careers than had been previously thought. As was indicated in the last chapter, this inclination to graduate school and to the academic life apparently represents a major social change. Although the materials used in this study are not suited to provide the kind of explanation that would be desirable, there seems to be some reason to suspect that this change is connected with the Americanization and the improved economic condition of the various Catholic ethnic groups. In this chapter we will investigate the plans and values of the four major Catholic ethnic groups among the June 1961 graduates and suggest that there are several complex processes occurring which offer some explanation of social change, but which require more detailed study. We will also offer a tentative explanation for the apparent declining Jewish interest in the academic life.

It seems reasonable to assume that before a group can produce graduate students it must first produce a substantial number of college graduates; further we might assume that there is a connection between family income and propensity to send young people to college. We might also suspect that even controlling for income, the college-going propensity may vary among ethnic groups because of the differential European background of the groups. Hence it could be argued that the lack of Catholic scholars in the past was related both to poverty and to ethnic background, and that even the elimination of poverty would not of itself lead to a situation where Catholics were producing their share of graduate students because of the tardiness of some of the ethnic groups in adjusting to the American attitude toward higher education. In an NORC study [1] done in 1957 of graduate students in the arts and sciences, it was discovered that Catholic students of Irish or German background were more likely to report that they took going to college for granted when they were in high school than were students of Polish or Italian background. The former were more likely also to have a higher estimate of their own abilities (Table 7.1). These differences persisted even under a control for family economic background. There is therefore some indirect evidence which would lead us to speculate that the current interest among Catholics in graduate schooling and in the academic life is due to the changing attitudes of the more recent immigrant groups as they become more fully assimilated into American culture.

Such a speculation would be confirmed if we could establish that the older groups were still more likely to send their children to college and hence to graduate school than the newer ones, even under a control for SES background. Unfortunately such a confirmation is not possible because, even though we know the nationality and SES of the June 1961 graduates, we do not have a very clear idea of the proportion of the ethnic groups in the general population nor of their distribution on SES indicators. There is some reason to suspect that the Poles and the Italians are still under-represented in the Catholic graduates with 28 per cent of the graduates having an Irish background, 20 per cent German, 13 per cent Italian and 9 per cent Polish.

Because of the lack of information on the total population, we are forced to hunt for clues in this analysis in the behavior of those who have in fact graduated from college. To simplify the procedure only males were studied and only those whose mother and father were of the same nationality (the total sample was used rather than the 10 per cent subsample).[2]

The first important point to be noted [3] (Table 7.2) is that the Irish and Italian graduates were considerably more likely to plan to go to graduate school in the autumn after their graduation than were the Germans or the Poles. Upper-income Irish and Italians were between 10 and 20 percentage points more likely to go than comparable groups from the German and Polish groups, with almost one half of the former groups planning immediate graduate school as opposed to about one third of the latter. Even though we have some reason to suspect that the Irish and the German Catholics are more likely to go to college, it would seem that among the college graduates the Irish and the Italians are the ones who are more likely to go to graduate school.

When we look at the career plans of the ethnic groups by SES [4] background, however, we see an interesting change in the picture (Table 7.3). It is precisely the Germans and the Poles who are most likely to plan arts and science careers, especially if they are upper SES; 21 per cent of the upper SES German males and 28 per cent of the Poles in the same group plan arts and science careers, as opposed to 13 per cent of the Irish and 12 per cent of the Italian. For the Poles and Germans this represents a nine per cent increase over their lower class compatriots, while for the Irish a four per cent decline and for the Italians an eleven per cent decline. What seems to be happening is that Poles and Germans from upper SES families are not nearly so attracted to law and medicine (10 per cent and 12 per cent respectively) as are Irish and Italians with the same background (26 per cent and 21 per cent respectively). Thus among the former groups the academic professions have more appeal to upper SES males and among the latter the free professions have more appeal. Among the lower class groups, the Poles seem especially interested in education, engineering and academic careers (with about one fifth of their total interested in each); the Italians over-choose arts and sciences and education in comparison with the Irish and the Germans; and the Germans are the most eager to be engineers (more than one forth planning such a career)—an inclination they share with their upper SES compatriots. Even though business is popular with all lower SES groups, it is the most popular with the Irish of whom two-fifths plan such a career.

It seems quite clear that there are very different patterns of occupational choice among the various ethnic groups within American Catholicism, even when controlling for financial background and even among college graduates. It seems very safe to assume that ethnicity is still a factor of major importance in American society and that social researchers can no longer ignore its operation.

There is a seeming paradox in the preceding paragraphs which must be explained: the Irish and the Italians are less likely to plan arts and science careers but more likely to plan graduate school, while the Germans and the Poles are more likely to plan arts and science careers but less likely to plan graduate school. The explanation underlines a very interesting phenomenon. In the upper SES groups (Table 7.4) the lead of the Germans and Poles in academic career plans is *not* reflected in any lead in plans to attend arts and science graduate schools in the coming autumn. Hence, the lead apparently consists mostly of male graduates who plan to continue their graduate studies at a later date. Those Irish and Italians who do plan academic careers are much more likely to actually begin the preparation of their careers in the coming autumn. On the other hand the lead of the Irish and Italians in plans for the free professions *is* reflected in plans to attend professional graduate school in the following autumn (the graduate school percentage for professionals in Table 7.4 is somewhat higher than the percentage planning free professional careers for each group because this school percentage also includes those going to graduate school in business administration). Thus, despite the over-choice of the academic life by the Poles and Germans, they actually lag behind the other two groups in immediate graduate plans because future academicians of Polish and German background are inclined to defer the beginning of their education, while the opposite does not seem to be true of the Irish and Italians who have contributed to their groups' over-choice of the free professions. The motivations behind this intriguing phenomenon are obscure, though they are probably intimately connected with the original career choices of the high SES members of the various Catholic ethnic groups.

Thus we might suggest that the increase in arts and science careers among American Catholics may well be related to the financial improvement of the German and Polish groups, an increase which is only in part offset by the decline of interest in such careers among Italians.

And on the other hand, the surprisingly large proportion of Catholic males who planned graduate school in the autumn after graduation is probably related to the increase in popularity of the free professions among upper class Irish and Italians, an increase whose impact on graduate school attendance is not completely offset by the tendency of Germans and Poles to delay the continuation of their academic-career preparation. The various balances at work in this complicated system may well be such that if the ethnic composition of the Catholic graduate population remained unchanged, there would be little variation in the proportion of arts and science careers or graduate students in years to come. Since it seems reasonable to suppose that both the Italian and Polish groups are under-represented, however, the increase in the proportion of these groups in college graduation classes in years to come will lead to a further improvement in Catholic orientation to higher study with the former raising the percentage level of professionals and the latter the level of academicians. All of this supposes, of course, that the patterns here reported continue to operate.

It is worth noting that we are not altogether prepared for the curious combination of groups. A similarity between Irish and Germans who were among the earlier arrivals would not have been surprising, but the similarity between Irish and Italians in career plans is unexpected. The need for further study of American ethnic groups seems quite clear.

Are the different patterns of career plans reflected in different occupational values? One is forced to reply that at least as far as the values are measured by the scale of occupational values in the present study (Table 7.5), the reflection is quite obscure. The Italians, especially the upper class Italians, seem to value money more than the Irish and the Germans, while the Poles value it somewhat less. This could be related to the choice of academia by the Poles and the free professions by the Italians, but there is then no explanation on this value scale for the behavior of the Irish and the Germans. Upper class Germans and Italians value creativity more than do the other groups, while upper class Poles, despite their academic plans, value it least. On the other "academic" value ("living and working in a world of ideas") the lower class Germans score highest and the lower class Poles the lowest; however, the Italians are close enough to the Germans so that the distinction between the two groups is not very strong even though they have very different inclinations toward the academic life. Thus in the distribution of percentages on values which correlate with academic career choice there is no clear pattern which might explain the choices of the various ethnic groups. The avoidance of high pressure is more important to the lower class of each ethnic group except for the Poles where it is slightly more important for the upper SES group. The desire for slow, sure progress is also a Polish trait with a full half of the upper SES Poles checking this item and two-fifths of the lower SES group. The Polish and German pattern of the upper SES group being more concerned about slow, sure progress is reversed among the Italians, where it is the lower group that has this concern. There is perhaps some connection between the desire for slow, sure progress and the tendency to turn away from the free professions.

There may also be a relation between the high scores of Italians and Irish upper SES males on "leadership" and their choice of the free professions, as well as between such choice and their high scores on "helpfulness" and "opportunity to work with people." To sum up, there seems to be a reflection on occupational values of the professional choice of upper SES Irish and Italians and some slight reflection of the upper SES German inclination to academia. There is, however, little explanation for the Polish interest in academia (unless it is viewed as a place for slow, sure progress) and little explanation of the Italian disinterest in academia (in the higher SES group) unless it be connected with their overvaluation of money. One is forced to suggest the possibility that the various ethnic groups may well see different values in the same career choices.

It is somewhat more easy to explain, by way of parenthesis, the decline of Jewish interest in academic life among upper SES Jews which was noted in an earlier chapter. An index of academic inclination was compiled from five values previously known to correlate either positively or negatively with academic career plans. Three values correlating positively were "opportunities to be original and creative," "opportunities to help others or to be useful to society," and "living and working in a world of ideas"; the negative values were "making a lot of money" and "chance to exercise leadership." Each Jewish respondent was scored on a scale from -2 to $+3$ points with a point being given for each positive value and a point subtracted for each negative value. Those scoring $+3$ or $+2$ were rated high on academic orientation, those scoring $+1$ were rated medium and the rest rated low. When the male Jews in the total sample (Table 7.6) were trichotomized on this scale, the differences in academic career choice between upper and lower income groups disappeared among "highs" and "lows" but not among the "mediums" in the academic orientation scale. Thus we can suggest that among male Jewish graduates social class produces a modification of occupational values which is in some fashion connected with a decline of Jewish inclination to academic careers. It should be noted that this decline merely brings the upper SES Jews to the same level of academic contributions as Gentiles, 17 per cent of the graduates choosing such a career among upper class Jews and among Gentiles in both upper and lower class. This 17 per cent represents a decline from 25 per cent among lower SES Jews.

The data reported in the last paragraph (and in this whole chapter) are obviously cross sectional; one cannot argue that they represent an historical process. It does not follow necessarily that the process of upward mobility has led American Jews to adopt attitudes toward the academic life which are similar to those of Gentiles. There is at least some suggestion in the data under consideration, however, that this might be the case. Under such circumstances it would be reasonable to assume that while in the future Jews will contribute academicians in their proportion in the general population, the years of over-contribution are coming to an end as the lower class base of this over-contribution is eroded. Whether a Jewish scholar will write *American Jewish Dilemma: An Inquiry into the Intellectual Life* remains to be seen.

This chapter has labored under one of the major restrictions that faces secondary analysis—the materials are simply not such as to give a clear answer to the questions asked. We are in a position to say that the new interest of Catholics in higher education is clearly connected with the "Americanization" of the various ethnic groups, a process which involves among other things an improvement in income and a change in values. We further observed that Irish and German Catholics are more likely to go to college while Irish and Italian Catholics are more likely to go to graduate school immediately and Polish and German Catholics are more likely to plan academic careers. The paradox involved in this finding is apparently connected with the tendency of the Polish and German graduates who plan an academic career to delay the beginning of their professional training. There did not seem to be a clear connection between social background and occupational values, which would explain the changes in the Catholic ethnic groups as neatly as the relative decline in academic interest among upper-status Jews could be explained. The final answers to the questions raised in this chapter must await a study designed specifically to investigate the operation of the ethnic factor in American society.

In this chapter we have reported findings on the career plans and interests of the various Catholic ethnic groups among the graduate population. One has the impression that some nationality groups, because of their historical background, are likely to put more emphasis on certain activities than other groups. It would seem that church-going is one area that is stressed by some groups more than by others. It would also seem reasonable to suppose that men are less likely than women to go to church frequently.[5]

Among the college graduates (Table 7.7) at least, the Irish Catholics are the most likely to report weekly church-going in all sex and income categories with some nine-tenths of the Irish in all groups so reporting. Nor is there much variation across sex (Table 7.8) or income lines. The Germans are the next most likely as a group with income having no effect on the weekly church practices of German men (some 89 per cent of them claiming to go every week); however, a more interesting fact is to be noted among German women. Upper SES women are more likely than men to go to church every week (94 per cent), but lower SES women are less likely to do so (81 per cent); there is no obvious explanation for this finding.

For the Poles there is little variation across income lines, but considerable variation across sex lines with four-fifths of the Polish men and nine-tenths of the Polish women reporting weekly Mass attendance. Among the Italians, however, there are differences across both SES and sex lines with about two-thirds of low SES Italian males going to church every week, approximately three-fourths of the high SES men and low SES women claiming weekly Mass attendance, and 86 per ment of the upper SES women reporting regular church-going.

Thus the Irish are the most likely to go to church and the least likely to be affected by sex or social class. The Germans are next most likely with the only variation occurring among upper SES females. The Poles are third in order with little income variation but some variation because of sex, and finally, the Italian propensity to go to church is affected by both income and sex.

It ought to be noted that all of the groups reported in this chapter are more likely to go to church than the average American Catholic—with the single exception of the low income Italian male; the national average as reported now in several studies is approximately 70 per cent. Thus it would appear that college education as well as an increase in income generally lead to an increase in church attendance, though both these factors probably operate differently among different ethnic groups.

NOTES

1. This study was reported in James A. Davis' *Stipends and Spouses* (Chicago: University of Chicago Press, 1962). I am grateful to Professor Davis for making the materials from this study available to me for re-analysis.

2. A control for generation (number of grandparents born in America) was used originally in this analysis, but produces little in the way of modification of the findings reported in this chapter. John Thomas has suggested to me that the important factor in determining change within ethnic groups is not the length of time a family has been in America, but the mobility it has experienced during these years. Our data confirm this suggestion.

3. The frequencies in Tables 7.2 to 7.4 are not in the same proportion as mentioned in the previous paragraph, since the percentages in the previous paragraph are based on father's ethnicity and the respondents analyzed in the rest of this chapter had parents from the same ethnic background. Of those in the sample, 55 per cent with Irish mothers had Irish fathers, 48 per cent of those with German mothers had German fathers, 70 per cent of those with Italian mothers had Italian fathers, and 71 per cent of those with Polish mothers had Polish fathers. In a future study of American ethnic groups it will be important to study the groups of mixed parentage also. In this chapter, however, they are excluded for simplicity and because none of

the mixed groups were sufficiently large to permit reliable analysis, especially when a control for parental income was introduced.

4. In this chapter the measure of SES is the income break at $7,500.

5. For a summary of the available data on church attendance among American Catholics see Andrew M. Greeley, "Some Information on the Present Situation of American Catholics," *Social Order* (April, 1963).

CHAPTER 8

Religious Changers in College

IN THE PRECEDING CHAPTER, we brought to a close our examination of the influence of the "religious factor" on the performance
and aspirations of June 1961 college graduates. We turn now to
a consideration of what might be called the "non-religious factor"
—religious change and religious apostasy. Justification for including this chapter comes from the fact that a study of religious
change will enable us to make a critical examination of certain
aspects of the Herberg-Lenski concept of the religious group as
a kind of super-ethnic group, a semi-*gemeineschaft* relationship
existing half way between the family and the state. If membership
in the religious community is an important means of social location
and an important communication network for the acquiring of
norms relevant to a wide range of activities, then religious change
should be relatively rare and should occur especially among those
people who already feel themselves alienated in some sense from
society. In an extremely interesting paper, Zelan [1] has suggested
a further conclusion; many of those who leave all organized religion will feel the need of finding a new religion or quasi-religion
of their own.

Four elements will make up this chapter. In the first section we will consider the fact of religious change and give apostasy and conversion rates for the five religious groups (including "others" and "nones"). In the second section, we will examine certain hypotheses (based largely on Zelan's work) about apostasy; then we will try to ascertain whether certain colleges are the cause of apostasy. Finally, we will turn to a consideration of the apostates from Catholicism and the converts to Catholicism, both because of our special interest in the Catholic group and because Catholicism is the only religion which makes a substantial amount of converts.

The Fact of Apostasy and Conversion

Some 14 per cent of the June 1961 seniors no longer consider themselves members of the religious group in which they were raised, 5 per cent had joined another group and 9 per cent had no religious preference. One is at something of a loss to say whether this is a high rate of religious change or not. The figure 14 per cent could be preceded by "only" or "as many as," depending on which side of the argument one chooses to place oneself. My own feeling is that considering the *détente* between modern science and religion, the non-religiousness of the current intellectual milieux, the large-scale apostasy of a good part of the European student class, and the unquestioned secularism of much of the American university atmosphere, a 14 per cent apostasy rate is rather small. No matter which side one chooses in the argument, it is at least interesting that in a religiously pluralistic society with no legal constraints on religious shifts, 86 per cent of the college graduates are still in the religious group in which they were raised. The ties which hold a person in his religious group still seem reasonably strong.

In Table 8.1 we see the apostasy and conversion rate for all five groups. Nine per cent of the Catholics, 15 per cent of the Protestants, 16 per cent of the Jews, 33 per cent of the "others," and 34 per cent of the "none" change their religion. Relatively few of the changers are converts to another religion. The largest absolute number of converts is the 49 Protestants (2 per cent of the total) who have become Catholics. The largest percentage of changes to another religion is from the "nones," 24 per cent of whom have become Protestants, and from the "others," 13 per cent of whom have become Protestants. The 56 converts to Catholicism meant that Catholics suffered the lowest net loss (2 per cent).

It seems reasonable to assume that the process of a change to another religion is somewhat different from the abandonment of all religions.

Zelan's Hypotheses

Let us now consider four hypotheses derived from the already cited work on apostasy of Joseph Zelan:

1. Apostasy is more likely to occur among graduates of high quality schools.

2. It is more likely to occur among lower class Jews and upper class Catholics.

3. It is likely to be correlated with alienation. (We will use two rather unsatisfactory measures of alienation—not being married and self-description.)

4. Apostates are likely to acquire a substitute "religion" of liberal intellectualism.

It seems true enough that the high quality schools (Table 8.2) are places not only of apostasy but of conversion. Apostates and converts are approximately twice as likely to come from the "A" quality schools as are other students (15 per cent for apostates, 11 per cent for the converts). It should be noted that this does not necessarily mean that these quality schools are either the cause or the occasion of religious change. It is arguable whether or not the elite colleges attract those whose religious ties are already weakening, if not actually destroyed, because they feel that it is at these schools that their problems can be resolved. We will return to this question in a later paragraph.

However, there does not seem to be much connection between social class (as measured by income over $7,500) and religious change (Table 8.3). There is practically no difference in the rates for the three major groups above or below the dividing line. Lower class is no safeguard from change, nor is upper class (at least as indicated by income) any cause of change.

On the other hand, there is strong confirmation for the suggestion that apostates are in some sense alienated people. Whether their apostasy cuts them off from their fellows or whether the personality traits that lead to apostasy also lead to the breaking of other ties is not clear. But apostates are much less likely to be married (Table 8.4) and more likely to describe themselves in somewhat morbid and alienated terms (Table 8.5). Thirty-eight per cent of the graduating seniors are married, but only 30 per cent of the apostates are married while 44 per cent of the converts are married. Perhaps the converts have by their conversion sufficiently adjusted their problems, so that they are eager to enter into closer relationships. Or, and what is more likely, the marriage situation is one of those decision-making points in life where a religious choice is likely to be made. Thus, one would not be more likely to be married because one was a convert, but one would be more likely to be a convert because one was married.

When it comes to self-description, apostates are much more likely to take a dim and gloomy view of their own personality than are other students, while converts usually are somewhere between the apostates and the others (although perhaps with a convert's zeal, they think of themselves as more idealistic than either group). The self-description of the apostates is that of an alienated man if there ever was one—less ambitious, less fun-loving, less cooperative, less easy-going, less good-looking, less happy, more lazy, more moody, less obliging, less poised, more rebellious. We would like to be able to probe more deeply into the social psychology of the apostate and the convert, but our data do not permit this. We must content ourselves with saying that, even though our indicators are very crude, the suggestion of a correlation between apostasy and alienation seems to be extremely plausible.

There is also some evidence in Tables 8.5 and 8.6 that apostates do turn to a religion of liberal intellectualism. They think of themselves as liberal and as intellectual to a greater extent than others in the graduating class. They are also more likely to plan a career in college teaching and research, to be more interested in creativity, ideas, and freedom in their jobs and less interested in dealing with people and helping others. They have done well academically (29 per cent in the upper fifth) and are planning to go to graduate school in large numbers (41 per cent), especially in the arts and sciences (28 per cent or more than twice as many as the sample proportion). Whether liberal intellectualism has indeed become a substitute religion, whether academia has become a new religion, is not absolutely clear, but the trends of the data are certainly suggestive.

Two questions can be asked: 1. Is intellectualism most common precisely for those who are alienated? 2. Do the most alienated ones also prove the most intellectual? If one argues that leaving a religion is a more alienation-producing experience for some people than for others, then it would follow that the need for a functional substitute is most pressing among these people. If we use "intellectual" as a self-description of intellectualism and the failure to describe oneself as "happy" as a proof of alienation, then we would argue that it would be precisely among the alienated (not happy) apostates that intellectualism increases. Table 8.7A confirms this hunch. Among the non-apostates, there is no difference between the "happy" and the "non-happy" in their inclination to describe themselves as "intellectual." But among the apostates, the non-happy are much more likely than the happy to describe themselves as "intellectual." (The same phenomenon occurs with regard to self-description as "liberal.") The numbers are small and the indicators are crude, but the findings were as predicted.

To probe the matter more deeply, we might argue that the apostates who are most likely to turn to liberal intellectualism would be those who had left the most behind in giving up their original religion. The person who had the most difficulty leaving a religion would be the one in most need of a functional substitute. We could further argue that those who had the most difficulty would be those who came from a group where apostasy was least likely to happen. Thus we would predict that the increase in alienation would be the greatest for the Catholic apostates; and that among the Catholic apostates, we would have the highest percentage increase in the self-rating as "intellectual." Actually this is what has occurred. The greatest difference in percentage of those not rating themselves as "happy" (38 per cent) occurs among the Catholic apostates, as does the greatest increase in percentage of those rating themselves as intellectuals (28 per cent). Among the Jews, there is the least increase in both categories (7 per cent decline in "happy" and 14 per cent increase in "intellectual"). We might argue then that it is easier for the Jews to leave their original religion, and that the need for a functional alternative is less pressing in their case.

One could conclude therefore that apostasy happens among all groups, though less among Catholics, but that it is not a major phenomenon. It seems connected with alienation and often leads to a "functional substitute" religion of liberal political outlook, intellectual values, and academic career. This new "religion" is especially popular with those for whom the alienation was most severe.

Selective Recruitment or Structural Effect

The key question we wish to consider in this chapter is the extent to which the schools are responsible for the religious change, either as a cause or at least as a provider of a substitute religion. Our first inquiry will be whether there is any connection between the religious atmosphere of the school and the apostasy rate. Each of the 119 schools was given a score on a religiosity scale depending on what percentage of the graduating seniors considered themselves to be religious. Thirty-three schools had a score of less than 50; 21 of these schools were in the class A or B (i.e., over 50) on the quality scale (only two schools—both women's colleges—in the A and B categories were over 50 on the religiosity index). Only six of the schools were not in the first or second strata of productivity of graduate students. The group could be described as being composed mainly of Eastern high prestige schools and Western state universities. The apostasy rates at high religiosity schools are 8 per cent, while such rates at low religiosity schools are 17 per cent. The apostasy rate is therefore twice as high at the low religiosity schools. The Catholic colleges were omitted from the following analysis.

Are these low religiosity schools responsible for the higher apostasy rate? In his *Great Aspirations* Davis suggests that the "pipe line theory" of college talent is most in accord with the facts. The prestige colleges do not take average students and turn them into scholars, but rather take bright students who are already oriented towards graduate study and merely confirm them in this previous plan. Might the same explanation be used of the inclination to desert one's family religion? Hence two theories might be applied to explain the influence of schools on religious change. The non-religious colleges may be having a structural effect on their students or they may be selectively recruiting them. To put it in another way, either the colleges are promoting (albeit perhaps unintentionally) apostasy or they are recruiting (with equal lack of intention) students who are already fairly well along the way towards apostasy. To be able to resolve this conflict with certainty, we would have to know something about the religious practice of the students before they came to college. However, there is a method which might give us some hint of whether college has actually produced a change in religious attitudes.

If apostasy is occurring in college and if an intellectual career is becoming a substitute for the lost faith, we would then expect that at the "apostasy" colleges, there would be a notable turnover from freshmen non-academic plans to senior academic plans for those who had left their religion. Thus we would predict that apostates in high apostasy colleges would be more likely to change their freshman plans and plan to attend arts and science graduate schools than non-apostates in these colleges and than apostates in low apostasy colleges. However (Table 8.9A), this phenomenon does not in fact occur; actually more changes take place at the *low* apostasy schools than at the high *even among the apostates*. In fact (Table 8.9B), there is some evidence for the contrary hypothesis. Apostates at both kinds of colleges were more likely to come as freshmen with arts and science careers in mind and to persist in such plans. However, there is no structural effect on the part of the high apostasy schools.

Apostates were much less likely to have "no-go" freshman plans, no matter what kind of school they went to. If a high arts and science graduate school orientation correlates with apostasy and if this orientation existed in the apostates when they came to col-ˈlege, it seems very unlikely that we can argue that the apostasy is the result of college influence. The formal break may indeed have occurred in college, but it seems highly probable that the personality constellations which seem to correlate with apostasy, as well as the alienation which seems to be closely connected with it, actually existed in the student before he came to college and that he chose the college he did because it would, among other things, provide an atmosphere in which he could work out his conflicts. In any case the data in this study provide no evidence that apostasy can be attributed to the colleges—even to the colleges where the atmosphere of religiosity is low.

In the final section of this chapter we will focus briefly on the question of changers to and from Catholicism. In the total weighted sample (1962 version) there were some 1031 apostates from Catholicism and 706 converts to Catholicism, which probably represents the largest number of such changers ever available for analysis. Since only indirect information can be obtained about the causes of conversion and apostasy, one must be content with reporting what social and demographic factors correlate with religious change and what ones do not.

There is also some question as to what comparison groups ought to be used in this analysis. Presumably both converts and apostates ought to be compared with the group whence they were most likely to come. Hence the apostates should be compared to the born Catholics and the converts to the born Protestants, since most of the converts to Catholicism were Protestants (Table 8.10). It is interesting to note that four-fifths of the converts were former Protestants and two-thirds of the apostates have no new religion.

First of all, we ought to note that there is no relationship between ✓ religious change (in or out of Catholicism) and academic performance or the various SES measures such as parental income, occupation and education. However, it is clear (Table 8.11) that both converts and apostates are more likely to be older and to be planning marriage than the non-changers. It is not too difficult to see that marriage is one of those crucial points in the life of a person where he must make up his mind as to his religious orientation and that of the family he is beginning. Hence oné may leave an old church and join a new one on the occasion of marriage. However, it is not at all clear why religious change should correlate with age. Two possible explanations could be offered. We might argue that it is age which increases the likelihood of apostasy and that since age also increases the possibility of marriage, it is natural that married people would be more inclined to be apostates. In such an argument age is the "cause" of apostasy and marriage the intervening variable. Or we might offer the reverse argument that marriage is the "cause" and that since married people are older, then apostates are going to be older too. In Table 8.12A we see that the first hypothesis is not supported. Within age classes apostates and converts are still more likely to be married than the groups from which they came. However, the matter is not so clear when we compare the age of the four groups within marital status categories (Table 8.12B). Converts and born Protestants are about the same age in each marital category, so it seems safe to say that there is no relation between age and religious change for this group; the independent variable is clearly marital status. For the apostates, however, the picture is different. Apostates are older than born Catholics in each marital status category. Thus age and marital status seem to be joint independent variables contributing to apostasy from Catholicism. These two factors seem to contribute about equally to apostasy. The correlation between age and apostasy with a control for marital status is .36, while the correlation between marriage and apostasy with a control for age is .33 (using Q coefficients).

The phenomenon reported in the last paragraph ought not to be too surprising since most of the apostates are people who have left one religion and have not joined another. Both age and marriage could be seen as contributing to such a change: age, because the exposure to the possibility of apostasy increases with age, and marriage, because it is a crucial point in the life cycle. However, converts not only leave an old religion but join a new one. It would seem reasonable to suppose that the passage of time, while it might increase a Protestant's tendency to leave his own religion, would hardly be likely to have much effect on his inclination to become a Catholic unless he found himself in a situation where he was going to marry a Catholic. Thus conversion correlates with marriage only while apostasy correlates both with marriage and with age.

Two other demographic factors correlate with religious change. Apostates are more likely to be male (71 per cent) than are born Catholics (60 per cent) and converts are more likely to be Negro (12 per cent) than are born Protestants (4 per cent). Thus the loss of the Church is proportionately greater among males than among females and the gain is proportionately greater among Negroes than among whites.

Does ethnic background have any connection with religious change? There is no such correlation among converts who are not greatly different on ethnicity than the American Protestant population (Table 8.13). There is a correlation, however, for apostasy, but it is a negative one; the Irish are less likely to be among the apostates than among the born Catholics. However, this 8 per cent difference does not correspond to any major contribution to apostasy by any other group.

There is only one correlation between religious change and hometown size. Apostates are more likely to be from cities over a half million and less likely to be from hometowns under 100,000 than are born Catholics (Table 8.14). Apostates are also less likely (by 8 per cent) to be from the North Eastern part of the country and from the North Central (6 per cent), but more likely to be from the West (by 10 per cent) than the born Catholics (Table 8.15). Conversion is more likely to be found among Protestants from the West and less likely among those from the South (Table 8.15). Proportionate Catholic losses are concentrated in the West but so are proportionate Catholic gains.

Conversion to Catholicism is then positively related to being married, to being a Negro and to being from the West. One might wonder whether religious conversion, connected as it seems to be with marriage, is an effective process from the viewpoint of the Church. There is food for thought in the fact that only 54 per cent of the converts to Catholicism report weekly church attendance— an average more than 30 per cent lower than that of the born Catholics. In Table 8.16 we see a very interesting sidelight in the conversion process which suggests that it is very closely connected with marriage. Seventy-eight per cent of those converts who are planning marriage in the coming fall are regular church-goers as opposed to 50 per cent of those who are married and 46 per cent of those who are single. We can thus suggest that the decline taking place in the change from engagement to marriage is related to marriage conversions which lack depth; however, this explanation does not account for the even lower rate of practice among those who are neither married nor planning marriage. It might be suggested that the convert, who is probably not used to the frequent church attendance demanded of Catholics, is more likely to go to church consistently when he (or she) has the good example of a fiancé (or fiancée). The single person lacks such example, while the married person appears less interested in following the example of his spouse. Thus a 50 per cent church attendance is the norm for the convert group and only the status of engagement furnishes motivation to increase the group's level to 75 per cent.

The typical convert to Catholicism is thus a Protestant who may well have entered the Church at the time of marriage and who is less likely to be a consistently practicing Catholic than those who were born in the Church. He is also more likely to be a Negro and from the West than is the born Protestant. The typical apostate, on the other hand, is more likely to be older and married (with both factors contributing equally), to be from a large city and from the West, and to be non-Irish, than is the born Catholic; he is also not inclined to be practicing any religion.

In this chapter we have noted that apostasy and conversion in college are relatively rare—in fact, surprisingly rare considering the relatively open nature of American society. We have also shown that there is a definite relationship between apostasy and an inclination to the academic life and have the suggestion that the causality seems to run from the former toward the latter, with intellectualism providing a substitute religion for the "alienated" apostate. There was little evidence that colleges caused apostasy, but it appeared that they were occasions where those who were inclined toward apostasy could find a functional substitute for religion and that some colleges were the occasion of more apostasy largely because of selective recruiting of people already oriented in this direction. Finally we noted that marriage and race were the most important factors contributing to conversion to Catholicism and that marriage and age were the most important factors contributing to apostasy from the Church. The religious practice of the converts was less than might be desired and the apostates had not yet joined any other church.

NOTES

1. Joseph Zelan, "Correlates of Religious Apostasy," unpublished MS, National Opinion Research Center, 1960.

CHAPTER 9

Religion and Society

IN THE PAST CHAPTERS we have reported a number of facts about the influence of religion on the career plans of college graduates, facts which were often at variance with what theory would have predicted. It is now time to indulge in some speculation of our own in an attempt to draw the facts together in some kind of coherent system.

At least three different theories could be used to describe the relationship between religion as a subcultural system [1] and society. In what we might call a simplified "Weberian" theory, religion influences the personality of its members and the members in their turn, acting under the influence of their religious values, influence the organization of the social system.[2] The second theory, which might trace its origin to the positivist followers of Marx or the functionalist disciples of Durkheim, would view the influence as flowing in the opposite direction: the social system would create certain "need dispositions" in the personalities of its participants, which "need dispositions" would in their turn lead to certain kinds of religious activity and belief. In the first theory religion is the independent variable; in the second it becomes an "epiphenomenon"—a dependent variable.

A third theory would view religion as neither necessarily an independent variable nor necessarily a dependent variable; rather it would see religion as a "correlate," as a "predictor" variable which is perhaps independent and perhaps dependent; but whose precise causal influence must be determined in each correlation and not as a matter of general principle. In this view, a person's religion could influence his personality organization which in turn would influence the role he plays in the social system. On the other hand, the role he plays in the social system could shape the value system he espouses (or that his children will espouse) and in turn affect the religious belief he professes. In such a theory, the relationship between culture, personality, and society are recognized to be so complex—especially when the factor of the past history of the culture or the society is introduced—that the sociologist is extremely hesitant to generalize about the direction of causality. His more immediate concern is prediction.

There is little reason to doubt that religion is a useful predictor variable in a study of American society. Differences in family values,[3] political attitudes,[4] and economic orientations [5] have been reported for the three major religious groups. Lenski found that in his survey religion was at least as efficient a predictor as social class. Two recent fertility studies found that religion was by far the most important predictor of family size.

However, not too much thought has been given to the question as to what there is in a religious group which causes differences across a range of dependent variables. Lenski defines a religion "as a system of beliefs about the nature of the forces ultimately shaping man's destiny and the practices associated therewith, shared by members of a group." [6] He views the religious group as a "network of informal, primary type relations" which constitute "segregated communications networks limited to the adherent of the same faith (and) facilitating the development and transmission of distinctive political and economic norms." [7] He insists that the norms which are communicated are not merely the result of the socio-economic condition of the religious group but also "reflect the exposure of past generations of believers to the social environments of other eras";[8] religions are "carriers of complex subcultures relevant to almost all phases of human existence" and "products of the social heritage of the group."[9]

Lenski's theory is certainly a useful contribution to the sociology of religion, and his proofs that religious variation cannot be dismissed merely as the result of the operation of current economic and social forces are quite convincing. However, at least one question remains to be answered: to what extent are the formal creed, code, and cult of a given religion responsible for the variations observed among members of the different groups? Are religious differences the result of the theology and the morality of a religion or are they the result of the social experiences of the group which are, in turn, the result of historical "accidents"? In some instances, the answers seem rather obvious: the connection between Catholic family morality and the Catholic birth rate seems obvious enough —especially when we learn that frequency of church attendance is correlated with family size. In other instances the answer is by no means so clear. Is the Jewish inclination to professional careers caused by any article of Jewish belief, or rather by the historical and cultural experiences of the Jewish group which indeed happened to a religious group but in no sense flowed from their religious creed? In other words, to what extent are the religious differences reported in so many studies the result of theology and to what extent are they the result of social history which has no direct connection with theology?

The writer was not convinced when entering this study and is now even less convinced that many of the differences which correlate with religion are specifically religious. (This feeling may result from the professional cynicism of the religious functionary who tends to feel that members of at least one church do their best to prevent their religious ideology from interfering with their daily lives.) Nothing in Lenski's volume or this work excludes the possibility of the explanation by socio-historical experience. Indeed, as we shall see, there is some slight confirmatory evidence for this latter explanation in the data we are analyzing. Some differences are obviously specifically religious; others seem to demand another explanation.

We might note that the explanation of Catholic and Jewish voting for Democrats, whereby the latter are viewed as the party of the minority group, would fit this socio-cultural experience theory.[10] A recent article by Scott Greer [11] on suburban Catholic voting patterns tends to confirm the notion that there are other social explanations, besides the rather gross measures of social class, for the Catholic allegiance to the Democratic party and that no specifically religious element need be introduced.

Some Explorations

There are no easy or short-cut methods for investigating these problems—especially with a body of data that was gathered for vastly different purposes. However a few tentative probings are possible. In the course of this book, we reported certain traits that correlated with religion (Table 9.1)—Catholics planned to work for large corporations; Jews valued creativity as an occupational value; Protestants were interested in elementary and secondary education. It might be asked whether these "religious" differences result from the religious creed, code, and cult of the group or from the group's historical experience. If it was a truly "ecclesiastical" difference, then the more devout one was in one's religion, the more likely one would be to possess the trait. Therefore, if we control for either self-description as "religious," we should find that, for example, the more Protestant one might be, the more likely one might be politically conservative. Obviously such measures are crude indeed, but they may give us some hints.

The first step then is to measure these traits against one's self-description as religious.

Denominational Traits

At least 31 traits are available for analysis (Table 9.1)—9

Protestant, 7 Catholic, and 15 Jewish. Each trait correlates with religion and maintains the correlation even when social, economic, and personality factors are controlled. In most instances the trait represents one group differing from the other two—for example, Jews scoring high on the choice of self-employment as opposed to the other groups. In some cases all three groups differ among themselves—thus, each group has a different score on graduate school plans.

The members of the three religious groups (Table 9.2) were divided into three categories according to their religiosity. Catholics and Protestants were separated into the very religious, the fairly religious; and the not religious. Since the distribution of the Jews on the scale was different and since the Jewish subsample was much smaller, a different division was necessary: the religious, the non-religious, and the "nones." (The last group were those who were raised Jews but no longer consider themselves Jewish in religion.) Such a division is not altogether at variance with theory because, as both Lenski and Glazer point out, the non-practicing Jews are still Jews, although the same could hardly be said of apostate Catholics or Protestants.

Table 9.2 presents data to test the hypothesis that the religious traits vary with religiosity. For a trait to be accepted as religious, it would be necessary for it to vary directly with religiosity for the group which scores high on it and not to vary with religiosity for the other groups (or at least to such a great extent).

Only in a very few instances is the hypothesis upheld. Only four traits—all of them Protestant—seem to be religiously correlated in the sense of the hypothesis. It can be said that education as a career, elementary education as an expected employment, drive, and the desire to help others are Protestant traits in some sense of the word.[12] A high score on the drive scale would fit the Protestant Ethic theory nicely. Social service and the helping of others is certainly part of the tradition of American Protestantism, though somewhat at variance with the strict "sola fide" doctrine. One might even fit the inclination to education, especially elementary education, into the Protestant tradition of service, all the more so since to a large extent the American public education system grew out of the Protestant "social improvement" impulse.

Control for Church Attendance

If church attendance is used as a measure of religiosity instead of self-description, the picture does not change very much (Table 9.3). The only Protestant traits which correlate with church attendance are the choice of an educational career and helping others as an occupational value. With virtually all the Jewish traits there is a negative correlation; those going irregularly to synagogue (less than two or three times a year) are more likely to score high on Jewish traits. One Catholic trait does have a positive association with weekly Mass attendance—business as a future career, but the association is not especially strong. There is no religious connection between Catholic church attendance and work for a large corporation.

The complete absence of religious correlation for Jewish and Catholic traits is surprising. Two possible explanations might be offered. First of all, the religiosity index might be worthless for these two groups. Certainly this is a possibility not to be rejected, particularly in view of Lenski's finding that the various component elements which he defined in religiosity do not correlate. However, it is worth noting that in the Lenski study there were few consistent correlation patterns for any of the religiosity indices with the exception of Catholic family values. While we cannot say with certainty that there is no correlation between religious involvement and the supposedly religious traits, we can say that we have some suggestive evidence for this conclusion—especially since there is at least persuasive data to support an alternative explanation of the differences between members of the various religious groups.

The second explanation is that traits are the result of the sociocultural experiences the various groups have had during their history. Stated more specifically, such an hypothesis would maintain that the deviations of Catholics and Jews from the American Protestant mode can be explained by the differential experiences the two groups had in the immigration and assimilation experience —the Jews as members of a highly developed middle class transplanted to a middle class culture, the Catholics as remnants of a peasant "folk" society transplanted into the midst of urban industrialism. In other words, there would be, in this hypothesis, nothing specific in Jewish doctrine or moral practice which would make the Jews more interested in earning money, but much in the two millennia of Jewish cultural experience would make this exceedingly reasonable. Nor would there be anything in the Catholic creed, code, or cult which would incline Catholics to work for large corporations more often than Protestants, but there might be much in the history of a group arriving at the threshold of economic and social success at this moment in America's history which would incline the group to regard the large company as an important means of upward mobility.

We would certainly hold with Lenski that religious groups are primary groups which form segregated communication networks limited to the adherents of the same faith and facilitating the development and transmission of distinctive political and economic norms, or, alternatively, distinctive role images. We would merely affirm that these differences do not flow from religious ideology but from cultural experience.

The Social Marginality Hypotheses

How could such an hypothesis be tested? There are no questions in our interview schedule which would perfectly fit our requirements. However, there are certain procedures which might give us "a hint of explanation." To the extent that one is physically isolated from the members of one's religious "communication network," there is some possibility that the norms the network carries would not come through so clearly. Thus, we might suggest that Protestants, Catholics, and Jews who are socially marginal to their religious groups might score less high on the religious traits than do their brothers. If you simply do not live in an area where there are, for example, very many Catholics or Jews, it might be much less likely that you will absorb the norms of your socio-religious community. The reason is not that you are a poorer Catholic or Jew religiously, but that you are, physically speaking, living on the margin of the Jewish or Catholic community.[13]

Therefore, we would expect, in this hypothesis, that Catholics from rural or small hometown background and Jews living in medium-sized cities (there were no rural or small-city Jews in the subsample) would decline in their respective religious traits, while Protestants in the same area would not decline in these traits or at least would not decline so much. The test was, therefore, applied to 25 per cent of the Catholics (N = 206) who live on farms or in towns under 50,000 and to the 23 per cent of the Jews (N = 61) who live in cities under 500,000. Table 9.4 presents the results.

In the first part of the table, dealing with Catholic traits, the first column shows the percentage for the "social-marginal" (small-town) Catholics and the second column gives the percentage for all the Catholics in the subsample. The third and fourth columns present comparable figures for Protestants. The fifth column is the "difference between the differences." Thus, the Catholic average on the first item is 33 per cent and the marginal Catholic score is 24 per cent for a difference of 9 per cent; the Protestant average is 28 per cent and the small-town Protestant average is 24 per cent for a difference of 4 per cent. The Protestant score declines 4 per cent, the Catholic score declines 9 per cent; the difference between the two declines is 5 per cent which is the number found in the fifth column.

In the second part of the table, the first column shows the percentage for Jews in medium cities (cities between 100,000 and 500,000)—the presumable social-marginal Jews. The second column reports on the large-city Jews. The third and fourth columns give the comparable Protestant data.

To establish the hypothesis, the figure in the first column must be lower than that in the second, while the figure in the third must not be lower than that in the fourth or not as much lower as the first is in relation to the second. Thus, in the first item, the first column is lower than the second, but the third is also lower than the fourth. However, the decrease is less sharp in the latter case so that the net difference is plus 5 per cent, and the hypothesis is supported.

In six of the eight Catholic traits and in twelve out of the sixteen Jewish traits, the predicted result occurs. In four of the Catholic traits and seven of the Jewish traits, the net difference is (difference between minority group scores minus difference between majority group scores) five or more percentage points. The other six cases are close, some of them very close indeed. The main burden of our argument, however, rests not so much on specific point differences on individual traits, but on the rather overwhelming *direction* of the data in favor of the hypothesis. The proof that these norms have something to do with the socially transmitted historical tradition is not absolutely conclusive, but the data are persuasive.

Thus, our social but not religious marginality hypothesis is dependent on two assumptions: (1) that the religiosity indicator we use is a valid measure of religious involvement, and (2) that the convergence of the scores in Table 9.4 in the direction of the hypothesis indicates that the Catholics and the Jews who live in areas where presumably there are few Catholics or Jews will be less likely to share certain distinctively Catholic or Jewish norms.

Some Speculations

If one might venture for a moment into the realm of speculation, it could be suggested that virtually all the traits listed in Tables 9.2 and 9.4 could be attributed to the past social history of the two groups as filtered through the immigration experience. What would happen, for example, to a Catholic group which had a "middle class tradition" like that which Glazer attributes to the Jews? Or what would happen to a Jewish group whose tradition had been that of peasant farmers? Would Armenian or Lebanese Catholics, for example, have scores in this survey more like Jews or like the main sample of Catholics? Where would some of the Asiatic Jewish groups who are migrating to Israel fit into the picture? What would come from a study of the various Orthodox Christian groups which have migrated to America? Their ideology, one would take it, is probably more like the Catholic than the Protestant or Jewish creeds. Would it be possible that the Ukranian Orthodox, for example, would have scores not dissimilar from that of the Polish Catholics, while the Greek Orthodox, coming from a tradition of mercantilism at least as old as that of the Jews, might have scores close to the Jewish scores? Even within the Catholic group there are possibilities that might be explored. Did the Irish, because of their command of the language, have an advantage in the struggle to become middle class Americans over, let us say, the Poles? Is it possible that the score of the Irish group on our indicators might be closer to that of the Jews? Is it possible that, even with the grosser social and economic variables controlled, those from an Irish cultural background might be more likely to go into self-employment than those from a Polish or Italian background? Would cross-cultural research show us that in some countries the occupational values of the three religious groups are arranged in different constellations?

It is time to call the preceding orgy of speculation to an end. The avenues of research suggested in the last paragraph would not be easy ones on which to journey. The precise meaning of ethnicity is by no means clear. One has the feeling that for all the books written on the assimilation—or acculturation, if you will—of the immigrant groups, we still know very little about the process, either about where it started, or where it has come to, or how it got there. One also has the disturbing feeling that with each passing year the task of unraveling all the twisted threads will grow more difficult. Indeed, one might be forgiven for suggesting that if sociologists do not soon put aside the outmoded melting pot assumption and return to the study of what is *happening* to the ethnic groups, then what may well be the most significant sociological experience that has gone on in America—or indeed anywhere anytime—will be forever beyond our comprehension.

In this chapter we have attempted to offer some explanation of the origins of traits that were specific to the three religious groups of June 1961 college graduates. We found that the traits did not vary directly with religiosity but did decrease among those members of the given group who existed on the social margins of the group. This led us to suggest that the religious groups are indeed communication networks which provide their members with norms and role images, but that these norms and images do not necessarily flow from religious ideology; in some instances, at least, they may rather be the result of the past cultural experience of the group which had no direct connection with the theology (official or popular) of the group. We then pointed out that all the existing differences between the minority religious groups and the main body of American college graduates could be explained in terms of the differential effects of the immigration experience on the Jewish and Catholic groups. We concluded by offering some possible methods of investigating this hypothesis.

If, of its very nature, this chapter is far from satisfactory to anyone, the non-sociologist will view it as unintelligible hair-splitting of the kind in which the medieval scholastics were wont to engage. The professional sociologist will be horrified by the crudity of the indices used. To protect ourselves from mayhem, perhaps we should insist once again that the analysis is extremely tentative. However, the justification for this kind of "stabbing in the dark" is strong: we are asking what a religious group is from the sociological viewpoint. We are suggesting that such a group is much more than a body of the faithful who profess a certain doctrine, worship with a certain cult, and adhere to a certain moral code.

It is also a community which has had certain historical experiences, a kind of super-ethnic group which transmits not only religious and quasi-religious values but all kinds of other values and inclinations which are not religious in the strict sense of the word and are in some cases opposed to the doctrinal values of the group. We are suggesting that all religious groups are a mixture of "elite" elements of value (the official religion) and "folk" elements (the historical accretion). We even go so far as to suggest that the past "anti-intellectualism" of American Catholics is a folk element which is now vanishing as American Catholics go through the socio-historical process of suburbanization and entry into the upper middle class.

NOTES

1. In a pluralist society, a religion would be described as a subculture both because a given religion involves only a certain number of people and because it involves only certain parts of the value system of its members.

2. Obviously such a model represents considerable simplification of Weber's complex, and at times difficult, thought on the subject.

3. Cf. Ronald Freedman, Pascal K. Whelpton, and Arthur A. Campbell, *Family Planning, Sterility, and Population Growth* (New York: McGraw-Hill, 1959); and Charles Westhoff, Robert Potter, Philip Sagi, and Elliot Mishler, *Family Growth in Metropolitan America* (Princeton: Princeton University Press, 1961).

4. Cf. Paul Lazarsfeld, Bernard Berelson, and Hazel Gaudet, *The People's Choice* (New York: Duell, Sloan, and Pearce, 1944); and Bernard Berelson, Paul Lazarsfeld and William N. McPhee, *Voting* (Chicago: University of Chicago Press, 1954).

5. Gerhard Lenski, *The Religious Factor* (New York: Doubleday, 1961).

6. *Ibid.*, p. 298.

7. *Ibid.*, p. 301.

8. *Ibid.*, p. 311.

9. *Ibid.*, p. 311.

10. Bernard Berelson, Paul Lazarsfeld and William N. McPhee, *Voting* (Chicago: University of Chicago Press, 1954).

11. Scott Greer, "Catholic Voters and the Democratic Party," *Public Opinion Quarterly* (Winter, 1961), pp. 611-26.

12. However, the other two religious groups also vary directly on these items, so that we cannot say with confidence that the effect results from Protestantism since the variation may be merely the result of religiosity as such and as Protestant religiosity. By the strictest standards, there are no traits that are religious in the sense that they vary directly only for one religious group.

13. Partial confirmation of this hypothesis comes from the studies on religious mixed marriages which seem to increase according to the social marginality of a member of a religious group with relation to his group. Cf. A. M. Greeley, "Religious Segregation in a Suburb" (unpublished M.A. thesis, University of Chicago, 1961), and Rudolph K. Hairle, "A Survey of the Literature on Religicus Intermarriage" (unpublished M.A. thesis, University of Chicago, 1961).

CHAPTER *10*

Conclusion

THE UNDERLYING SUBJECT of this book has been cultural accommodation. We have been asking in effect whether American Catholics can go through the process of higher education, share the values of the American intellectual tradition and still remain faithful members of the Church. All the evidence presented suggests that they can, even if they do not attend Catholic colleges. The occupational values and career plans of the Catholic graduate are not such that one could argue that Catholicism inhibits his interest in economic activity nor his intellectual curiosity. The Catholic graduate comes from similar economic, social and demographic backgrounds as the average American, and there is no evidence that he comes from a group less likely to send its young people to college. The Catholic parity with the average American in inclination to the intellectual life holds up under a vast variety of controls. Male Catholics from large cities with an upper SES background are no less inclined to the choice of an academic career than is anyone else.

Nor have we been able to find any evidence that Catholics do not plan to get a Ph.D., nor to continue in graduate school, nor to use their academic training in research careers. Finally there does

137

not seem to be any Catholic fear of the physical sciences nor appreciable apostasy from the faith among those planning to be scholars.

The impact of Catholic education seems to be in the area of church attendance (though the impact is not as great as might have been expected) and in the development of certain life values, though the colleges seem to contribute more to the formation of these values than do the Catholic high schools. There was nothing to substantiate the hypothesis that the graduates of Catholic colleges had different career plans or occupational values than did the graduates of other colleges, and hence, no evidence for the alleged inferiority of Catholic colleges—when compared with the American norm instead of with the elite schools, as they so often are. Indeed, there was some evidence to lead us to suspect that the faculties at the Catholic schools were making special efforts to channel their promising graduates into academic careers.

The implications of these findings were so much at odds with those reported in other studies that we suggested we might be witnessing an advanced stage of a major social change in American Catholicism, a change which has accompanied the emergence of American Catholics as the social, political, and economic equals of their fellow Americans. Though in the nature of the data available to us the fact of this change could not be proved definitively, it seemed to be a highly plausible hypothesis. Again tentative evidence indicated that the new position of Catholics in higher education was related to the development of the Catholic ethnic groups, a development which was not yet complete and which was going on in some fascinating patterns which demanded further study. Finally, we suggested, again very tentatively, that many of the differences which still exist and which may have existed in the past among religious groups pertain to the cultural history of the members of a group in a given society rather than to the theological stance of the Church. The facts about the career plans and values of Catholic graduates seem beyond dispute. The explanation of these facts as well as their implication are still tentative, both because of the nature of the data at our command and because of the fact that the June 1961 graduates are just beginning their professional careers.

Myths die hard, especially religious myths. There have been several studies in recent years which have hinted that the economic and social state of American Catholics was little different than that of anyone else and even some that suggested that they might not be more anti-intellectual than anyone else. Yet these studies received no headlines, whereas a study of one city with a small sample that suggested the contrary became the object of much publicity. Intellectuals (whether Catholic or not) are often tempted to get so engrossed in their theories that facts, whether collected by statisticians or merely by observation, tend to become unimportant. The myths said that since Catholics were a separate religious and ethical enclave in American society, they could not do as well economically or intellectually as other Americans. That they were able to do as well politically seemed to be irrelevant.

The data reported in this book can hardly claim to have destroyed the myths. It is to be hoped, however, that the myths have been called into serious question, that they will not be repeated with as much blind certitude as they have enjoyed in the past.

Clearly, the later stages of the acculturation process of the Catholic immigrant groups is not definitively studied in this book; nor is the question of the quality and effect of Catholic higher education closed. These fascinating subjects need much more careful investigation, investigation which one hopes will be marked by more data collection and less pontification than have certain earlier efforts.

I have spoken before about the need for continuing critical examination of American Catholicism and especially its educational and intellectual contribution which at least to the present has left much to be desired. I have said before that I am not attempting to canonize American Catholicism or its educational system. I am not denouncing self-criticism or denying the important service rendered by the self-critics of the past decade and a half. I am merely pointing out that criticism ought to be based on fact, that it cannot ignore the highly dynamic nature of American Catholicism, and that it cannot judge the reality of the present by the fact of the past. Some of these observations have already been dismissed in certain Catholic circles as conservative. I should have thought that the conservative was the one who made blind acts of faith in the myths of the past and ignored the facts of the reality of the present; but then one gets into complex questions as to who the self-critic is and is not and these questions are, perhaps fortunately, beyond the scope of the survey research and certainly beyond the scope of the present book.

APPENDICES

APPENDICES

APPENDIX I

TABLES

TABLE 2.1

SUMMARY OF DEMOGRAPHIC DIFFERENCES AMONG THREE RELIGIOUS GROUPS (RSS)

	Protestant	Catholic	Jew	Statistical Significance		
				P-C	P-J	C-J
Age 22 or over	59	53	34	01	01	01
Male	57	64	61	01	no	no
White	94	99	100	05	no	no
Hometown over 500,000	24	39	79	01	01	01
North East Area	23	55	68	01	01	01
Commuting distance from school	27	43	59	01	01	01
Married	29	14	19	01	01	no
Have children (% of those married)	63	70	21	no	01	01
Three or more children in family of origin	31	37	11	01	01	01

The N's on the various items in summary tables vary from item to item because of the slightly different NA rate on each dependent variable. However, the approximate N for Protestants is 2007, for Catholics 833, and for Jews 272.

TABLE 2.2

AGE AND RELIGION (RSS)

	Protestant	Catholic	Jew
19 or under	-	-	1
20	3	4	17
21	38	43	48
22	28	25	19
23 to 24	13	12	6
25 to 29	12	12	6
30+	6	4	3
	100 (2001)	100 (830)	100 (268)

TABLE 2.3

PERCENTAGE MALE AND RELIGION (RSS)

Protestant	Catholic	Jew
57 (2007)	64 (833)	61 (272)

TABLE 2.4

RELIGION AND RACE (RSS)

	Protestant	Catholic	Jew
White	94	100	99
Negro	4	-	1
Oriental	1	-	-
Other	1	-	-
	100 (2007)	100 (272)	100 (833)

TABLE 2.5

RELIGION AND HOMETOWN (RSS)

	Protestant	Catholic	Jew
Farm	28	12	-
Metropolitan Area			
Suburb			
More than 2 million	8	13	19
500,000 to 2 million	9	10	11
100,000 to 499,999	8	8	5
Less than 100,000	8	11	5
Central City			
More than 2 million	3	8	45
500,000 to 2 million	4	8	7
100,000 to 499,999	7	10	5
50,000 to 99,999	4	5	1
10,000 to 49,999	11	9	2
Less than 10,000	10	4	0
	100 (1994)	99 (823)	98 (270)

TABLE 2.6

RELIGION BY REGION DURING
HIGH SCHOOL (RSS 1962)

	Protestant	Catholic	Jew
New England	24	13	6
Middle Atlantic	22	43	70
East North Central	21	21	9
West North Central	11	9	2
South	25	6	2
Mountain and West	15	6	10
Alaska, Hawaii, Canada and other	2	2	1
	100 (1715)	100 (681)	100 (228)

TABLE 2.7A

RELIGION AND MARITAL STATUS (RSS)

	Protestant	Catholic	Jew
Single, not married before fall	56	74	69
Single, will be married before fall	14	12	12
Married, children	18	10	4
Married, no children	11	4	15
Ex-married	1	0	-
	100 (1981)	100 (827)	100 (268)

TABLE 2.7B

RELIGION AND FAMILY SIZE (RSS)

	Protestant	Catholic	Jew
Only child	14	12	15
One other	31	25	47
Two other	24	25	26
Three or more	31	37	11
	100 (2007)	99 (853)	99 (272)

TABLE 2.8

SUMMARY OF SOCIAL AND ECONOMIC DIFFERENCES AMONG
THREE RELIGIOUS GROUPS (RSS)

	Protestant	Catholic	Jew	Statistical Significance		
				P-C	P-J	C-J
Father went to college	43	34	44	01	no	01
Mother went to college	39	27	32	01	05	no
Parental occupation, professional or managerial	46	47	67	no	01	01
Income over $7,500	45	46	57	no	01	01

TABLE 2.9

RELIGION AND EDUCATIONAL BACKGROUND (RSS)

	Protestant	Catholic	Jew
A. Father			
Eighth grade or less	20	27	18
Part High School	15	18	18
High School graduate	22	20	20
Part College	15	12	16
College graduate	14	11	11
Graduate degree	13	11	17
	100 (1993)	99 (829)	100 (272)
B. Mother			
Eighth grade or less	13	21	10
Part High School	14	18	18
High School graduate	33	33	40
Part College	19	14	15
College graduate	16	12	13
Graduate degree	4	1	4
	99 (1997)	99 (830)	100 (270)

TABLE 2.10

RELIGION AND INCOME (RSS)

	Protestant	Catholic	Jew
Less than $5,000	19	16	9
$5,000 to $7,499	25	26	21
$7,500 to $9,999	16	17	17
$10,000 to $14,999	14	13	17
$15,000 to $19,999	5	10	4
$20,000	9	5	20
No idea	11	12	13
	99 (1967)	99 (824)	101 (270)

TABLE 2.11

CURRENT RELIGION AND PARENT'S OCCUPATION
AS COMPARED WITH DISTRIBUTION OF OCCUPATION
BY RELIGION IN NATIONAL POPULATION[a] (RSS)

	Protestant		Catholic		Jew	
	College Graduate	National	College Graduate	National	College Graduate	National
Upper[b]	46	21.3	47	21.0	67	53.6
Middle[c]	29	30.0	32	33.8	26	31.8
Lower[d]	13	34.1	20	37.0	7	13.3
Farm	11	14.5	2	8.4	0	1.3
	99	99.9	101	100.2	100	100

Ratio of Percentage in Graduation Class to Percentage
in National Population by Occupation and Religion

	Protestant	Catholic	Jew
Upper	2.2	2.2	1.2
Middle	0.98	0.97	0.86
Lower	0.38	0.54	0.53
Farm	0.78	0.25	-

[a]The national distribution is based on figures compiled for Donald J. Bogue, Population of the United States (Glencoe: The Free Press, 1957), p. 703, from survey materials at the National Opinion Research Center.

[b]Managers and proprietors.   [c]Clerical, sales, craftsmen.

[d]Semi-skilled, unskilled, and service.

TABLE 2.12

SES BY RELIGION (RSS)

	Protestant	Catholic	Jew
Male			
Blue collar, no college, $7,500-	32	29	12
Blue collar, no college, $7,500+	8	12	4
Blue collar, part-college, $7,500-	2	1	1
White collar, no college, $7,500-	11	11	14
Blue collar, part college, $7,500+	2	2	2
White collar, no college, $7,500+	12	16	27
White collar, part college, $7,500-	7	5	4
White collar, part college, $7,500+	26	24	34
	100 (1119)	100 (515)	98 (161)
Female			
Blue collar, no college, $7,500-	24	26	6
Blue collar, no college, $7,500+	7	8	5
Blue collar, part college, $7,500-	4	2	
White collar, no college, $7,500-	7	10	15
Blue collar, part college, $7,500+	1	1	2
White collar, no college, $7,500+	14	19	25
White collar, part college, $7,500-	7	4	6
White collar, part college, $7,500+	35	29	41
	99 (833)	99 (291)	100 (100)

TABLE 2.13

RELIGION AND BACKGROUND CHARACTERISTICS (TWS)

Hometown	SES	Sex	Catholic	Protestant	Jew
Large (over 100,000)	High	Male	18	13	39
		Female	12	12	22
	Low	Male	20	8	18
		Female	8	4	9
Small (under 100,000)	High	Male	10	16	5
		Female	8	13	7
	Low	Male	14	21	1
		Female	9	12	0
			99 (13,020)	99 (30,405)	101 (4306)

TABLE 2.14

SUMMARY OF DIFFERENCES ON PERSONALITY SCALES
AMONG THREE RELIGIOUS GROUPS
(PER CENT SCORING HIGH) (RSS)

	Protestant	Catholic	Jew	Statistical Significance		
				P-C	P-J	C-J
Drive	54	47	47	01	05	no
Sophistication	18	21	25	no	no	no
Emotionality	11	13	19	no	05	05
Intellectual-Idealism	17	22	26	05	01	no
Extroversion	37	36	45	no	01	01

TABLE 2.15

SUMMARY OF DIFFERENCES ON ORIENTATIONS (RSS)

	Protestant	Catholic	Jew	Statistical Significance		
				P-C	P-J	C-J
Favorable to modern art	49	43	44	no	no	no
Conventional	56	57	45	no	01	01
Religious	70	84	40	01	01	01
Liberal	44	50	66	01	01	01

TABLE 2.16A

RELIGION AND ATTITUDE TOWARDS
MODERN ART (RSS)

	Protestant	Catholic	Jew
Very favorable	14	11	18
Fairly favorable	35	32	26
Neither	25	27	37
Fairly unfavorable	18	18	12
Very unfavorable	8	11	17
	100 (1958)	99 (820)	100 (107)

TABLE 2.16B

RELIGION AND CONVENTIONALITY (RSS)

	Protestant	Catholic	Jew
Very conventional	8	9	5
Fairly conventional	48	48	40
Neither	15	15	18
Fairly unconventional	22	22	27
Very unconventional	6	6	10
	99 (1961)	100 (214)	100 (869)

TABLE 2.17

RELIGION AND POLITICAL ORIENTATION (RSS)

	Protestant	Catholic	Jew
Very liberal	9	11	16
Fairly liberal	35	39	50
Neither	14	18	17
Fairly conservative	34	27	17
Very conservative	8	6	-
	100 (1955)	101 (810)	100 (267)

TABLE 2.18

RELIGION AND RELIGIOSITY (RSS)

	Protestant	Catholic	Jew
Very religious	18	32	4
Fairly religious	52	52	36
Neither	13	6	19
Fairly non-religious	12	6	23
Very non-religious	5	5	17
	100 (1972)	101 (816)	99 (268)

TABLE 2.19

RELIGIOUS ATTENDANCE (RSS 1962)

	Protestant	Catholic	Jew
Weekly	30	81	4
Several times a month	20	4	4
Once a month	15	3	6
Two or three times a year	23	7	50
Once a year	4	1	17
Never	7	4	19
	99 (1667)	100 (675)	100 (225)

TABLE 2.20A

MOST SATISFACTION (RSS 1962)

	Protestant	Catholic	Jew
Career plans	27	27	24
Family relationships	63	59	71
Leisure time recreational activities	3	2	7
Religious beliefs or activities	7	15	1
Participation as a citizen in affairs of your community	1	1	1
Participation in activities directed toward national or international betterment	2	2	1
	103 (1717)	106 (679)	105 (226)

TABLE 2.20B

WORRY BY RELIGION (61) (RSS 1962)
(PER CENT REPORTING WORRY)

	Protestant	Catholic	Jew
	1740	696	232
My children's health and development	6	6	3
Ability to make friends	7	7	7
Physical Health	8	10	5
Finances	39	37	32
Loneliness	13	12	12
Dating, relations with opposite sex	15	15	20
Goals in life	30	34	34
Relations with spouse	5	4	6
Career plans	36	41	39
School studies this year	13	13	28
Emotional state	8	9	12
Relations with parents	7	10	14
World conditions	24	23	26
Relations with in-laws	4	3	8
My job	22	23	19
Other problems	4	4	5
None	15	17	17

TABLE 3.1

RELIGION AND SCHOOL QUALITY (RSS)

	Protestant	Catholic	Jew	None
A	6	3	13	13
B	6	9	13	12
C	49	66	59	55
D	39	21	16	20
	100 (2007)	99 (833)	101 (272)	100 (102)

TABLE 3.2

RELIGION AND AREA OF SCHOOL (RSS)

	Protestant	Catholic	Jew
North East	23	55	68
North Central	32	31	14
South	28	6	6
West	17	7	12
	100 (2007)	99 (833)	100 (272)

TABLE 3.3

RELIGION AND DISTANCE FROM SCHOOL (RSS)

	Protestant	Catholic	Jew	None
Within commuting distance	27	43	59	36
Four hours drive or less	43	31	17	29
More than four hours drive, same state	8	6	7	12
Different state	21	20	17	24
	99 (1999)	100 (827)	100 (272)	101 (108)

TABLE 3.4

RELIGION AND CAMPUS RESIDENCE (RSS)

	Protestant	Catholic	Jew	None
Fraternity or sorority	13	5	9	8
Dorm or other campus housing	37	33	16	20
Off campus	37	27	32	55
With parents	14	36	41	23
	101 (1981)	101 (821)	98 (272)	106 (108)

TABLE 3.5

RELIGION AND PLACES WHERE FRIENDS WERE MET (RSS)

	Protestant	Catholic	Jew	None
Before I came	31	32	40	30
Dorm or rooming house	54	44	28	38
Fraternity or sorority	34	20	37	20
Campus activity	35	36	25	19
Classes in major	70	72	66	68
Classes not in major	31	40	37	32
Other	7	8	10	8
None here	1	1	1	4
	263 (1992)	253 (824)	244 (272)	219 (107)

TABLE 3.6

RELIGION AND PURPOSES OF COLLEGE (RSS)

	Protestant	Catholic	Jew	None
A. Objective (What you think)				
1. Basic education and appreciation of ideas	65	65	65	63
2. Having a good time	2	0	2	3
3. Career training	33	28	21	37
4. Learning to get along with people	16	17	19	12
	116 (1989)	110 (823)	107 (272)	115 (106)
B. Projective (What others think it is)				
1. Basic education and appreciation of ideas	35	44	27	34
2. Having a good time	26	18	29	27
3. Career training	37	38	41	42
4. Learning to get along with people	8	9	7	6
	116 (1958)	109 (804)	118 (265)	119 (104)

TABLE 3.7

RELIGION AND SCHOOL LOYALTY (RSS)

	Protestant	Catholic	Jew	None
Very strong	33	34	28	12
Like it	44	37	43	51
Mixed feelings	16	22	19	24
Don't like it	4	5	7	12
Strongly dislike	2	1	2	1
	99 (1979)	99 (825)	99 (258)	100 (115)

TABLE 3.8

EVALUATION OF UNDERGRADUATE SCHOOLS
BY RELIGION AND BY SEX (RSS 1962)
(Per Cent Rating School as "Excellent")

Item	Male			Female		
	Protes-tant	Catho-lic	Jew-ish	Protes-tant	Catho-lic	Jew-ish
Teaching	25	24	26	21	30	20
Courses	29	29	46	27	29	35
Research facilities	27	27	41	28	26	33
Student housing . .	24	24	25	28	35	46
Caliber of students	19	21	26	22	28	18
Caliber of faculty .	43	43	59	38	48	46
N = ...	976	434	143	762	243	89

TABLE 3.9

GRADES BY RELIGION (RSS)

	Protestant	Catholic	Jew
Male			
A, A-	7	5	4
B+, B	21	21	24
B-, C+	55	54	55
C, C-, D+	17	21	18
	100 (1119)	101 (515)	101 (101)
Female			
A, A-	10	5	6
B+, B	33	30	36
B-, C+	49	54	47
C, C-, D+	8	10	13
	100 (846)	99 (302)	102 (102)

TABLE 3.10A

SUBJECTIVE RANK BY RELIGION (RSS)

	Protestant	Catholic	Jew
Top 10%	24	25	24
Top Quarter but not top 10%	25	23	30
Second Quarter	30	30	30
Third Quarter	12	17	14
Lowest Quarter	8	6	2
	99 (2007)	101 (833)	100 (272)

TABLE 3.10B

RELIGION AND ACADEMIC PERFORMANCE (RSS)

	Protestant	Catholic	Jew
High	19	15	26
Medium	36	38	37
Low	45	47	36
	100 (1972)	100 (826)	89 (265)

TABLE 3.11

COURSE REACTIONS BY RELIGION (RSS)

	Protestant	Catholic	Jew	Statistical Significance		
				P-C	P-J	C-J
Course reactions:						
Science interesting	34	33	37	no	no	no
Math interesting	32	34	37	no	no	no
Bio. interesting	44	37	37	01	05	no
Soc. Sci. interesting	63	65	68	no	no	no
English interesting	49	54	37	01	01	01

TABLE 3.12

RESEARCH EXPERIENCE OF
COLLEGE GRADUATES BY RELIGION (RSS)

	Protestant	Catholic	Jew
No research experience	62	60	58
Own project	12	12	15
Other	26	28	27
	100 (2007)	100 (833)	100 (272)

TABLE 3.13

SUMMARY OF DIFFERENCES ON FUTURE PLANS

	Protestant	Catholic	Jew	Statistical Significance		
				P-C	P-J	C-J
Graduate school next year	28	34	47	01	01	01
Career Employer:						
Large Company	25	33	26	01	no	no
Small Company	7	11	21	no	01	01
Self	7	8	14	no	05	05
Education	36	27	27	01	01	no
Career Occupation:						
Science	7	6	8	no	no	no
Social Sci. and Hum.	10	10	10	no	no	no
Medicine	2	3	6	no	05	05
Law	2	3	10	no	05	05
Engineering	7	8	8	no	no	no
Education	34	26	27	01	01	no
Business	15	23	17	01	no	01
Other professions	16	12	6	05	01	01
Other	7	5	8			

TABLE 3.14

RELIGION AND GRADUATE SCHOOL PLANS (RSS)

	Protestant	Catholic	Jew
Next year	28	34	47
Later	47	44	37
Never	25	22	16
	100 (2007)	100 (833)	100 (272)

TABLE 3.15

PER CENT GOING TO GRADUATE SCHOOL
OF THOSE WHO HAD PLANNED TO GO (TWS 1962)

		Male			Female		
		Protes-tant	Catholic	Jew	Protes-tant	Catholic	Jew
High API	G	$93_{(1337)}$	$90_{(622)}$	$96_{(431)}$	$78_{(716)}$	$78_{(328)}$	$85_{(129)}$
	F	$18_{(539)}$	$24_{(229)}$	$40_{(63)}$	$16_{(1038)}$	$22_{(315)}$	$16_{(147)}$
Medium API	G	$84_{(1916)}$	$84_{(991)}$	$90_{(390)}$	$65_{(899)}$	$59_{(520)}$	$73_{(179)}$
	F	$17_{(1789)}$	$16_{(790)}$	$24_{(181)}$	$13_{(2526)}$	$16_{(782)}$	$17_{(230)}$
Low API	G	$72_{(1367)}$	$72_{(901)}$	$82_{(300)}$	$53_{(516)}$	$51_{(265)}$	$60_{(101)}$
	F	$16_{(3348)}$	$18_{(1762)}$	$25_{(241)}$	$12_{(2167)}$	$17_{(783)}$	$23_{(159)}$

G = Planned to go in fall of 1961.
F = Planned to go in future.

TABLE 3.16

RELIGION AND FUTURE CAREER

Long-run Career Field	Male					Total	
	Protes-tant	Roman Catholic	Jew-ish	Other	None	Per cent	N
Total	59	27	8	3	3	100	25,054
Chemistry . .	54	31	10	2	2	99	607
Physics . . .	55	28	9	2	6	100	435
Geo. Phy. Sci.	67	15	8	2	8	100	199
Mathematics .	60	22	11	3	4	100	473
Other Phy. Sci.	62	21	8	2	6	99	85
Civil Engineer	65	21	4	5	6	101	596
Chemical Engr.	56	27	10	4	4	101	310
Elect. Engr. . .	61	24	7	4	4	100	1,160
Mech. Engineer	65	25	5	1	4	100	507
Eng. General.	57	28	8	3	4	100	429
Other Engineer	60	28	6	3	4	101	769
Medicine . . .	49	23	23	2	3	100	1,162
Dentistry. . .	56	21	21	2	1	101	187
Pharmacology	41	23	32	3	1	100	220
Other Health .	51	29	12	2	7	101	118
All Health Fields Except Medicine . . .	48	24	24	2	2	100	525
Biology. . . .	62	23	1	4	9	99	69
Bio. Chem. .	51	31	13	.2	4	101	85
Microbiology.	62	26	12	0	0	100	58
Zoology. . . .	79	13	3	3	1	99	67
All Other Bio. Sci. . . .	66	15	9	5	4	99	234
Agriculture .	80	13	0	7	1	101	261
Forestry. . .	81	12	0	3	5	101	176
Farming . . .	89	4	0	4	3	100	104
All Agricul-ture & Vet. Medicine . . .	81	12	1	5	2	101	585
Elem. Educ. .	74	14	4	4	5	101	342
Secondary Educ., Sci.. .	68	21	2	3	5	99	650
Secondary Educ., Non-Sci..	66	24	5	3	2	100	1,483

TABLE 3.16—Continued

Long-run Career Field	Female					Total	
	Protes-tant	Roman Catholic	Jew-ish	Other	None	Per Cent	N
Educ. Admin.	66	27	2	3	1	99	664
All Other Educ..	69	20	5	3	3	100	829
Clinical Psych.	65	14	16	1	4	100	153
Other Psych.	50	28	13	2	7	100	251
Pol. Sci. . . .	53	36	6	2	4	101	340
Economics . .	59	21	7	7	6	100	180
Sociology. . .	65	18	7	4	6	100	89
Other Soc. . . Sci.	82	5	9	0	5	101	66
Fine Arts . .	68	16	9	3	4	100	368
English . . .	45	37	11	3	4	100	296
History . . .	53	35	5	3	4	100	284
Languages . .	64	23	5	4	3	99	118
Philosophy. .	51	22	16	7	3	99	99
Architecture.	56	28	9	2	5	100	288
Journalism. .	51	26	12	7	3	99	296
Other Hum. .	55	31	3	0	10	99	99
Theology. . .	76	17	3	3	1	100	778
Business. . .	55	32	8	2	2	99	4,650
Accounting. .	54	33	8	3	2	100	1,316
Advertising .	54	31	11	1	3	100	351
Public Adm. .	51	40	4	1	4	100	381
Law.	42	34	19	2	3	100	1,612
Social Work .	62	24	6	5	3	100	207
Mil. Service .	71	25	2	1	2	100	395
Other Misc. Professions .	57	23	6	6	8	100	114
Total . . .	63	23	9	2	3	100	18,300
Chemistry . .	49	37+	6	1	6	99	172
Physics . . .	63	28+	7	0	2	100	54
Mathematics.	64	22	5	4	5	100	188
Other Phy. Sci.	81	19	0	0	0	100	26

TABLE 3.16 (continued)

Long-run Career Field	Female					Total	
	Protes- tant	Roman Catholic	Jew- ish	Other	None	Per Cent	N
Engineering .	48	42	0	3	6	99	31
Medicine. . .	45	42	7	4	2	100	89
Nursing . . .	72	21	1	5	1	100	780
Med. Tech.. .	72	21	3	3	2	101	190
Other Health.	73	20	6	1	1	101	296
Biology. . . .	66	21	11	1	1	100	87
Bio. Chem.. .	56	34	6	1	3	100	70
Microbiology.	61	18	11	1	10	101	94
All Other Bio. Sci. . . .	50	34	6	7	4	101	188
Elem. Educ. .	67	18	9	4	2	100	4,396
Secon. Educ., Science . . .	64	27	6	3	1	101	617
Secon. Educ., Non-Science .	65	24	5	4	2	100	2,850
Other Educ. .	69	20	7	3	1	100	1,869
Clin. Psych. .	61	10	26	2	2	101	147
Other Psych..	44	36	13	4	3	100	156
Sociology. . .	39	37	12	7	5	100	59
Pol. Sci. . . .	54	32	10	1	3	100	175
All Other Soc. Sci. . . .	43	36	12	7	3	101	75
Fine Arts . .	71	14	8	3	3	99	545
English. . . .	64	23	8	1	5	101	425
Languages . .	46	33	5	11	6	101	197
Other Hum. .	67	23	8	1	1	100	172
Journalism. .	59	21	10	4	5	99	214
Lib. Science .	71	13	4	7	4	99	217
All Business .	66	21	7	2	4	100	1,000
Social Work .	65	19	11	2	3	100	561
Law	42	31+	20	4	4	101	55
Home Econom.	81	13	2	3	0	99	340
Other Misc. Professions .	79	16	1	1	3	100	149
Housewife . .	59	31	8	1	1	100	1,816

N = ... 43,354
NA and No Equivalent 3,525
Not Applicable 955
Total Weighted N = ... 47,834

TABLE 3.17

RELIGION AND EXPECTED EMPLOYER (RSS)

	Protestant	Catholic	Jew
Large company	25	33	26
Small company	7	11	21
Family business	2	3	4
Self-employed	7	8	14
Research organization	7	7	10
College	12	12	11
Educational system	36	27	27
Other education	-	-	-
Federal government	14	14	15
State or local government	5	7	4
Hospital, church, or welfare	9	6	4
Other	3	3	3
	127 (2007)	131 (833)	139 (272)

TABLE 3.17A

RELIGION AND OCCUPATIONAL ACTIVITY (RSS)

	Protestant	Catholic	Jew
Teaching	52	45	43
Research	27	24	32
Administration	38	49	31
Service	22	25	37
None of these	6	6	2
	145 (2007)	149 (833)	145 (272)

TABLE 3.18A
OCCUPATIONAL IMAGE: RESEARCH CHEMIST (RSS)

	Protestant	Catholic	Jew
	Male		
Very interested	42	39	54
No ability	58	63	48
Need more money	6	8	26
No personality	28	33	34
No challenge	3	2	1
	N = 1076	504	159
	Female		
Very interested	39	44	51
No ability	76	75	82
More money	2	2	6
No personality	34	37	26
No challenge	1	-	-
	N = 822	295	100

TABLE 3.18B
OCCUPATIONAL IMAGE: COLLEGE PROFESSOR (RSS)

	Protestant	Catholic	Jew
	Male		
Very interested	63	67	61
No ability	13	14	15
Need more money	30	35	52
No personality	9	9	14
No challenge	4	6	8
	N = 1049	487	155
	Female		
Very interested	63	70	19
No ability	18	25	19
Need more money	14	16	18
No personality	10	11	13
No challenge	1	1	1
	N = 791	276	93

TABLE 3.18C

OCCUPATIONAL IMAGE: HIGH SCHOOL TEACHER (RSS)

	Protestant	Catholic	Jew
Male			
Very interested	45	42	27
No ability	4	5	7
Need more money	58	62	75
No challenge	26	28	42
N = 1091	529	169	
Female			
Very interested	63	68	58
No ability	3	5	6
Need more money	27	23	27
No challenge	8	8	12
N = 811	304	97	

TABLE 3.18D

OCCUPATIONAL IMAGE: MEDICINE (RSS)

	Protestant	Catholic	Jew
Male			
Very interested	38	38	50
No ability	51	56	42
Need more money	2	2	1
No personality	13	14	16
No challenge	2	2	3
N = 1087	503	159	
Female			
Very interested	49	54	58
No ability	67	66	71
Need more money	1	1	2
No personality	19	20	19
No challenge	-	-	-
N = 824	287	98	

TABLE 3.18F

OCCUPATIONAL IMAGE: ENGINEER (RSS)

	Protestant	Catholic	Jew
Male			
Very interested	45	41	37
No ability	41	48	51
Need more money	2	5	13
No personality	13	14	21
No challenge	5	5	9
	N = 1030	480	155
Female			
Very interested	15	20	19
No ability	80	84	82
Need more money	1	1	2
No personality	29	33	27
No challenge	4	5	2
	N = 792	286	98

TABLE 3.18G

OCCUPATIONAL IMAGE: BUSINESS EXECUTIVE (RSS)

	Protestant	Catholic	Jew
Male			
Very interested	54	67	61
No ability	12	9	9
Need more money	2	2	0
No personality	17	15	16
No challenge	7	7	8
	N = 1048	496	158
Female			
Very interested	36	37	33
No ability	33	40	24
Need more money	3	1	2
No personality	33	37	29
No challenge	10	10	13
	N = 783	281	103

TABLE 3.19

OCCUPATIONAL VALUES AND RELIGION (RSS)[a]

	Protestant	Catholic	Jew	P-C	P-J	C-J
				Statistical Significance		
Making a lot of money	21	27	38	01	01	01
Chance to be creative	50	50	64	no	01	01
Helpful to others	68	61	60	01	01	no
Avoid high pressure	15	17	15	no	no	no
World of ideas	39	35	50	no	01	01
Freedom from supervision	18	17	21	no	no	no
Slow and sure progress	33	32	25	no	05	no
Leadership	34	40	40	01	no	no
Same area	4	8	9	05	05	no
New area	10	11	11	no	no	no
Work with people, not things	57	55	56	no	no	no
N =	(2007)	(833)	(272)			

[a]Answer to question: "Which of these characteristics would be important to you in picking a career?"

TABLE 4.1

GRADUATE PLANS BY BACKGROUND CHARACTERISTICS
BY RELIGION (RSS)
Per Cent Going in Fall of 1961

	Male			Female		
	Protestant	Catholic	Jew	Protestant	Catholic	Jew
Large City:						
High SES	44(248)	48(159)	55(161)	29(200)	28(96)	44(60)
Low SES	39(161)	39(161)	55(48)	24(92)	28(67)	35(23)
Small City:						
High SES	35(304)	38(94)	36(14)	15(248)	29(74)	27(18)
Low SES	26(431)	21(115)	0	16(263)	22(67)	

TABLE 4.2

CAREER PLANS BY BACKGROUND
CHARACTERISTICS BY RELIGION (RSS)
Per Cent Choosing Arts and Science Careers

	Male			Female		
	Protes-tant	Catholic	Jew	Protes-tant	Catholic	Jew
Large City:						
High SES	22(248)	18(159)	12(103)	25(260)	28(96)	29(60)
Low SES	18(161)	20(161)	28(48)	14(92)	15(67)	13(23)
Small City:						
High SES	19(304)	12(94)	7(14)	16(248)	23(74)	23(18)
Low SES	17(431)	11(115)	0	9(265)	7(67)	

TABLE 4.3

CAREER PLANS BY BACKGROUND
CHARACTERISTICS BY RELIGION (RSS)
Per Cent Choosing Law and Medicine

	Male			Female		
	Protes-tant	Catholic	Jew	Protes-tant	Catholic	Jew
Large City:						
High SES	12(248)	18(159)	38(103)	0(260)	1(96)	0(60)
Low SES	7(161)	10(161)	9(48)	1(92)	0(67)	4(23)
Small City:						
High SES	13(304)	16(94)	28(14)	0(248)	2(74)	0(18)
Low SES	4(431)	7(115)	0	0(263)	2(67)	

TABLE 4.4

CAREER PLANS BY BACKGROUND
CHARACTERISTICS BY RELIGION (RSS)
Per Cent Choosing Education

	Male			Female		
	Protes-tant	Catholic	Jew	Protes-tant	Catholic	Jew
Large City:						
High SES	11(248)	7(159)	4(103)	48(260)	41(96)	64(60)
Low SES	25(161)	15(161)	13(48)	59(92)	57(67)	74(23)
Small City:						
High SES	15(304)	12(94)	0(14)	58(248)	53(74)	56(18)
Low SES	27(431)	22(115)	0	68(263)	69(67)	

TABLE 4.5

CAREER PLANS BY BACKGROUND
CHARACTERISTICS BY RELIGION (RSS)
Per Cent Choosing Business

	Male			Female		
	Protes-tant	Catholic	Jew	Protes-tant	Catholic	Jew
Large City:						
High SES	30(248)	35(159)	30(103)	10(260)	15(96)	7(60)
Low SES	19(161)	28(161)	9(48)	5(92)	10(67)	4(23)
Small City:						
High SES	26(304)	36(94)	43(14)	3(248)	4(74)	11(18)
Low SES	19(431)	34(115)		6(263)	3(67)	

TABLE 4.6

CAREER EMPLOYER BY BACKGROUND
CHARACTERISTICS BY RELIGION (RSS)
Per Cent Choosing Corporation With More Than 100 Employees

	Male			Female		
	Protes-tant	Catholic	Jew	Protes-tant	Catholic	Jew
Large City:						
High SES	42(248)	41(159)	31(103)	17(260)	14(96)	14(60)
Low SES	41(161)	54(161)	38(48)	5(92)	9(67)	0(23)
Small City:						
High SES	35(304)	30(94)	29(14)	12(248)	20(74)	13(18)
Low SES	27(431)	43(115)	25(1)	7(263)	5(167)	

TABLE 4.6A

CAREER EMPLOYER BY BACKGROUND
CHARACTERISTICS BY RELIGION (RSS)
Per Cent Choosing Primary or Secondary Education

	Male			Female		
	Protes-tant	Catholic	Jew	Protes-tant	Catholic	Jew
Large City:						
High SES	10(248)	7(159)	5(103)	54(260)	42(96)	64(60)
Low SES	23(161)	15(161)	9(48)	57(92)	61(67)	75(23)
Small City:						
High SES	17(304)	12(94)	0(14)	60(248)	60(74)	60(18)
Low SES	27(431)	24(115)	0(1)	71(263)	67(167)	

TABLE 4.7

OCCUPATIONAL VALUES BY BACKGROUND
CHARACTERISTICS BY RELIGION (RSS)
Per Cent "Money"

	Male			Female		
	Protestant	Catholic	Jew	Protestant	Catholic	Jew
Large City:						
High SES	30(248)	38(159)	56(103)	12(260)	16(96)	18(60)
Low SES	25(161)	28(161)	46(48)	7(92)	12(67)	8(23)
Small City:						
High SES	29(304)	35(94)	36(14)	10(248)	12(74)	33(18)
Low SES	26(431)	30(115)		13(263)	24(167)	

TABLE 4.8

OCCUPATIONAL VALUES BY BACKGROUND
CHARACTERISTICS BY RELIGION (RSS)
Per Cent "Original and creative"

	Male			Female		
	Protestant	Catholic	Jew	Protestant	Catholic	Jew
Large City:						
High SES	59(248)	58(159)	61(103)	59(260)	53(96)	68(60)
Low SES	55(161)	49(161)	62(48)	52(92)	46(67)	76(23)
Small City:						
High SES	47(304)	41(94)	43(14)	56(248)	56(74)	72(18)
Low SES	42(431)	43(115)	50(2)	42(263)	51(167)	

TABLE 4.9

OCCUPATIONAL VALUES BY BACKGROUND
CHARACTERISTICS BY RELIGION (RSS)
Per Cent "People rather than Things"

	Male			Female		
	Protestant	Catholic	Jew	Protestant	Catholic	Jew
Large City:						
High SES	46(248)	46(159)	54(103)	71(260)	68(96)	72(60)
Low SES	45(161)	50(161)	35(48)	68(92)	64(67)	64(23)
Small City:						
High SES	46(304)	45(94)	64(14)	72(248)	64(74)	61(18)
Low SES	46(431)	46(115)	75(3)	72(263)	82(167)	

TABLE 4.10

DENOMINATION AND SES (RSS)
(Per Cent High)

Catholic	Baptist	Episco-palian	Lutheran	Meth-odist	Presby.	Congreg.
49(833)	36(307)	81(186)	42(245)	54(473)	69(112)	67(206)

TABLE 4.11

DENOMINATION AND GRADUATE SCHOOL PLANS (RSS)

	Catho-lic	Bap-tist	Epis.	Lutheran	Meth-odist	Presby.	Cong.
Arts and Sciences	16	10	13	10	14	13	12
Total Going	34	26	31	22	29	29	27

TABLE 4.12

CAREER PLANS BY DENOMINATION (RSS)

	Catho-lic	Bap-tist	Epis.	Lutheran	Meth-odist	Presby.	Cong.
Science	6	6	9	7	6	7	7
Humanities & Soc. Sci.	10	6	11	8	10	8	12
Medicine	3	2	3	1	2	2	2
Law	7	2	4	2	3	2	1
Engineering	8	8	7	8	8	7	6
Education	26	37	24	42	36	33	23
Business	23	16	13	12	14	17	19
Other Prof.	12	16	18	14	15	17	26
Other	5	8	10	6	5	6	4
	100	101	99	100	99	99	100

TABLE 4.13

VALUES BY DENOMINATION (RSS)

	Catho-lic	Bap-tist	Epis.	Lutheran	Meth-odist	Presby.	Cong.
Money	27	18	21	20	19	23	24
Creativity	50	40	64	55	50	49	55
People	55	55	51	64	60	58	55

TABLE 4.14

ACADEMIC PERFORMANCE BY DENOMINATION (RSS)
(Per Cent in Upper Half)

Catholic	Baptist	Episco-palian	Lutheran	Meth-odist	Presby.	Congreg.
52	43	62	55	55	60	64

TABLE 4.15

SEX AND DENOMINATION (RSS)
(Per Cent Male)

Catholic	Baptist	Episco-palian	Lutheran	Meth-odist	Presby-terian	Congrega-tionalist
60	59	53	57	57	50	54

TABLE 4.16

FALL PLANS BY DENOMINATION (RSS)
(Per Cent Going to Graduate School)

Catholic	Baptist	Episco-palian	Lutheran	Meth-odist	Presby-terian	Congrega-tionalist
			Male			
36(529)	32(173)	40(97)	26(135)	37(265)	37(132)	27(60)
			Female			
29(304)	20(116)	20(84)	21(99)	21(200)	23(133)	28(51)

TABLE 4.17

FUTURE CAREER BY DENOMINATION (RSS)

	Catholic	Baptist	Epis.	Lutheran	Methodist	Presby.	Cong.
Male							
Science and Soc. Sci.	16	13	16	16	20	18	16
Medicine and Law	13	8	12	4	9	11	4
English	14	16	15	15	15	15	10
Education	13	24	16	31	18	10	10
Business	33	23	22	22	22	28	33
Other Prof.	10	16	19	13	15	19	26
N =	529	168	89	124	255	127	58
Total	99	100	100	101	99	101	99
Female							
Science and Soc. Sci.	19	11	30	15	12	12	24
Medicine and Law	1		2		1		
English							1
Education	53	61	41	62	65	62	41
Business	9	9	7	2	5	9	4
Other Prof.	17	19	20	20	17	17	29
N =	304	111	76	98	192	124	49
Total	99	100	100	99	100	100	99

TABLE 4.18

SELECTED OCCUPATIONAL VALUES BY DENOMINATION (RSS)

	Catho-lic	Bap-tist	Epis.	Lutheran	Meth-odist	Presby.	Cong.
				Male			
Money	33	22	30	27	24	34	31
Orig. & Creat.	49	40	67	58	48	47	42
People	47	49	41	53	50	43	44
N =	(529)	(173)	(97)	(135)	(265)	(132)	(60)
				Female			
Money	16	11	12	12	11	12	8
Orig. & Creat.	52	38	64	50	54	49	61
People	69	65	64	82	74	77	65
N =	(304)	(116)	(84)	(99)	(200)	(133)	(81)

TABLE 4.19

API BY DENOMINATION (RSS)
Per Cent Upper Half

Catholic	Baptist	Episco-palian	Lutheran	Meth-odist	Presby-terian	Congrega-tionalist
			Male			
47	45	60	49	49	53	58
(529)	99(173)	100(97)	100(135)	100(265)	132(100)	100(60)
			Female			
62	56	65	63	62	67	68
(304)	100(116)	100(84)	99(99)	100(200)	99(133)	99(51)

TABLE 5.1

SUMMARY OF DEMOGRAPHIC AND
SOCIAL DIFFERENCES AMONG CATHOLICS IN
CATHOLIC SCHOOLS AND OTHER SCHOOLS

	Catholic College	Other College
Male	57	69
Large city	48	35
Not married or planning marriage before fall	81	68
Father went to college	40	26
Mother went to college	37	21
Income over $7,500	50	42
Father Prof. or Man.	54	42
SES index high	57	41
	N = 448	395

TABLE 5.2

SUMMARY OF ATTITUDINAL ORIENTATIONS
AMONG CATHOLICS (RSS)

	Catholic College	Other College
Liberal	45	53
Religious	92	76
For Modern Art	43	43
Conventional	57	57

TABLE 5.3

SUMMARY OF PLANS AND PERFORMANCE
FOR CATHOLICS BY SCHOOL TYPE (RSS)

	Catholic College	Other College
High academic	15	15
Graduate school in fall	36	33
Occupational choice:		
Science	6	7
Soc. Sci. and Humanities	10	10
Medicine	3	3
Law	7	3
Engineering	6	11
Education	25	28
Business	24	23
Other profession	15	10
Other	4	5
Career employer:		
Large Company	33	26
Education	23	29

TABLE 5.4

GRADUATE PLANS BY SCHOOL TYPE (RSS)

Students	Ivy League	High Quality Private	Midwest	Big Ten	Catholic
Total Graduate	52	63	32	26	36
Arts and Science	21	25	15	9	15
N =	81	140	339	211	448

TABLE 5.5

OCCUPATIONAL VALUES
FOR CATHOLICS BY SCHOOL TYPE (RSS)

	Catholic College	Other College
Making a lot of money	26	27
Chance to be creative	48	51
Helpful to others	64	59
Avoid high pressure	14	19
World of ideas	32	37
Freedom from supervision	13	22
Slow and sure progress	26	38
Leadership	39	41
Same area	9	6
New area	9	15
People not things	58	52

TABLE 5.6

EVALUATION OF UNDERGRADUATE SCHOOL BY
CATHOLICS BY SCHOOL TYPE (RSS 1962)

Worry	Male		Female	
	Catholic College	Other College	Catholic College	Other College
Teaching. . .	26	23	37	21
Curriculum .	20	36	31	26
Research . .	14	37	22	30
Housing . . .	25	22	39	30
Students . . .	26	16	35	20
Faculty. . . .	44	41	56	37
N = . . .	200	242	141	112

TABLE 5.7

RELIGIOUS PRACTICE BY CATHOLIC
FROM CATHOLIC AND OTHER COLLEGES (RSS)

	Catholic College	Other College
A. Apostasy Rates (RSS)		
	1% (428)	12% (405)
B. Church Attendance (RSS 1962)*		
Weekly	93	77%
Several times a month	3	6
Once a month	1	5
Two or three times a year	3	10
Once a year or never	0	3
	100(338)	101(316)

*The difference in N's is due to the lower response rate in the 1962 questionnaire.

TABLE 5.8

LIFE SATISFACTIONS AND
SELECTED WORRIES BY SCHOOL TYPE (RSS 1962)

	Catholic College	Other College
Main Life Satisfaction:		
Career	21	32
Family	57	60
Leisure Time	1	4
Religion	22	8
Civic Affairs	1	2
National or International Affairs	2	2
Worries:		
Finances	49	60
Life Goals	55	47
Career Plans	42	52

TABLE 5.9

SOCIAL AND DEMOGRAPHIC DIFFERENCES
AMONG CATHOLIC GRADUATES
BY EDUCATIONAL BACKGROUND (RSS)

	Catholic High School	All Catholic	Catholic College	All Non-Catholic
% Male	69	60	57	68
% From hometown under 100,000	38	39	47	50
% Over 23	42	15	19	38
% Low SES	54	42	46	60
N =	109	303	145	296

TABLE 5.10

ATTITUDES BY EDUCATIONAL BACKGROUND (RSS)

	Catholic High School	All Catholic	Catholic College	All Non-Catholic	Sample*
% Conventional	54	58	63	52	55
% Liberal	61	44	47	52	49
% Very loyal to school	22	40	48	25	32

*All students regardless of religion.

TABLE 5.11

COURSE REACTIONS BY EDUCATIONAL BACKGROUND (RSS)

	Catholic High School	All Catholic	Catholic College	All Non-Catholic	Sample
Chemistry & Physics:					
Took	69	50	46	66	63
Interesting	42	29	30	37	36
Mathematics:					
Took	72	63	62	72	72
Interesting	30	37	37	36	34
Biology:					
Took	48	45	44	65	65
Interesting	37	32	38	47	43
Social Science:					
Took	94	88	91	92	94
Interesting	64	71	67	65	66
English:					
Took	97	96	98	95	97
Interesting	47	61	62	48	52

TABLE 5.12

FALL GRADUATE SCHOOL PLANS
BY EDUCATIONAL BACKGROUND (RSS)

	Catholic High School	All Catholic	Catholic College	All Non-Catholic	Sample
Arts and Sciences	12	13	10	12.5	12
Professional	15.5	17.5	20	14.5	16
Other	4	4	5	4.5	5
Total	31.5	34.5	35	31.5	33

TABLE 5.13

FUTURE CAREER BY EDUCATIONAL BACKGROUND (RSS)

	Catholic High School	All Catholic	Catholic College	All Non-Catholic	Sample
Science	9	7	2	5	7
Social Science & Hum.	11	10	10	9	8
Medicine	6	3	3	2	5
Law	1	6	8	4	3
Engineering	11	6	6	11	14
Education	28	20	31	28	24
Business	18	28	17	21	11
Other Prof.	6	4	16	10	16
None, etc.	10	5	6	9	13

TABLE 5.14

OCCUPATIONAL VALUES BY EDUCATIONAL BACKGROUND (RSS)

	Catholic High School	All Catholic	Catholic College	All Non-Catholic	Sample
Money	29	28	24	27	24
Orig. and Creat.	50	47	48	53	51
Helpful	61	62	65	58	65
Avoid Press.	21	16	12	19	16
Ideas	40	31	32	36	39
Freedom	21	13	15	22	18
Slow, Sure Progress	46	26	28	36	33
Leadership	41	38	41	42	41
Same Area	5	11	8	6	7
Different Areas	17	7	10	14	13
People	49	57	60	53	56

TABLE 5.15

CHURCH ATTENDANCE OF CATHOLICS
BY EDUCATIONAL PATTERN (RSS)

	All Catholic	Catholic College	Catholic High School	All Non-Catholic
Regular Mass*	95	93	85	72
Irregular Mass	4	4	6	10
Apostate	1	3	9	18

*Weekly or several times a month.

TABLE 5.16

EXPECTED MOST LIFE SATISFACTION FOR CATHOLICS
BY EDUCATIONAL PATTERN (RSS)

	All Catholic	Catholic College	Catholic High School	All Non-Catholic
Career	22	21	39	30
Family	57	59	51	63
Leisure	1	0	4	4
Religion	23	21	9	8
Civic Affairs	1	0	1	2
Betterment	1	3	0	2
	105 (240)	104 (91)	104 (110)	109 (206)

TABLE 5.17

SELECTED WORRIES BY EDUCATIONAL PATTERN (RSS)

	All Catholic	Catholic College	Catholic High School	All Non-Catholic
Finances	50	46	59	61
Life Goals	54	57	43	49
Career Plans	42	43	53	51
World Conditions	30	27	19	26

TABLE 6.1

CAREER FIELD OF SCHOLARS BY RELIGION (TWS)

	Protestant	Catholic	Jew
Physical Science	30	32	33
Biological Science	14	11	9
Social Science	20	18	25
Humanities	36	39	32
	100 (2159)	100 (970)	99 (489)

TABLE 6.2

GRADUATE SCHOOL PLANS BY RELIGION (TWS)

Graduate Field Open	N	% Prot.	Roman Cath.	% Jew	% None	% Other	Total
Other (cr)	3038	72.6	16.7	4.5	3.6	3.5	100.1
Soc. Work (*)	724	62.1	24.0	9.6	1.3	3.1	100.1
N. A. (0)	2127						
Chemistry (1)	864	53.4	32.2	9.1	4.0	1.2	99.9
Physics (2)	727	59.7	23.1	8.9	4.7	3.7	100.1
Geo.-Geog. (3)	272	72.6	16.2	5.0	2.7	3.5	100.0
Mathematics (4)	902	60.8	23.6	10.0	8.4	1.4	100.0
Phy., other (5)	158	53.5	14.6	14.0	10.2	7.6	99.9
English (10)	3060	56.7	27.0	7.9	4.2	4.3	100.1
Medicine (20)	1440	47.0	27.0	21.2	2.4	2.4	100.0
Nursing (30)	438	68.4	24.2	1.6	1.6	4.2	100.0
Health, oth. (31)	669	62.1	21.7	12.0	1.8	2.3	99.9
Biol. (40)	363	69.9	20.2	5.2	2.9	1.7	99.9
Biochemistry (41)	188	45.2	41.9	9.7	2.9	0.5	100.2
Botany (42)	106	74.5	7.8	1.0	6.9	9.8	100.0
Microbiology (43)	132	14.6	21.5	11.5	2.3	0	99.9
Physiology (44)	98	56.7	22.7	11.3	2.1	7.2	100.0
Zoology (45)	158	81.5	11.6	2.1	2.1	2.8	100.0
Bio., other (46)	290	64.1	21.4	8.6	2.4	3.4	99.9
Clin. Psy. (50)	375	55.0	21.0	20.2	2.4	0.5	100.0
Other Psyc. (51)	285	53.7	22.8	11.8	8.5	3.3	100.1
Economics (52)	470	48.1	35.4	8.4	4.8	3.3	100.0
Political Sci. (53)	690	52.2	30.9	9.5	4.4	2.9	99.9
Soc. (54)	379	58.9	23.7	11.3	2.2	4.0	100.1
Soc. other (55)	288	59.0	18.4	10.1	4.7	7.9	100.1
Fine Arts (60)	1429	67.6	16.2	9.6	4.1	2.7	100.2
English (61)	1201	53.3	31.3	11.2	1.8	2.4	100.0
History (62)	1142	58.2	28.7	7.1	3.0	3.0	100.0
Language (62)	726	51.8	30.6	9.2	5.5	3.0	100.1
Philo. (64)	205	45.0	35.4	13.1	3.0	4.5	100.0
Hum., other (65)	201	58.6	27.2	5.8	5.8	2.6	100.0
Educ. (70)	11691	65.4	22.4	6.7	2.0	3.5	100.0
Bus. (80)	4561	53.0	34.4	8.2	2.3	2.1	100.0
Law (90)	2456	43.5	35.1	17.5	2.5	1.5	100.0
Total	41853						

TABLE 6.3

CAREER FIELDS OF CATHOLIC SCHOLARS
BY SCHOOL TYPE (TWS)

	Catholic	Other
Physical Science	30	33
Biological Science	6	15
Social Science	20	16
Humanities	44	36
	100 (482)	99 (488)

TABLE 6.4

CAREER ACTIVITIES OF SCHOLARS BY RELIGION (TWS)

	Protestant	Catholic	Jew
Teaching	73	73	76
Research	62	60	73
Administration	17	17	16
Service	8	9	15
None of these	2	2	4
	(2159)	(970)	(489)

TABLE 6.5

CAREER ACTIVITIES OF CATHOLIC SCHOLARS
BY SCHOOL TYPE (TWS)

	Catholic	Other
Teaching	72	70
Research	57	62
Administration	18	15
Service	8	11
None of these	2	2
	N = (482)	(488)

TABLE 6.6

POTENTIAL PH.D.'S IN KNAPP SAMPLE AND NORC SAMPLE

	Knapp Rank Order	NORC Rank Order	Net Change in Rank
School A......	61	13	+48
School B......	73	23	+50
School C......	65	39	+26
School D......	57	46	+ 9
School E......	55	55*	0
School F......	46	55*	- 9
School G......	62	55*	+13

*Tie in last three schools.

TABLE 6.7

CHURCH ATTENDANCE OF
ARTS AND SCIENCE GRADUATE STUDENTS (TWS)

	Protestant		Catholic		Jew	
	Grad. Stud.	All Prot.	Grad. Stud.	All Cath.	Grad. Stud.	All Jew
Regular Church Attendance*	36	65	73	85	36	68
Irregular Church Attendance	33	20	16	6	37	16
Apostates	31	15	11	9	27	16

*For Catholics, weekly; for Protestants, at least once a month; for Jews, two or three times a year.

TABLE 6.8

PERCENTAGE REPORTING INFLUENCE OF "FACULTY ADVISER"
IN MAKING CAREER DECISION FOR CATHOLIC
AND OTHER SCHOOLS BY API SCORE (TWS)

API	Arts and Sciences	Professional	Not Going
Catholic Schools*			
High	61 (241)	45 (198)	49 (652)
Not high	58 (340)	43 (754)	48 (4580)
Other Schools**			
High	53 (126)	38 (108)	40 (331)
Not high	65 (105)	43 (172)	49 (2187)

*Weighted N = 6765 (representing all Catholic school graduates in survey).

**N = 3029 (all graduates of non-Catholic colleges in 10% representative subsample).

TABLE 6.9

PER CENT REPORTING INFLUENCE OF
"OTHER FACULTY MEMBERS" IN
MAKING CAREER DECISION BY API SCORE
AND SCHOOL TYPE (TWS)

API	Arts and Sciences	Professional	Not Going
Catholic Schools*			
High	80 (241)	69 (198)	53 (652)
Not high	67 (340)	50 (754)	56 (4580)
Other Schools**			
High	69 (126)	43 (108)	49 (331)
Not high	75 (105)	55 (172)	54 (2187)

*Weighted N - 6765.
**N = 3029.

TABLE 6.10

PER CENT REPORTING INFLUENCE OF FACULTY ADVISER AND
OTHER FACULTY MEMBERS IN PUBLIC AND PRIVATE
NON-CATHOLIC SCHOOLS BY API (TWS)

API	Public Schools			Private Schools (non-Catholic)		
	Arts and Sciences	Profes-sional	Not Going	Arts and Sciences	Profes-sional	Not Going
Faculty Adviser*						
High	68 (52)	39 (33)	37 (152)	48 (74)	36 (75)	45 (180)
Not high	53 (46)	48 (84)	54 (1274)	64 (59)	47 (88)	52 (912)
Other Faculty Members**						
High	80 (52)	66 (33)	37 (152)	66 (74)	51 (75)	50 (180)
Not high	66 (46)	68 (84)	54 (1274)	77 (59)	54 (88)	52 (912)

*Public N = 1641   **Public N   = 1641
Private N = 1388   Private N = 1388
Total N = 3029   Total N = 3029

TABLE 6.11

INFLUENCE OF ADVISORS AND OTHER FACULTY BY API
AS REPORTED BY STUDENTS IN NON-CATHOLIC
DENOMINATIONAL COLLEGES WITH HIGH (OVER 80)
STUDENT RELIGIOSITY SCORE (TWS)

API	Arts and Sciences	Professional	Not Going
	Advisor		
High	85 (7)	55 (11)	47 (47)
Not high	75 (60)	56 (81)	50 (367)
	Other Faculty*		
High	70 (7)	72 (11)	70 (47)
Not high	41 (60)	75 (81)	57 (367)

*N = 573

TABLE 6.12

PER CENT OF THOSE CHOOSING ACADEMIC CAREERS
WHO WERE RECRUITED TO THOSE CAREERS
WHILE THEY WERE IN COLLEGE BY API
FOR CATHOLIC AND NON-CATHOLIC COLLEGES (TWS)

API	Catholic Colleges*	Other Colleges**
High	41 (123)	28 (76)
Not high	31 (305)	40 (179)

*All Catholic college graduates in survey.
**Ten per cent subsample.

TABLE 6.13

INFLUENCE OF FACULTY MEMBERS ON RECRUITING
OR RETAINING STUDENTS FOR ACADEMIC CAREERS
BY API FOR CATHOLIC AND NON-CATHOLIC
COLLEGES (PER CENT REPORTING FACULTY
INFLUENCE IN CAREER DECISION) (TWS)

API	Recruits	Retained
	Catholic Colleges*	
High	90 (51)	68 (72)
Not high	60 (94)	55 (211)
	Other Colleges**	
High	78 (23)	73 (53)
Not high	51 (70)	69 (109)

*N = 428.
**N = 259.

TABLE 7.1

DIFFERENCES BETWEEN IRISH-GERMAN
AND POLISH-ITALIAN CATHOLICS
IN 1957 STUDY OF GRADUATE STUDENTS

	Irish-German (N = 556)	Polish-Italian (N = 147)
College taken for granted when in high school	43	30
High estimate of own abilities	33	23

TABLE 7.2

PERCENTAGE PLANNING TO GO TO
GRADUATE SCHOOL IN AUTUMN OF 1961 FOR
CATHOLIC ETHNIC GROUPS (TWS 1962) BY SES
(Males Only)

	Parental Income	
	Under $7,500	Over $7,500
Irish	30 (461)	48 (480)
German	32 (359)	34 (280)
Italian	39 (468)	45 (310)
Polish	26 (182)	29 (127)

TABLE 7.3

CAREER PLANS FOR CATHOLIC ETHNIC GROUPS BY SES (TWS 1962)
(Males Only)

Career Plans	Irish		German		Italian			
	-$7,500	+$7,500	-$7,500	+$7,500	-$7,500	+$7,500	-$7,500	+$7,500
Academia . .	17	13	12	21	23	12	19	28
Professions .	29	26	4	12	6	21	3	10
Education . .	12	6	11	4	21	12	19	7
Engineering .	6	7	27	22	14	7	21	10
Business . . .	40	36	33	31	24	33	30	35
Others	16	12	13	10	12	15	8	10
Total . . .	100	100	100	100	100	100	100	100
N = ...	461	480	359	280	468	310	182	127

TABLE 7.4

CAREER PLANS AND GRADUATE SCHOOLS PLANS
FOR CATHOLIC ETHNIC GROUPS IN UPPER SES
(Males Only)

Ethnic Group	Academic Field		Professional Field	
	Per cent planning career	Per cent planning graduate school in autumn of 1961	Per cent planning career	Per cent planning graduate school in autumn of 1961
Irish (N = 480)	13	14	26	32
German (N = 280)	21	11	12	24
Italian (N = 310)	12	12	21	29
Polish (N = 127)	28	16	10	16

TABLE 7.5

OCCUPATIONAL VALUES FOR CATHOLIC ETHNIC GROUPS
(MALES ONLY) BY SES (TWS 1962)

Occupational Value	Irish		German		Italian		Polish	
	-$7,500	+$7,500	-$7,500	+$7,500	-$7,500	+$7,500	-$7,500	+$7,500
Money	34%	33%	30%	34%	35%	39%	28%	28%
Creativity	45	40	47	56	52	51	42	37
Helpful	53	57	51	44	60	55	51	35
Avoid pressure	23	11	20	12	16	14	17	20
Ideas	30	30	40	38	35	35	24	33
Freedom	21	24	20	19	24	21	27	24
Slow, sure progress	30	28	41	31	30	40	51	40
Leadership	42	56	48	51	46	59	39	44
Same area	6	10	14	17	15	12	7	9
Different area	11	6	7	8	8	8	9	15
People	44	53	41	46	50	56	35	40
Total	339%	348%	359%	356%	371%	390%	330%	325%
N =	461	480	359	280	468	310	182	127

TABLE 7.6

INFLUENCE OF PARENTAL INCOME AND ACADEMIC
ORIENTATION ON THE CHOICE OF AN ARTS AND
SCIENCE CAREER AMONG JEWISH MALES
(Per Cent Choosing Arts and Science)

High Academic Orientation	
Less than $7,500	More than $7,500
42 (276)	39 (515)
Medium Academic Orientation	
26 (293)	18 (384)
Low Academic Orientation	
8 (325)	6 (780)

TABLE 7.7

CHURCH ATTENDANCE FOR CATHOLICS
BY MAJOR ETHNIC GROUP,
BY SEX, BY SES (TWS 1962)
(Per Cent Attending Weekly)

Ethnic Group	Male		Female	
	-$7,500	+$7,500	-$7,500	+$7,500
Irish	89 (462)	93 (483)	95 (166)	96 (273)
German	89 (360)	89 (280)	94 (159)	81 (105)
Polish	80 (183)	78 (127)	91 (122)	90 (59)
Italian	66 (468)	72 (305)	78 (204)	86 (166)

TABLE 7.8

CHURCH ATTENDANCE FOR CATHOLICS
BY MAJOR ETHNIC GROUP BY SEX
(Per Cent Attending Weekly)

Ethnic Group	Male	Female
Irish	91 (945)	96 (439)
German	89 (640)	89 (264)
Polish	79 (310)	91 (181)
Italian	68 (773)	83 (370)

TABLE 8.1

RELIGIOUS CHANGERS BY RELIGIOUS GROUPS (RSS)

Original religion	Present Religion					Total
	Protestant	Catholic	Jew	Other	None	
Protestant	85	2	0	2	11	100 (2007)
Catholic	2	91	0	1	6	100 (833)
Jew	1	0	84	2	13	100 (272)
Other	13	2	2	67	16	100 (108)
None	24	2	1	7	66	100 (110)

TABLE 8.2

SCHOOL QUALITY INDEX FOR APOSTATES,
CONVERTS, AND TOTAL SAMPLE (RSS)

	Apostates	Converts	Sample
A	15	11	6
B	9	7	8
C	54	59	54
D	23	24	32
	101 (304)	101 (175)	100 (3397)

TABLE 8.3

APOSTASY RATES FOR THREE RELIGIOUS GROUPS
BY INCOME (PER CENT CHANGING) (RSS)

	Protestant	Catholic	Jew
High	11 (875)	5 (375)	11 (81)
Low	12 (871)	6 (345)	12 (153)

TABLE 8.4

APOSTATES, CONVERTS, AND OTHERS
BY MARITAL STATUS (RSS)

	Apostates	Converts	Total Sample
Single	70	56	62
Married or planning marriage	30	44	38
	100 (304)	100 (175)	100 (3397)

TABLE 8.5

APOSTATES AND CONVERTS
ON SELECTED ADJECTIVES (RSS)

	Apostates	Converts	Others
Ambitious	44	59	56
Athletic	27	31	32
Cooperative	50	57	62
Cultured	24	25	20
Easy-going	31	31	36
Fun-loving	37	45	46
Good-looking	21	27	22
Happy	31	43	49
Idealistic	39	50	33
Intellectual	37	28	21
Lazy	17	14	9
Moody	35	36	23
Obliging	22	31	29
Poised	18	27	24
Rebellious	18	20	9
N =	304	175	3397

TABLE 8.6

SELECTED CHARACTERISTICS
FOR APOSTATES AND CONVERTS (RSS)

	Apostate	Convert	Sample
Per Cent Liberal	56	48	48
Ideas as Purpose of Education	76	73	67
Career Activity:			
Research and college	40	25	19
Education	22	30	33
Federal Government	19	13	14
Occupational Values:			
Money	30	21	24
Creativity	65	60	61
Others (help)	50	65	65
Ideas	57	47	39
Leadership	36	41	41
People	40	54	56
Freedom	24	24	18
High API	29	19	18
Graduate School (total)	41	27	32
Arts and Sciences	28	15	14
Professional	16	12	18
N =	304	175	3397

TABLE 8.7

INTELLECTUALITY BY APOSTASY
BY HAPPINESS (PER CENT INTELLECTUAL)
(RSS)

	Apostates		Non-apostates	
Happy	Not Happy		Happy	Not Happy
30 (27)	40 (77)		19 (273)	19 (267)

TABLE 8.8

NOT HAPPINESS AND INTELLECTUALITY FOR THREE
MAJOR RELIGIOUS GROUPS (RSS)

	Per Cent Not Happy			Per Cent Intellectual		
	Apostate	Non-Apostate	Diff.	Apostate	Non-Apostate	Diff.
Protestant	65 (209)	50 (1675)	15	35 (209)	18 (1675)	17
Catholic	80 (48)	42 (748)	38	47 (48)	19 (748)	28
Jew	57 (31)	50 (227)	7	39 (31)	25 (227)	14

TABLE 8.9A

APOSTASY AND CHANGE TO A LIBERAL ARTS CAREER
BY APOSTASY RATE OF SCHOOL
(Per Cent Changing from Careers Not Requiring Graduate School
to Liberal Arts Careers Requiring Graduate School)

	Apostates	Non-Apostates
High apostasy schools	6 (116)	4 (561)
Low apostasy schools	7 (566)	8 (1865)

TABLE 8.9B

	Apostates	Non-Apostates
High apostasy schools	30 (166)	21 (561)
Low apostasy schools	25 (166)	14 (1865)

TABLE 8.10

OLD RELIGION OF CONVERTS AND NEW RELIGION
OF APOSTATES FOR CATHOLICS
INVOLVED IN RELIGIOUS CHANGE

	Converts	Apostates
Protestant	79	24
Jew	3	1
Other	6	8
None	13	66
	100 (706)	100 (1031)

TABLE 8.11

SELECTED DEMOGRAPHIC INFORMATION
ON APOSTATES AND CONVERTS (1962)

	Apostates (1031)*	Born Cath. (683)	Converts (706)*	Born Prot. (1740)**
% Over 25	31	16	28	18
% Male	71	60	58	57
% Negro	2	1	12	4
% Married or planning marriage	44	27	59	44

*TWS   **RSS

TABLE 8.12A

MARITAL STATUS OF RELIGIOUS CHANGERS BY AGE
(Per Cent Married or Planning Marriage)

	Apostates	Born Catholics	Converts	Born Protestants
Over 25	73 (315)	60 (105)	86 (191)	77 (309)
Under 25	32 (701)	20 (591)	47 (502)	36 (1405)

TABLE 8.12B

AGE OF RELIGIOUS CHANGERS BY MARITAL STATUS
(Per Cent Over 25)

	Apostates	Born Catholics	Converts	Born Protestants
Married	51 (454)	33 (186)	40 (406)	37 (746)
Not Married	15 (562)	9 (510)	11 (287)	9 (968)

TABLE 8.13

APOSTASY AND CONVERSION BY ETHNIC GROUP

	Apostates	Born Cath.	Converts	Born Prot.
Anglo-Saxon	18	14	41	44
Irish	15	23	11	9
German	19	20	29	27
Italian	14	12		
Polish	6	6		
Other	28	25	20*	20**
	100	100	101	100

*12% American Negro   **3% American Negro

TABLE 8.14

APOSTASY AND CONVERSION BY HOMETOWN SIZE

	Apostates	Born Cath.	Converts	Born Prot.
Over Half Million	46	39	26	24
100,000 - 500,000	16	18	15	15
Under 100,000	26	30	35	33
Farm or Open Country	13	12	25	28
	101	99	101	100

TABLE 8.15
APOSTASY AND CONVERSION BY REGION OF COUNTRY

	Apostates	Born Cath.	Converts	Born Prot.
New England- Middle Atlantic	48	56	30	27
North Central	23	29	28	31
South	7	6	15	25
Mountain and West	16	6	22	16
Other*	6	3	5	2
	100	100	100	101

*Foreign-born, Alaska, Hawaii, etc.

TABLE 8.16

CHURCH ATTENDANCE FOR CONVERTS
TO CATHOLICISM BY MARITAL STATUS
(Per Cent Going Weekly)

Single	46 (277)
Marriage by next autumn	78 (119)
Married	50 (263)

TABLE 9.1

DISTINCTIVE RELIGIOUS TRAITS

Trait	Item
Protestant	
1. High not going to graduate school	Fall plans
2. Education	Future career
3. Other professional	Future career
4. Elementary education	Career employer
5. No pressure	Occupational value
6. Slow sure progress	Occupational value
7. High academic performance	Academic performance index
8. Per cent conservative	Political orientations
9. Drive	Drive scale (from self-description)

TABLE 9.1 (continued)

Trait	Item

Catholic
1. High going to graduate school . Fall plans
2. Intellectual. . . . . Intellectual ideal scale (self-description)
3. Business . . . . Future career
4. Large corporation . . . . . . Career employer
5. Low academic performance . . Academic performance index
6. Per Cent liberal . . . . Political orientations
7. Per Cent against modern art . Artistic orientation

Jewish
1. High going to graduate school . Fall plans
2. Science . . . . Future career
3. Medicine . . . . Future career
4. Law. . . . . Future career
5. Small companies . . . . Career employer
6. Self-employment. . . . . Career employer
7. Chance to make money. . . . . Occupational value
8. Chance to be creative . . . . . Occupational value
9. Working in world of ideas . . . Occupational value
10. High academic performance. . Academic performance index
11. Per Cent liberal . . . . Political orientation
12. Per Cent unconventional. . . . Conventionality orientation
13. High sophistication . . . . . . Personality scales (from self-description)
14. High emotionality . . . . . . Personality scales
15. High extroversion . . . . . . Personality scales
16. High intellectual . . . . . . Personality scales

TABLE 9.2

RELIGIOUS TRAITS BY RELIGIOSITY (RSS)

N's	Protestant	Catholic	Jew
High religious	346	259	105
Medium religious	985	417	122
Low religious	337	141	41

		High Religious	Medium Religious	Low Religious
A. Protestant Traits				
1. High go graduate school	Protestant	27	23	30
	Catholic	36	30	38
	Jew	47	49	54
2. Education	Protestant	45	35	24
	Catholic	28	25	20
	Jew	33	25	22
3. Other professional	Protestant	22	15	12
	Catholic	28	25	20
	Jew	33	25	22
4. Elementary education	Protestant	43	34	25
	Catholic	29	23	25
	Jew	32	26	20
5. Helpful	Protestant	82	67	64
	Catholic	74	46	54
	Jew	73	56	55
6. Slow sure progress	Protestant	27	37	34
	Catholic	31	29	30
	Jew	23	34	17
7. High API	Protestant	16	16	21
	Catholic	15	16	15
	Jew	19	30	31
8. Per Cent conservative	Protestant	46	36	42
	Catholic	34	31	31
	Jew	22	11	25
9. Drive scale	Protestant	62	53	52
	Catholic	52	38	42
	Jew	55	48	44

TABLE 9.2 (continued)

		High Religious	Medium Religious	Low Religious
B. Catholic Traits				
1. High go				
2. Intellectual	Protestant	22	13	15
	Catholic	25	16	25
	Jew	18	30	35
3. Business	Protestant	7	16	19
	Catholic	20	28	15
	Jew	24	15	15
4. Large corporation	Protestant	10	24	32
	Catholic	29	34	29
	Jew	21	29	20
5. Low API	Cf. Table 9.2A.			
6. Per Cent liberal	Protestant	30	44	38
	Catholic	47	50	54
	Jew	67	70	60
7. Per Cent against modern art	Protestant	27	25	23
	Catholic	18	31	27
	Jew	20	13	
C. Jewish Traits				
1. High go				
2. Science	Protestant	7	7	6
	Catholic	6	6	6
	Jew	7	7	10
3. Medicine	Protestant	2	2	3
	Catholic	2	4	3
	Jew	5	8	5
4. Law	Protestant	1	1	7
	Catholic	3	6	8
	Jew	7	12	12
5. Small company	Protestant	9	14	21
	Catholic	15	26	22
	Jew	12	13	12
6. Self-employment	Protestant	1	2	3
	Catholic	2	4	1
	Jew	4	4	1

TABLE 9.2 (continued)

		High Religious	Medium Religious	Low Religious
C. Jewish Traits (continued)				
7. Chance to make money	Protestant	14	18	30
	Catholic	18	18	39
	Jew	36	38	39
8. Chance to be creative	Protestant	48	48	47
	Catholic	49	47	54
	Jew	64	66	70
9. Working in a world of ideas	Protestant	35	35	37
	Catholic	33	30	50
	Jew	47	51	57
10. High API	Cf. Table 9.2A.			
11. Per Cent liberal	Cf. Table 9.2B.			
12. Per Cent unconventional	Protestant	24	19	33
	Catholic	19	21	54
	Jew	43	38	75
13. Sophistication	Protestant	13	10	13
	Catholic	18	11	13
	Jew	15	19	10
14. Emotionality	Protestant	8	18	15
	Catholic	8	23	23
	Jew	18	20	27
15. Extroversion	Protestant	61	61	65
	Catholic	63	63	61
	Jew	58	74	77

TABLE 9.3

RELIGIOUS TRAITS BY CHURCH ATTENDANCE (RSS)

	Protestant		Catholic		Jew	
	Regular*	Irreg.	Regular**	Irreg.	Regular†	Irreg.
Graduate Plans	24	33	34	32	48	52
Academic Performance (Per Cent High)	18	22	16	10	26	30
Educational Career	40	29	27	24	27	27
Business Career	19	28	31	26	26	27
Occupational Values:						
Money	15	24	23	31	34	44
Creativity	45	55	48	61	64	67
Help	73	63	65	49	62	60
Ideas	35	42	33	50	47	59
Slow sure progress	35	33	31	37	28	23
Self-employed	5	8	8	11	11	19
	(773)	(791)	(513)	(120)	(141)	(80)

*Monthly **Weekly †Yearly

TABLE 9.4

RELIGIOUS TRAITS BY SOCIAL MARGINALITY (RSS)

Catholic Traits	Catholics		Protestants		Net Differ- ence
	Small- Town	Average	Small- Town	Average	
1. High go	24	33	24	28	+5
2. Intellectual	15	22	15	17	+5
3. Business	22	24	15	15	+2
4. Large corporation	23	33	21	25	+6
5. Modern art	29	29	24	26	-2
6. Liberal	48	50	44	44	+2
7. High API	90	85	82	80	-8
8. Religiosity	77	80	74	70	+7
	N = (206)	(830)	(1060)	(2007)	

Jewish Traits	Jews		Protestants		Net Differ- ence
	Medium	Large	Medium	Large	
1. High go	36	50	30	37	+7
2. Science	7	9	8	8	+2
3. Medicine	2	7	2	3	+4
4. Law	3	10	3	3	+7
5. Small company	25	18	9	10	-8
6. Self-employment	15	15	5	7	-2
7. Make money	36	40	20	20	+4
8. Creative	53	63	54	59	+5
9. World of ideas	41	51	38	43	+5
10. High API	21	27	18	27	-5
11. Liberal	64	67	42	44	+1
12. Unconventional	28	40	28	35	+7
13. Sophistication	18	16	13	13	-2
14. Emotionality	14	21	13	13	+7
15. Extroversion	28	31	23	23	+3
16. Intellectual	15	30	20	20	+15
	N = (63)	(209)	(460)	(480)	

APPENDIX II

COLLEGE TALENT INDEX

The College Talent Index (CTI) is a measure designed to classify colleges and universities on the basis of the average intellectual ability of the student body. It is based primarily on average scores of students in a particular college or university on the National Merit Scholarship Qualifying Test (NMSQT) plus a composite index constructed from several institutional characteristics of the colleges or universities which indicate the degree of admissions selectivity and emphasis on academic quality. The CTI yields a four point classification from Class A schools at the top through Class D schools at the bottom.

Construction of the CTI

First, all schools in the sample were ranked on the basis of the average NMSQT score for students attending each college out of a 10 per cent random sample of all high school students scoring above the 64th percentile on the 1959 NMSQT. These means[1] are based on the scores of students who entered each college in the fall of 1959 and thus are not exact estimates of the average intellectual ability of 1961 seniors. However, assuming that most colleges have not varied widely in two years, these data may be taken as a fairly accurate estimate of the intellectual level of the student body of each college during the college experience of this year's graduating class.

The reliability of these estimates was tested by NMSC (National Merit Scholarship Corporation) for its small samples (N=15-24). The correlation in 37 colleges between the mean NMSQT scores and the mean SAT (Standard Achievement Test) scores from the previous year for the entire freshman class was .92. In order to obtain data on as many of our schools as possible, the sample size was lowered to 7 students from the 10 per cent random sample enrolled in the 1959 freshman class. In schools where there were less than 7 students who were in the NMSC 10 per cent sample, the mean NMSQT scores were felt to be too unreliable to use and classification was made on the basis of the composite index of institutional characteristics described below.

Second, a composite index of institutional characteristics was constructed by counting the presence of each of the following characteristics as 1 and its absence as 0:
1. Membership in the College Entrance Examination Board;
2. A local chapter of Phi Beta Kappa;
3. Institutional expenditure of fifty dollars or more per year per student on library facilities;
4. Application deadline of July 1 or earlier for admission to fall term.

---

[1] Raw scores were converted to a 9 point equal-interval scale with scores ranging from 0 to 8. The mean scores for 114 schools in the study on which data were available ranged from 1.16 to 7.23.

Presence of these characteristics was felt to be indicative of emphasis on intellectual quality, while absence of such characteristics represents a relative lack of interest in intellectual quality and a lack of selectivity in accepting students for enrollment. Schools were rated on a 5 point scale, 0-4 on the composite index. The degree of correlation between the composite index and the NMSQT ratings for these cases where all information was available is seen below in Table 1:

Table 1

Composite Index Score

NMSQT Rating	4	3	2	1	0	N
= 4.50	7	3				10
3.50-4.49	4	4	1	1	1	11
2.50-3.49		9	18	10	4	41
2.00-2.49		2	1	8	11	22
= 1.99			1	2	7	10
						94

Third, the CTI was constructed by combining ratings on the NMSQT with those on the composite index as follows:

For all schools with NMSQT scores based on N=7 or larger:

Class A = NMSQT scores = 4.50
Class B =   "   "   = 3.50-4.49
Class C =   "   "   = 2.50-3.49
Class D =   "   "   = 2.49

EXCEPTION:

NMSQT scores 2.00-2.49 are placed in Class C if they are also scored 1, 2, or 3 on the combined index; schools in this range NMSQT are classified as Class D if they score 0 of the combined index.

Schools with NMSQT scores based on N=6 or less, or on which no NMSQT data are available, are classified as follows:

Class C = 1, 2, or 3 on combined index
Class D = 0 on combined index

There were 21 schools classified on this basis.

By these criteria the 135 schools fell into the four classes as follows:

Class A = 11 schools
Class B = 12   "
Class C = 71   "
Class D = 41   "

A list of schools by class is appended.

Use of the CTI

The CTI was used to adjust the meaning of grades at different levels of schools. On a rather arbitrary basis the following equivalence tables were constructed:

Academic Performance				
High	B- & up	B & up	B+ & up	A- & up
Middle	C & C+	C+ & B-	B- & B	B & B+
Low	C- & D+	C & down	C+ & down	B- & down

On the basis of the above adjustments it is estimated that the sample will yield approximately the following percentages:

	Unweighted	Weighted
Highs	20%	18%
Middles	40%	27%
Lows	40%	55%

The estimates on the left were made of the basis of unweighted sample estimates. Since weighting primarily will increase the size of the schools in Class C and D, this will probably have the effect of increasing the per cent of lows at the expense of the middles and, to a lesser extent, the highs.[2]

---

[2]Sources of data used in construction of College Talent Index:

1. NMSQT scores were supplied by Doctor Alexander Astin of the National Merit Scholarship Corporation

2. College Board membership data were supplied by Mrs. Ann K. Pasanella of the College Entrance Examination Board.

3. Data on Phi Beta Kappa chapters from the Phi Beta Kappa Bulletin, Vol. 23, February 20, 1960.

4. Data of library expenditure from Library Statistics of Colleges and Universities, 1959-60, Part I: Institutional Data (U. S. Department of Health, Education, and Welfare, Office of Education, CE-15023). The relevant statistic is the expenditure on library facilities per student, column 16 in Table 1, pp. 6-49.

5. Data on closing date for admission application were taken from the catalogues of each individual college.

APPENDIX III
OTHER INDICES USED IN THIS STUDY

Occupational Index

The Occupational Index used in this study was composed in the following fashion:

Science. — Astronomy, astrophysics, chemistry, physics, geography, geology, oceanography, metallurgy, meteorology, mathematics and statistics, anatomy, biology, biochemistry, botany, biophysics, entomology, genetics, microbiology, pathology, pharmacology, physiology, and zoology (N = 241).

Social Sciences and Humanities. — Clinical psychology, social psychology, industrial psychology, experimental psychology, anthropology, archaeology, economics, political science, sociology, fine and applied arts, English, creative writing, classical languages and literature, history, modern language and literature, and philosophy (N = 333).

Engineering. — Aeronautical, civil, chemical, electrical, industrial, metallurgical, and mining (N = 278).

Education. — All primary or secondary educational fields and physical education, musical education, and art education (N = 1040).

Business. — Advertising, public relations, accounting, secretarial science, personnel, and other business (N = 565).

Other professional. — Agricultural science, forestry, farming, architecture, city planning, journalism, radio, television, library science, theology, religion, public administration, foreign service, social work, home economics, military service, dentistry, nursing, optometry, pharmacy, physical therapy, occupational therapy, veterinary science, medical technician, and dental hygiene (N = 478).

Law. — N = 91.

Medicine. — N = 126

Other. — Not listed, no answer, housewife (N = 246).

The SES scale was composed in the following fashion:

	Parental Occupation	Father's Education	Family Income
1	Blue collar and service and farm	No college	Less than $7500
2	Blue collar and service and farm	No college	More than $7500
3	Blue collar and service and farm	Part college	Less than $7500
4	Blue collar and service and farm	Part college	More than $7500
5	White collar	No college	Less than $7500
6	White collar	No college	More than $7500
7	White collar	Part college	Less than $7500
8	White collar	Part college	More than $7500

Upper class was composed of 4, 6, 7, and 8.

Drive Scale

The drive scale was composed of the following adjectives:

     Positive: Ambitious, energetic, hard-driving

     Negative: Lazy, easy-going.

Low score.—A negative adjective and no positive adjective.

Medium score.—One positive and no negative or two positive and one negative.

High score.—Two or three positive and no negative.

Sophistication Scale

The sophistication scale was composed of the following adjectives: poised, good-looking, and sophisticated. A low score had none of the adjectives, a medium score one adjective and a high score two or three adjectives.

Emotionality Scale

The emotionality scale was composed of the following adjectives: high-strung, impetuous, rebellious, moody. A low score had none of the adjectives, a medium score one of the adjectives and a high score two or more adjectives.

Extroversion Scale

The extroversion scale was composed of the following adjectives:

     Positive: Outgoing, talkative, witty, fun-loving

     Negative: Calm, reserved, shy, quiet.

The score was determined by the presence of a positive punch and the absence of a negative punch. Thus scores ran from 0 to 8. Cutting points were at 3 and 5.

Intellectual-Idealism

The Intellectual-Idealism scale was composed of the following adjectives: cultured, idealistic, intellectual. A low score was indicated by no check, a medium by one, and a high score by two or three checks.

APPENDIX IV

THE SAMPLE DESIGN

Delimitation of the Universe

The universe for the survey was defined to include:

All students completing the requirements for their baccalaureate degrees during the Spring term (semester, quarter, or trimester) of 1961 and upon whom such degrees
were conferred at the end of that term by an eligible institution of higher learning.

A number of the concepts employed in the foregoing are in need
of explanation:

Baccalaureate recipients were here defined as including all those
receiving a first-level earned degree of a type normally based on at
least four years of degree-credit work beyond the high school level
with the exception of those receiving a first-level degree from a professional school requiring at least two years of undergraduate work
prior to admission. The decision to exclude the specified set of first-
professional degree recipients derived from the focus of the surveys on
graduate educational plans. It was felt that, in practice, the degrees
granted by professional schools of the type here excluded were generally terminal. The largest groups excluded under this provision are
recipients of M.D., D.D.S., L.L.B., and B.D. degrees. Groups like these
did not appear to fit into the study design very well. The excluded first-
level degree recipients amounted to about eight or nine per cent of the
total first-level degree recipients during the 1960-1961 academic year.
While the rule under which they were excluded was admittedly arbitrary, it most certainly served to delimit a universe for the study which
was more nearly congruent with the study objectives than one in which
all recipients of first-professional degrees would be included.[1]

---

[1]See W. C. Eells and H. A. Haswell, Academic Degrees (OE-
54008, Bulletin 1960, No. 28, Government Printing Office, Washington,
1960) and W. E. Tolliver, Earned Degrees Conferred 1959-1960 (OE-
54013-60, Circular No. 687, Government Printing Office, Washington,
1962) for an elaboration of these problems. Beginning with the 1960-
1961 earned degree statistics, the Office of Education will be making a
distinction between baccalaureate and first-professional degrees only
slightly different from the one made in the present survey. Statistics

The restriction of the universe to Spring convocation degree recipients was due to two rather different considerations. First of all, many of the students who received their degrees in August of 1960 or during the Winter of 1960-1961 might be expected to have already embarked, by the time of the survey in April, 1961, along a line of postgraduate activity. Some were already serving in the military establishment, some were in graduate school, some were working at regular jobs, and others were full-time housewives. A questionnaire dealing with plans for the first year out of college did not seem appropriate for mid-year graduates and yet their special problems did not seem to be of sufficient interest to warrant the design and administration of a special retrospective questionnaire. Second, it was anticipated that it would be quite difficult to locate these individuals and to elicit their cooperation.

This combination of circumstances made it appear prudent to exclude mid-year (including Summer session) graduates from the scope of the inquiry. The problem then became one of defining a mid-year graduate. A number of institutions hold only one convocation a year while others have only Summer session and Spring convocations. But there are students at such institutions who complete their degree requirements at the end of the Autumn semester and are then free to enter into their postgraduate activities in February. Even though they do not receive their degrees until June, their status is essentially identical to that of students from multiple convocation institutions who are graduated in mid-year. It was thus decided to include in the survey only students who were still in the process of completing their baccalaureate degree requirements during the Spring term. This included all students who were formally registered as well as some students who were not registered but were working on undergraduate honor theses, engaged in required practice teaching, or fulfilling some other type of internship requirement. On the basis of a special survey of college registrars, we estimate that approximately 75 per cent of all those receiving baccalaureate degrees during the period from July, 1960 through June, 1961 did not complete the requirements for their degrees until the Spring term of 1961 and were thus included within the scope of the present research. Our more detailed estimates appear in the following table:

---

for baccalaureate and first-professional degrees involving four years of <u>academic</u> credit will for the first time be separated from the statistics for professional degrees requiring five or more years of <u>academic</u> credit. Thus, the only discrepancy between the NORC and the Office of Education classifications will be in the handling of participants in the relatively rare five-year programs leading to bachelor degrees in Engineering and the five-year bachelor degree programs in fields like Architecture and Forestry. The relatively small number of recipients of degrees under such programs were considered as eligible for the NORC survey but will be combined with recipients of first-professional degrees in fields like Law, Medicine, Dentistry, and Divinity in the Office of Education Series.

PERCENTAGE DISTRIBUTION OF STUDENTS RECEIVING
BACCALAUREATE DEGREES FROM JULY, 1960 THROUGH
JUNE, 1961 BY PERIOD DURING WHICH DEGREE
REQUIREMENTS WERE COMPLETED*

Summer, 1960** 12%	
"Regular students"	10
Summer session only	2
Autumn-Winter, 1960-61** 13	
Spring, 1961 . . . . <u>75</u>	
100%	

*Based on March, 1961 survey of registrars
at the 135 institutions in the NORC sample. The
estimates are so weighted as to provide an un-
biased estimate for 1960-1961 graduates of all
U.S. institutions of higher learning.
**About one-sixth to one-fifth of those
completing their requirements mid-year (i.e.,
about four or five per cent of all graduates)
were in attendance at schools with a single
convocation and therefore did not actually receive degrees until the end of the Spring term.

The distributions of a number of characteristics among the students completing their requirements mid-year unquestionably differ
appreciably from the comparable distributions among those finishing in
the Spring. We know, for instance, that the mid-year students were
disproportionately in attendance at Southern and public institutions,
while the Spring students were disproportionately from Northeastern
and private institutions. There are quite probably many concomitant
differences between the two groups of students arising out of the variation among institutions in terms of regulations and customs with regard
to the phasing of the various academic junctures as well as more idio-
syncratic factors which cause a student to deviate from the time pattern
conventional at his own institution. Thus, in generalizing from the current sample, we suggest the rather conservative approach of limiting
projections to those 1960-1961 graduates who completed their baccalaureate requirements during the Spring term of 1961.[2]

---

[2]Some notion of the possible danger involved in projections from
the present survey to the total 1960-1961 graduating class can be gained
from the following rather extreme hypothetical example.

Assume that 30 per cent of the Spring students but only
10 per cent of the mid-year students planned to enroll for
graduate courses during 1961-1962. Then, a projection to
the entire 1960-1961 class from the survey of Spring students would show 106,000 students planning to enroll while
a survey of the entire class would have resulted in a pro-

An "eligible institution" for purposes of this study was one which was listed in Part 3 (Higher Education) of the 1957-1958 Office of Education Education Directory as being accredited by one of the six regional accrediting associations (including institutions with only provisional accreditation). Also included were those baccalaureate-degree-granting institutions which were not accredited by a regional accrediting association but which were listed in the Directory as having an enrollment of five hundred or more students.[3]

The use of the foregoing sampling frame resulted in the exclusion from the survey universe of certain types of students who might properly have been included:

1. Students who received at the end of the Spring term of 1961 a baccalaureate degree from an institution which had not had a baccalaureate-degree program in 1956-1957.

2. Students who received at the end of the Spring term of 1961 a baccalaureate degree from an institution which was listed in the 1957-1958 Directory as not being accredited by one of the regional accrediting associations and which were listed in that Directory as having a total enrollment of less than five hundred students.

3. Students who received at the end of the Spring term of 1961 a baccalaureate degree from an institution which had a baccalaureate-degree program in 1956-1957 but which did not meet the criteria for inclusion in the Directory.[4]

---

jection of 88,000. Thus, the projection derived from the Spring students alone would be about 20 per cent too high.

This example may be highly unrealistic. Twenty percentage points may be a substantially larger difference than one would ever find between the mid-year and Spring students with respect to any variable of consequence. Unfortunately, we are aware of no data which would enable us to estimate the magnitude of parametric differences between the two populations. Thus, caution in the scope of projections is advisable, particularly where relatively small proportions of the total population are characterized by the property in question.

[3] The enrollment figures were for the Fall of 1956. They presumably included all students enrolled for courses beyond the high school level but exclude students who were enrolled only for correspondence courses.

[4] See page one of the previously cited Directory for the criteria. Given the leniency of the standards for inclusion in the Directory, this source of loss was probably totally inconsequential. Excluded institutions would appear to have been primarily "diploma mills," the degrees from which were recognized as legitimate by practically no legitimated institutions connected with higher education.

Since the statistics pertaining to earned degrees conferred during 1960-1961 will not be available until the Summer of 1963, it is impossible at present to make a precise estimate of the number of legitimate baccalaureate degree recipients excluded from the survey universe. Our best guess is that the exclusions amount to somewhere between five and ten per cent of the hypothetically complete universe. A more precise estimate will be made at such time as the requisite conferment data become available.

The Sample

A two-stage sampling scheme was followed in the selection of students. The first stage involved the selection of 135 of the 1,039 institutions defined as eligible for the purposes of this study.[5]

Clustering by school was accepted in preference to a single-stage sample wherein students would be subsampled from each of the 1,039 schools. One reason for this decision was the necessity of employing field representatives at each of the schools from which students were being taken in order to insure the accuracy of the subsampling process within the school and to maximize the rate of questionnaire completion. The costs of employing field representatives at all 1,039 schools would have been prohibitive. The second reason for clustering was the intention to analyze certain of the data on a school-by-school basis. For this purpose, it was deemed desirable to select a relatively large number of cases from each of the schools falling into the sample. Of course the fewer schools in the sample the larger the "take" from each school (given a fixed total sample size) but the larger the sampling variance of estimates pertaining to the entire universe. Balancing the two pres-

---

[5] A number of arbitrary decisions were involved in the formation of primary sampling units. It is difficult to determine the limits of a particular institution in situations where several rather distinct colleges are affiliated in such a way that they can be viewed as either components of a larger university or separate schools. Since the expected values of estimates to the universe of graduates are not affected by the manner in which primary samplings are formed, expediency in terms of the field operation was allowed to govern the process. A few examples follow:
1. Harvard and Radcliffe were treated as one.
2. Brown and Pembroke were treated as one.
3. Columbia and Barnard were treated as one.
4. Tulane and Newcomb were treated as one.
5. Brooklyn Center, Brooklyn College of Pharmacy, and C. W. Post College were treated as one.
6. The Minneapolis and Duluth Campuses of the University of Minnesota were treated as one.
7. The various branches of the University of California were each treated separately.
8. The various branches of the College of the City of New York were each treated separately.

sures toward a smaller number of primary sampling units against the pressure toward the minimization of the variance of over-all estimates, a first-stage sample of 135 was felt to be more or less optimal.

Each institution was first allocated into one of four strata on the basis of an index reflecting the postgraduate educational activities of its recent graduates. Values with respect to each of eight variables were determined for each of the 1,039 schools. The value with respect to a given variable for a given school was the number of individuals who had received a baccalaureate degree from that school and who:

1) were awarded a Ph.D. during 1957, 1958, or 1959 in Mathematics, Physics, Astronomy, Chemistry, or an Earth Science.
2) were awarded a Ph.D. during 1957, 1958, or 1959 in Botany, Phytopathology, Biochemistry, Genetics, Microbiology, Physiology, or a related field, Zoology, in some other Biological Science, or in a Medical Science.
3) were awarded a Ph.D. during 1957, 1958, or 1959 in Engineering.
4) were awarded a Ph.D. during 1957, 1958, or 1959 in Sociology, Anthropology, Archeology, Economics, Geography, or Psychology.
5) were awarded a Ph.D. during 1957, 1958, or 1959 in History, a Foreign Language, English, or Philosophy.
6) were awarded a Ph.D. or Ed.D. in Education during 1957, 1958, or 1959.
7) enrolled as a freshman in an American medical school during one of four selected academic years between 1949 and 1955.
8) enrolled as a freshman in an American dental school at some time between 1951 and 1957.

The schools were ranked with respect to each of these eight variables independently. The four strata were then defined as follows:

I. One of the 25 top schools with respect to one or more of the eight variables.
II. Not in Stratum I, but with a rank between 26 and 100 with respect to one or more of the eight variables.
III. Not in Strata I or II, but had a value of two or more per year with respect to one or more of the eight variables.
IV. Not in Strata I, II, or III.

Within each of the above strata, the institutions were allocated into two groups on the basis of whether they were under public or under private control. Within each of the resulting eight strata, the institutions were ordered with respect to a measure of size and institutions were generally sampled systematically with probability proportionate to the measure of size. In the case of several strata, it was necessary to sample with equal probability a substratum composed of the smallest schools, in order to avoid intricate weighting at the tabulation stage of the survey.

The measure of size was usually the number of 1958-1959 bachelor degrees awarded by that school as reported in the 1960 edition of the American Council of Education's <u>American Universities and Colleges</u>.[6] Frequently, separate figures appeared for bachelor degrees and for first professional degrees. For institutions where all professional degrees granted were clearly of the type which were being treated as baccalaureate degrees in the present survey,[7] the measure of size was the sum of the bachelor and first professional figures. For each of the 111 institutions thought to grant some first professional degrees which were to be excluded from the survey, a letter was sent to the registrar requesting the total count of bachelor degrees and first professional degrees of the type to be included in the survey granted by his institution during the 1958-1959 academic year. The figure supplied by the registrar was then used as the measure of size.

The following table shows how the universe and the sample were distributed with respect to the eight strata:

DISTRIBUTION OF THE UNIVERSE AND THE SAMPLE WITH RESPECT TO THE EIGHT STRATA

Index of Postgraduate Activities	Public Control			Private Control		
	Universe		Sample	Universe		Sample
	Number of Schools	Total Measure of Size	Number of Schools	Number of Schools	Total Measure of Size	Number of Schools
I	35	69,414	22	31	32,613	22
II	66	56,334	20	92	38,085	20
III	113	44,684	10	204	40,614	11
IV	138	26,571	10	360	36,592	20
Total. .	352	197,003	62	687	147,904	73

---

[6]In the relatively rare instances when no data were available in the ACE volume with respect to the number of degrees conferred by a given school, the data appearing in the Office of Education's <u>Earned Degrees</u> volume for 1957-1958 were employed.

[7]In other words, the institution had no medical, dental, law, divinity, or other professional school which granted first professional degrees of the type being excluded from the present survey.

The number of schools selected from a given stratum was arbitrary. The numbers were arrived at by trying to balance the needs of the anticipated school-by-school analysis against the need to avoid a complex system of weights.

A field representative was assigned to each of the 135 schools. His first task was to collect the previously cited data pertaining to the number of degrees of various types conferred at each convocation during the academic year. This information was necessary for the establishment of the over-all sampling rate for the survey. The next task of the field representative was to assemble a list of all seniors who were completing their baccalaureate requirements during the Spring term and who, it was anticipated, were going to be graduated at the end of that term. Officials at every one of the 135 selected institutions cooperated with the field representative in assembling the list of eligible seniors and granted general approval of the survey.

Prospective baccalaureate degree recipients from institutions in Strata I and II were sampled at a rate of .288 while those from institutions in Strata III and IV were sampled at a rate of .096. The differential sampling rates were adopted because among the chief objectives of the survey was the estimation of parameters pertaining to graduating seniors who were planning to go on for graduate study in particular academic fields. Even though the stratification was based on the absolute numbers of eventual Ph.D.'s produced by a school rather than its per capita productivity, there was reason to believe that the rate of graduate study would be appreciably higher among Strata I and II baccalaureates than among those from Strata III and IV. While the employment of differential sampling rates undoubtedly increased the sampling variance of most estimates pertaining to the total cohort of graduating seniors, it was felt that this disadvantage would be more than compensated by the gains in the precision of estimates pertaining to certain relatively rare graduate fields.

For any given school, the subsampling rate for students was the ratio of the over-all sampling rate for the school's stratum to the school's probability of being selected. This procedure automatically compensated for any disproportionality between the measure of size which had been assigned to the school at the primary stage of selection and the actual number of students found to be eligible for inclusion in the survey. The assigned measures of size were, of course, quite imperfectly related to the actual sizes owing to differences among the schools in the magnitude of the changes which had taken place from 1958-1959 to 1960-1961 in the sizes of their graduating classes. In addition, schools varied markedly in the proportion of graduates completing the requirements for the baccalaureate degree during a term other than the Spring one. Nevertheless, the disproportionality resulting from these factors introduced no appreciable bias in the estimates derived from the sample. The primary consequence was a considerable variation among schools in the number of students selected for the sample and quite probably a slight increase in the sampling variance of the survey statistics, even though they are all of the ratio type.

At sixty of the schools, <u>all</u> eligible seniors were to be taken into the sample because the probability of the school was either less than or equal to the student sampling rate which had been set for the school's stratum. At the remaining seventy-five schools, a sample of eligible seniors was drawn at a rate computed in the manner indicated in the preceding paragraph. The actual sampling procedures employed varied from school to school. A copy of the field representatives' sampling instruction appears at the end of this appendix.

As was anticipated, lists of eligible seniors assembled during March and April turned out to contain a number of false positives, individuals who failed to meet at least one of our criteria of eligibility. The most frequent types of false positives were cases where the student himself did not (in April, May, or June) think that he would graduate at the end of the current term.[8] Of the 36,013 completed questionnaires returned prior to the survey deadline, 2,231 were from individuals who appeared to be ineligible for the survey. These questionnaires were omitted from all tabulations.

In making estimates from the sample, two types of weighting are necessary. The returns from schools the probabilities of which were less than the sampling rates for their strata had to be so weighted as to bring the probability of a student in such a school up to the stratum level. This most frequently occured with respect to III and IV strata schools. Many of the schools in those strata had been sampled at a rate of .0555 and it was thus necessary to weight their returns by a factor of 1.723 to bring the probability for their students up to the over-all stratum sampling rate (.096).

In addition to the above initial weighting, the returns from all III and IV schools were weighted by a factor of three to compensate for the differential sampling rates between strata. Thus, the range of weights among schools was from 1 to 5.169 and averaged 1.677.

Since the eligibility status of many of the students who were sent questionnaires but did not return them is not known, it is impossible to make a precise estimate of the survey completion rate. Assuming that the proportion of non-respondents with unknown eligibility status who were in fact ineligible was the same as the proportion of ineligibles among those who did respond, the weighted completion rate for the survey was 85 per cent. Since the non-respondents from the 1961 survey are being followed up with fair success in NORC's periodic surveys of the Spring, 1961 cohort, it may soon be possible to form at least a fair impression of the direction and magnitude of the non-response bias in the original survey.

---

[8]See Question 43 of the questionnaire. A later questionnaire (Spring, 1962) was pre-tested on a sample of the 1961 respondents who had not expected to be graduated in the Spring of 1961. While the expectations of the vast majority had in fact been correct, some of the respondents were graduated in Spring, 1961, in spite of their pessimism in response to Question 43.

APPENDIX V

LISTING OF SAMPLE COLLEGES AND UNIVERSITIES

SAMPLE OF COLLEGES AND UNIVERSITIES
FOR SURVEY OF 1961 GRADUATING CLASS
(Alphabetical Listing)

College or University	Number Eligible Students Sampled	Per cent Responding
Alabama, University of—University ..	471	62
Albion College—Albion, Michigan. . . .	171	100
Arkansas State College—Jonesboro. . .	197	72
Arkansas, University of—Fayetteville .	365	64
Atlantic Union College—South Lancaster, Massachusetts.	50	98
Auburn University—Auburn, Alabama. .	178	82
Beloit College—Beloit, Wisconsin. . . .	147	98
Blackburn College—Carlinville, Illinois	41	100
Boston College—Chestnut Hill, Massachusetts	533	91
Boston University—Massachusetts . . .	396	73
Briar Cliff College—Sioux City, Iowa. .	25	100
Bridgewater College—Bridgewater, Virginia	74	93
Brooklyn College—New York City. . . .	593	90
Brooklyn, Polytechnic Institute of— New York City	209	72
Brown University (and Pembroke College)—Providence, Rhode Island. . . .	584	77
California, University of—Berkeley. . .	595	87
California, University of—Los Angeles.	487	82
Carnegie Institute of Technology— Pittsburgh, Pennsylvania	230	97
Case Institute of Technology— Cleveland, Ohio	260	84
Chico State College—Chico, California .	264	91
Cincinnati, University of—Ohio	762	89
Clark University—Worcester, Massachusetts	105	99
Cleary College—Ypsilanti, Michigan . .	19	79
Clemson Agricultural College— Clemson, South Carolina	329	99
Colorado State University—Fort Collins	427	88
Colorado, University of—Boulder. . . .	501	82
Columbia University—New York City. .	382	79
Concordia Teachers College— Seward, Nebraska	114	99
Cornell University—Ithaca, New York .	447	84

COLLEGES AND UNIVERSITIES (Continued)

College or University	Number Eligible Students Sampled	Per cent Responding
Dartmouth College—Hanover, New Hampshire	236	91
Delaware, University of—Newark	350	45
De Paul University—Chicago, Illinois	324	99
Detroit, University of—Michigan	177	84
Drexel Institute of Technology— Philadelphia, Pennsylvania	356	72
Eastern Michigan University— Ypsilanti, Michigan	461	86
Eastern Oregon College—La Grande	63	81
Eastern Washington College of Education—Cheney	157	79
Evansville College—Evansville, Indiana	160	99
Florence State College—Florence, Alabama	116	100
Fordham University—New York City	574	73
Fort Valley State College—Fort Valley, Georgia	98	83
Fresno State College—Fresno, California	425	68
Greenville College—Greenville, Illinois	101	100
Hamline University—St. Paul, Minnesota	146	98
Harvard University—Radcliff College— Cambridge, Massachusetts	491	75
Haverford College—Haverford, Pennsylvania	110	57
Hawaii, University of—Honolulu	624	96
Hebrew Teachers College—Brookline, Massachusetts	23	100
Henderson State Teachers College— Arkadelphia, Arkansas	113	90
Holy Cross, College of the—Worcester, Massachusetts	353	96
Hood College—Frederick, Maryland	98	100
Hunter College—New York City	647	61
Huron College—Huron, South Dakota	38	97
Illinois Institute of Technology—Chicago	155	93
Illinois, University of—Urbana	480	76
Indiana University—Bloomington	447	77
Iowa State University of Science and Technology—Ames	437	94
Kansas, University of—Lawrence	619	94

COLLEGES AND UNIVERSITIES (Continued)

College or University	Number Eligible Students Sampled	Per cent Responding
Kentucky, University of—Lexington . . .	427	87
Lake Erie College—Painesville, Ohio. .	80	86
Lake Forest College—Lake Forest, Illinois	104	94
Langston University—Langston, Oklahoma	63	86
Le Moyne College—Syracuse, New York	204	100
Long Beach State College—California. .	179	83
Long Island University—Brooklyn, New York.	434	69
Los Angeles State College—California .	309	80
Lycoming College—Williamsport, Pennsylvania.	107	79
Manhattanville College of the Sacred Heart—Purchase, New York.	143	100
Marquette University—Milwaukee, Wisconsin	386	96
Maryland, University of—College Park .	594	68
Mary Washington College— Fredericksburg, Virginia	224	93
Massachusetts,Institute of Technology, Cambridge, Massachusetts	206	88
McKendree College—Lebanon, Illinois .	47	77
Memphis State University—Memphis, Tennessee	256	91
Merrimac College—North Andover, Massachusetts	148	92
Miami, University of—Coral Gables, Florida.	419	94
Michigan State University—East Lansing, Michigan	453	94
Michigan, University of—Ann Arbor . .	588	93
Mills College of Education— New York City	29	100
Minnesota, University of—Minneapolis .	409	88
Minnesota, University of—Duluth Campus	78	78
Mississippi Southern College— Hattiesburg.	180	96
Mississippi State University—State College, Mississippi.	481	86
Montclair State College—Upper Montclair, New Jersey.	383	54
New York, City College of— New York City	519	95

COLLEGES AND UNIVERSITIES (Continued)

College or University	Number Eligible Students Sampled	Per cent Responding
New York, State University of:		
College of Education at Buffalo	418	93
College of Education at Fredonia . . .	146	92
New York University—New York City. .	385	74
North Carolina, University of—Chapel Hill.	407	94
Northland College—Ashland, Wisconsin.	53	81
Northwestern University—Evanston, Illinois	393	54
Notre Dame of Maryland, College of— Baltimore	87	100
Notre Dame University—Notre Dame, Indiana.	790	85
Oberlin College—Oberlin, Ohio	288	99
Ohio State University—Columbus	504	82
Ohio Wesleyan University—Delaware. .	350	81
Oklahoma Baptist University—Shawnee.	172	73
Oklahoma, University of—Norman . . .	420	86
Oregon State University —Corvallis. . .	614	88
Oregon, University of—Eugene	534	84
Pasadena College—Pasadena, California	104	99
Pembroke State College—Pembroke, North Carolina.	63	100
Pennsylvania State University— University Park	624	92
Pennsylvania, University of— Philadelphia	417	70
Pittsburgh, University of—Pennsylvania	233	71
Princeton University—Princeton, New Jersey	245	86
Rensselaer Polytechnic Institute— Troy, New York	238	81
Rochester Institute of Technology— Rochester, New York	238	75
St. Benedict, College of—St. Joseph, Minnesota	50	100
St. Bonaventure University—St. Bonaventure, New York	194	98
St. Scholastica, College of—Duluth, Minnesota	65	91
Sam Huston State Teachers College— Huntsville, Texas	221	94
San Jose State College—San Jose, California	422	93

COLLEGES AND UNIVERSITIES (Continued)

College or University	Number Eligible Students Sampled	Per cent Responding
South Dakota, State University of— Vermillion	247	92
Southeastern State College—Durant, Oklahoma	117	97
Southern California, University of— Los Angeles	297	73
Southern Illinois University— Carbondale	391	83
Southern Methodist University— Dallas, Texas	529	54
Southern University—Baton Rouge, Louisiana	180	92
Stanford University—Stanford, California	413	88
Susquehanna University—Selinsgrove, Pennsylvania	85	100
Sweet Briar College—Sweet Briar, Virginia	87	100
Syracuse University—Syracuse, New York	294	31
Texas, University of—Austin	412	80
Tulane University—New Orleans, Louisiana	171	69
Ursinus College—Collegeville, Pennsylvania	178	100
Wagner College—Staten Island, New York	255	100
Washington University—St. Louis, Missouri	543	69
Washington, University of—Seattle . . .	481	89
Wayne State University—Detroit, Michigan	470	89
Western Kentucky State College— Bowling Green	237	86
Western State College of Colorado— Gunnison	109	100
Williams College—Williamstown, Massachusetts	269	99
Wisconsin, University of—Madison . . .	520	88
Wyoming, University of—Laramie . . .	450	77
Xavier University—Cincinnati, Ohio . .	270	96

SUMMARY OF SCHOOL RESPONSE RATES

Per cent Return	N	Per cent of Schools	Cumulative Per cent of Schools
96 - 100	37	27.2	27.2
91 - 95	24	17.6	44.8
86 - 90	21	15.4	60.2
81 - 85	16	11.8	72.0
76 - 80	12	8.8	80.0
71 - 75	11	8.1	88.9
66 - 70	6	4.4	93.3
61 - 65	3	2.2	95.5
60 or less	6	4.4	99.9
	136*	99.9%	

*Totals 136 rather than 135 because of separate field operations at University of Minnesota, Duluth and University of Minnesota, Minneapolis.

SCHOOLS WITH LESS THAN 60 PER CENT RESPONSE

School	Per cent
Haverford College	57
Northwestern University	54
Montclair State College	54
Southern Methodist University	54
University of Delaware	45
Syracuse University	31

APPENDIX VI

SURVEY QUESTIONNAIRE (1961)

NATIONAL OPINION RESEARCH CENTER

UNIVERSITY OF CHICAGO
5720 WOODLAWN AVENUE · CHICAGO 37 · ILLINOIS

April, 1961

Dear Student:

National Opinion Research Center, a non-profit research organization affiliated with the University of Chicago, has been asked by three Federal agencies, the U.S. Office of Education, The National Science Foundation, and the National Institutes of Health, to survey the career plans of seniors in American colleges and universities.

You are one of 40,000 students in 135 schools who have been chosen by scientific probability sampling methods to participate in this study.

The research is designed to yield important information on the relationships between college experiences and career plans.

The questionnaire requires 30 minutes or so to fill out. Please answer the questions as frankly and accurately as you can. Your answers will be absolutely confidential, and no individual student's answers will be revealed in the reports, which will be based on statistical tabulations.

Almost all of the questions can be answered by drawing a circle around one or more numbers or letters in the right hand margins of the questionnaire. Thus:

> I am now-- (Circle one.)
>
> A student in high school 1
>
> A student in college . . . . . . ②
>
> A student in graduate or pro-
> fessional school X

NOTE: After each question there are instructions in parentheses. Please follow these instructions closely as they are very important for data processing.

    A.   If it says "(Circle one.)," draw a circle around only the one number or letter which best describes your answer, even though one or more other alternatives might be relevant.

    B.   If it says "(Circle one in each column.)" or "(Circle one in each row.)," please look to see that you have circled one and only one number or letter in each of the appropriate rows or columns.

    C.   If it says "(Circle as many as apply.)," circle as many or as few numbers or letters in the columns or rows as you think are relevant.

If you are interested in the results of this study, please write a letter or card requesting a copy of the results to National Opinion Research Center, 5720 South Woodlawn, Chicago 37, Illinois, after October, 1961.

Thank you very much for your help.

Sincerely,

James A. Davis

James A. Davis
Study Director

Survey 431

I. Plans For This Coming Fall

1. What will you be doing this Fall?

   Circle the number which describes what you will be doing this Fall.
   If you expect to be doing two things simultaneously, circle both. If
   you are considering two alternative plans, circle only the more probable.

   Working full time at a type of job which I expect to be my long run career
   field 2   (9)

   Non-career military service 3   1

   Working full time at a civilian job which will probably not be my long run
   career field 4

   Housewife 5

   Graduate study in an arts and science field (physical science, biological
   science, social science, humanities) 6

   Graduate study in a professional field (law, medicine, engineering,
   education, agriculture, social work, etc.) 7

   Other (Circle and specify:_____ . . . 8

2. How definite are the plans you circled in question 1? (Circle one.)

   Quite definite X   (10)
   Fairly definite, but subject to change. . . . 0   y
   Quite indefinite 1

3. If you are considering a set of alternative plans, different from the ones you
   circled in question 1, indicate them by circling the appropriate numbers below,
   using the categories from question 1.

   If you have no alternative plans in mind, circle the number nine below.

   2   3   4   5   6   7   8   9   (11)
                                             1

4. At the time you entered college, what were your plans for study beyond the bachelor's
   degree? (Circle one.)

   I planned to go into a line of work which requires graduate or
   professional training X   (12)

   I planned to go on for graduate or professional training, but I didn't
   have a specific field in mind 0   y

   I planned to stop at the bachelor's degree 1

   I didn't have any definite plans 2

5. Have you applied for admission to any graduate or professional school for the coming
   year? (Circle one.)

   *No, and I do not expect to go to school next year 4   (13)
   **No, but I do expect to go to school next year 5   9
   ***Yes, I applied to one school 6   IF 4,
   ***Yes, I applied to 2 or 3 schools 7   SKIP
   ***Yes, I applied to 4 or more schools 8   TO
                                                                        COL.
                                                                        23

   *IF "NO, AND DO NOT EXPECT TO GO TO SCHOOL NEXT YEAR": SKIP TO QUESTION 7.

   **IF "NO, BUT I DO EXPECT TO GO TO SCHOOL NEXT YEAR": SKIP TO QUESTION 6.

   ***IF "YES": PLEASE ANSWER a, b, AND c.

   a. How many schools accepted you? (Circle one.)

      None 0   (14)
      One 1   4
      More than one 2

2

b. How many schools rejected your application? (Circle one.)

None 5	(15)
One 6	9
More than one 7	

c. Have you any applications pending? (Circle one.)

Yes 0	(16)
No 1	y

6. Did you apply (or were you nominated) for financial support (scholarship, fellowship, assistantship, etc.) for this Fall? (Circle one.)

*No 7	(17)
**Yes 8	9

*IF "NO": Did you not apply because-- (Circle any which apply.)

I had no intention of going to school at the time applications were due . 0   (18)
I wouldn't need any support of this type 1   y
The amount I could get would have been too little 2
The duties attached would have been unsatisfactory 3
I didn't think I could get any 4
It didn't occur to me to apply 5
Other (Circle and specify:_____) . . . 6

**IF "YES": PLEASE ANSWER a, b, c, AND d.

a. To where did you apply or was your nomination sent? (Circle one or more.)

The school I will (probably) attend 0	(19)
Other schools or schools 1	y
Other source (government, private foundation, etc.) . 2	

b. Which ones offered you aid? (Circle one or more.)

The school I will (probably) attend 4	(20)
Other school or schools 5	9
Other source (government, private foundation, etc.) . 6	
No offers 7	

c. Which of the following do you expect to receive next year? (Circle one or more.)

Scholarship for part tuition 1	(21)
Scholarship for full tuition 2	9
Fellowship for tuition plus an amount under $1,000. . 3	
Fellowship for tuition plus $1,000 or more 4	
Teaching assistantship 5	
Research assistantship 6	
No financial support of this type 7	
Don't know yet 8	

d. From which of the following source or sources do you expect to receive financial aid (scholarship, fellowship, assistantship, etc.)? (Circle one or more.)

No financial aid of this type expected. 1	(22)
School I will attend 2	0
Private foundation, philanthropic organization, etc.. 3	
U.S. Federal government:	
National Defense Act 4	
National Science Foundation 5	
Public Health Service - National Institutes of Health 6	
Other 7	
State or local government (U.S.) 8	
Other (Circle and specify:_____). 9	

3

ARE YOU SURE OR FAIRLY SURE THAT YOU WILL BE ATTENDING GRADUATE OR PROFESSIONAL SCHOOL
NEXT YEAR? (ACADEMIC YEAR 1961-1962)?

    IF YES: PUT A CHECK IN THIS BOX AND SKIP TO QUESTION 13 . . . .

IF YES,
SKIP TO
COLUMN
32

    IF NO: ANSWER QUESTIONS 7 THROUGH 12.

7. If there were no obstacles in terms of finances, grade records, getting admitted,
    etc., would you <u>like</u> to go on for graduate or professional study in the future?
    (Circle one.)

                                                Yes . . . . 2 <u>(23)</u>

                                                Maybe 3   5

                                                  No 4

8. Do you expect to go on for graduate or professional school sometime in the
    future? (Circle one.)

                                            No . . . . 5 <u>(24)</u>

                                         Probably not 6   9

                                       *Probably yes 7

                                         *Yes 8

    <u>*IF "PROBABLY YES" OR "YES"</u>: PLEASE ANSWER a AND b.

    a. Do you expect that your future employer will send you or pay for your future
        studies? (Do not count savings from your pay or anticipated veteran's
        benefits.) (Circle one.)

                                                Yes . . . . 0 <u>(25)</u>

                                             No 1   y

    b. When will you start your graduate or professional studies?
        Make your single best prediction. (Circle one.)

                                          Academic Year

                                        '62 - '63 . . . . 0 <u>(26)</u>

                                        '63 - '64 1   y

                                        '64 - '65 2

                                        '65 - '66 or after 3

                                      No specific date in mind . . . 4

9. Do you have a definite job (including military service) lined up after
    graduation? (Circle one.)

                                  Yes . . . . 6 <u>(27)</u>

                                  No, but I intend to be working 7   9

                                  No, I do not intend to be working . . . 8

10. Since you've been in college, have you at any time considered going on for
     graduate study or considered an occupation which would require professional
     training beyond a bachelor's degree? (Circle one.)

                                  I never thought of it . . . . 2 <u>(28)</u>

                                  I thought about it, but I never considered it seriously 3   1

                                  I considered it seriously, but decided against it 4

                                  I do plan to go on, but not next year 5

11. To what extent did immediate financial obstacles (not doubts about the long run
     economic value of further study) affect your decision regarding graduate or
     professional school <u>next year</u>? (Circle one.)

                                Financial obstacles had nothing to do with it . . . . 6 <u>(29)</u>

                                *Financial obstacles played some part in my decision . 7   9

                                *Financial obstacles are the major reason I am not
                                  going on for further study next year 8

* Please answer question at top of next page.

*Listed below are some selected types of financial assistance. Circle any type which in itself (not in combination with the others) would have made it possible for you to go on to graduate or professional school next year.

Tuition Scholarship 0   (30)
Fellowship for tuition plus $1,000 cash 1   9
Loan for tuition which would not have to be
    paid back until I was out of school 2
Loan for tuition plus living expenses which would
    not have to be paid back until I was out of school. 3
10-20 hour a week job as a teaching or research
    assistant 4
Financial help from my parents 5
Payment of all my current debts for undergraduate
    education 6
None of these 7

12. Which of the following best explains why you do not anticipate going to graduate or professional school next year? (Circle any which apply.)

No desire to do so . . . . y   (31)
Can get a desirable job without further schooling 0   SP
Financial obstacles 1
Low grades in college 2
Family responsibilities 3
I would rather get married 4
I want to get practical experience first 5
I don't think I have the ability 6
I lack the necessary undergraduate course prerequisites . . . 7
I'm tired of being a student 8
Military service 9
I will be in a company training program which provides
    the equivalent X

SKIP TO QUESTION 18, "FIELDS AND CAREERS"   SKIP TO
                                                            COLUMN
                                                            38

IF YOU ARE SURE OR FAIRLY SURE THAT YOU WILL BE ATTENDING GRADUATE OR PROFESSIONAL SCHOOL NEXT YEAR, ANSWER QUESTIONS 13-17.

13. Have you decided upon the specific school you will attend? (Circle one.)

                        Yes 7   (32)
                        No 8   9

14. Write below the name of the school that you will most probably attend next Fall.

_____   _____   _____
(Name of School)   (City)   (State or Country)
a. Is the above school the one you are now attending? (Circle one.)

                        Yes 4   (33)
                        No 5   6

15. If you were absolutely free to choose (ignoring finances, admissions, etc.) would you prefer to-- (Circle one.)

Go to the same school I expect to attend next year 0   (34)
*Attend a different school. 1   y

IF "ATTEND A DIFFERENT SCHOOL": Did any of the following prevent you from
attending the school you would really prefer? (Circle any which apply.)

Wasn't offered any financial support (scholarship, fellowship,
assistantship) 2   (35)

Was offered support, but it was too little 3   9

Was refused admission or didn't apply because I thought I
would be refused 4

Financial obstacles other than scholarship, assistantship,
etc. 5

Limited to schools in a particular community 6

Other (Circle and specify:_____) . . . 7

16. If you were absolutely free to choose (ignoring finances, admissions, etc.)
would you prefer to--   (Circle one.)

Study in the same field I will be in 0   (36)

*Study in a different field 1   y

IF "STUDY IN A DIFFERENT FIELD": Did any of the following prevent you from studying
in the field which you really prefer? (Circle any which apply.)

Wasn't offered any financial support (scholarship, fellowship,
assistantship) 2   (37)

Was offered support, but it was too little 3   9

Was refused admission or didn't apply because I thought I
would be refused 4

Financial obstacles other than scholarship, assistantship,
etc. 5

Limited to schools in a particular community 6

Other (Circle and specify:_____) . . . 7

17. In terms of your finances during the next academic year when you are in graduate
or professional school, from which of the following sources do you expect to
receive $200 or more? (Circle any which apply.)

Full time job 1   (38)

Part time job other that teaching or research assistantship . . . 2   9

Withdrawals from savings 3

National Defense Education Act Loan 4

Other Loan 5

Parents or relatives 6

Income from spouse's employment 7

Other (Circle and specify:_____) . . 8

IMPORTANT

The following list of fields is to be used in answering Questions 18 through 24.
Read the instructions for these questions found on page 8 before using the list.

Business and Administration
92 Accounting
90 Advertising, Public Relations
9X Military Service, Military Science
97 Secretarial Science (or employed as a
secretary)
72 Industrial or Personnel Psychology
91 All other business and commercial fields
(Business Administration, Marketing,
Insurance, Finance, Industrial Relations, etc.)
93 Public Administration (or employed as
government administrator if not
covered by other fields)

Engineering
10 Aeronautical
11 Civil (including Agricultural, Architec-
tural, Civil, Sanitary)
12 Chemical (including Ceramic)
13 Electrical
14 Engineering Science, Engineering Physics,
Engineering Mechanics
15 Industrial
16 Mechanical (including Naval Architecture
and Marine, Welding, Textile)
17 Metallurgical
18 Mining (including Mining, Geological,
Geophysical, Petroleum)
1X Engineering, General and other specialties

Physical Science (NOTE: Secondary School Science Teaching is classified under Education)
01 Astronomy, Astrophysics
02 Chemistry (excluding Biochemistry which is 32)
03 Physics (excluding Biophysics which is 34)
04 Geography
05 Geology, Geophysics
06 Oceanography
07 Metallurgy
08 Meteorology (Atmospheric sciences)
OX Physical Science, General and other specialties

09 Mathematics and Statistics (NOTE: Secondary School Mathematics Teaching is classified under Education)

Education (NOTE: Junior College, College and University Teaching should be coded by Field of Specialization, not as Education)
50 Elementary (including Kindergarten and Nursery School)
Secondary--Academic Subject Fields
51 English
52 Modern Foreign Languages
53 Latin, Greek
54 History, Social Studies
55 Natural Science (General, Physics, Chemistry, Biology, etc.)
56 Mathematics

Specialized Teaching Fields
57 Physical Education, Health, Recreation
58 Music Education
59 Art Education
60 Education of Exceptional Children (Including Speech Correction)
61 Agricultural Education
62 Home Economics Education
63 Business Education
64 Trade and Industrial Education (Vocational)
65 Industrial Arts Education (Non-Vocational)
66 Counseling and Guidance
67 Educational Psychology
68 Administration and Supervision
6X Education, General and other specialties

Health Professions
20 Dentistry or Pre-Dentistry
21 Medicine or Pre-Medicine
22 Nursing
23 Optometry
24 Pharmacy
25 Physical Therapy
26 Occupational Therapy
27 Veterinary Medicine or Pre-Veterinary
28 Medical Technology or Dental Hygiene
2X Other Health Fields

Biological Sciences
30 Anatomy
31 Biology
32 Biochemistry
33 Botany and Related Plant Sciences (Plant Pathology, Plant Physiology, etc.)
34 Biophysics
35 Entomology
36 Genetics

37 Microbiology (including Bacteriology, Mycology, Parasitology, Virology, etc.)
38 Pathology
39 Pharmacology
40 Physiology
41 Zoology
3X Other Biological Science Fields

Agricultural and Related Fields
45 Agricultural Sciences (including Animal Husbandry, Agronomy, Farm Management, Horticulture, Soil Science, Soil Conservation, etc.)
46 Forestry, Fish and Wild Life Management
27 Veterinary Medicine
47 Farming (Code as occupation only, not as field of study)

Psychology (NOTE: Code Psychiatry as Medicine 21)
70 Clinical Psychology
66 Counseling and Guidance
67 Educational Psychology
71 Social Psychology
72 Industrial and Personnel Psychology
73 Experimental and General Psychology
74 Other Psychological Fields

Social Sciences
75 Anthropology, Archeology
76 Economics
04 Geography
83 History
77 Area and Regional Studies
78 Political Science, Government, International Relations
93 Public Administration
79 Sociology
96 Social Work, Group Work
7X Social Science, General and Other

Humanities
80 Fine and Applied Arts (Art, Music, Speech, Drama, etc.)
81 English, Creative Writing
82 Classical Languages and Literatures
83 History
84 Modern Foreign Languages and Literatures
85 Philosophy
8X Humanities, General and Other Fields

Other Fields and Occupations
86 Architecture, City Planning
94 Foreign Service (Code as occupation only, not field of study)
98 Home Economics (Code either as a field of study or as an occupation if you mean working as a home economist for pay)
99 Housewife (Code as occupation only, not as field of study)
87 Journalism, Radio-Television, Communications
95 Law, Pre-Law
88 Library Science, Archival Science
96 Social Work, Group Work
89 Theology, Religion (Employment as a Clergyman or religious worker)

X0 Field of Study or Job Which has no Near Equivalent in This List (If you use this code, please describe your field in a word or two under the questions where it applies.)

X1 Do not expect to be either employed full time or to be a Housewife (Code only for questions about careers, not for field of study.)

7

II. Fields and Careers

**IMPORTANT
NOTE:**

On pages 6 and 7 of this questionnaire is a list of fields of study
and employment. Each one can be used to describe a field of study or a
type of job. Thus, for example, in questions about fields of study,
"Psychology" means college courses in psychology; in questions about
careers, "Psychology" means the occupation of psychologist.

When you have chosen the field or occupation from the list which is your
answer to one of the questions below, please write the two numbers or
letters of that field in the double box at the end of that question. For
example, if "Clinical Psychology" is now your major field, write its code
number (70) in the boxes at the end of question 18 thus:

7 | 0

18. Present major field?

    If you have a joint major, give the one with the most course credits.   (39-40)
                                                                                                X X

19. Previous major field?

    If you have not shifted majors, write "yy" in the boxes.

    If you have several previous majors, give the <u>first</u> one in which
    officially registered.   (41-42)
                                                                                                X X

20. Future graduate or professional major?

    If you do not plan to ever go to graduate or professional school,
    write "yy" in the boxes.

    If you plan study in several fields, give the <u>main</u> one.   (43-44)
                                                                                                X X

21. Anticipated career field?

    Please give what you expect to be your long-run career and ignore
    any school, stop-gap job, or temporary military service which
    might precede it.

    If you are a woman, use "Housewife (99)" only if you do not expect
    to work full time until your children are grown.   (45-46)
                                                                                                X X
    In addition to writing the code in the boxes, please describe your
    anticipated career in a few words here:_____

22. Possible alternative career field?

    If none, write "yy" in the boxes.

    If your alternative has the same code number as the one to
    question 21, write "yy" in the boxes.

    If more than one alternative, give the most likely only.   (47-48)
                                                                                                X X

23. Career preference when you started college?

    Give your single strongest preference even if it was vague or if
    there were several alternatives.

    If absolutely no preference, write "yy" in the boxes.   (49-50)
                                                                                                X X

24. Any alternative career field seriously considered during college which is not
    mentioned in questions 21, 22, or 23?

    If none, write "yy" in the boxes.   (51-52)
                                                                                                X X

    > NOTE: THE NEXT THREE QUESTIONS REFER TO YOUR ANSWER
    > TO QUESTION 21 (ANTICIPATED CAREER FIELD). IF YOU
    > CODED "99" OR "X1" AS YOUR ANSWER TO QUESTION 21,
    > PLEASE SKIP TO QUESTION 28. OTHERWISE, ANSWER ALL
    > THREE QUESTIONS.

25. Which of the following will be your most likely employer when you begin full time work in your anticipated career field? (If you have a definite expectation, circle one; if not, circle the most likely possibilities.)

Private company with 100 or more employees	y
Private company with fewer than 100 employees or professional partnership .	X
Family business	0
Self-employed	1
Research organization or institute	2
College or University or Junior College	3
Elementary or Secondary School or School System	4
Other educational institutions (e.g. Technical Vocational School). .	5
Federal Government (U.S.)	6
State or Local Government	7
Hospital, Church, Clinic, Welfare Organization, etc.	8
Other (Circle and specify:_____). . .	9

(53)
SP

26. How do you feel about the occupation which you checked as your anticipated career field? (Circle one.)

I strongly prefer it to any other	0
I could be tempted by one or more alternatives	1
I would prefer one or more alternatives	2

(54)
y

27. The following activities cut across a number of specific jobs. Which ones do you anticipate will be an important part of your long run career work? (Circle any which apply.)

Teaching	3
Research	4
Administration	5
Service to patients or clients.	6
None of these	7

(55)
9

28. Regardless of your career plans now, when you first enrolled as a freshman in college did you have-- (Circle one.)

One particular kind of work in mind	5
Two or more alternative kinds of work in mind.	6
No specific career plans at that time	7
Planned to be a housewife	8

(56)
9

29. Which of these characteristics would be very important to you in picking a job or career? (Circle as many as apply.)

Making a lot of money	y
Opportunities to be original and creative	X
Opportunities to be helpful to others or useful to society	0
Avoiding a high pressure job which takes too much out of you	1
Living and working in the world of ideas	2
Freedom from supervision in my work	3
Opportunities for moderate but steady progress rather than the chance of extreme success or failure	4
A chance to exercise leadership	5
Remaining in the city or area in which I grew up	6
Getting away from the city or area in which I grew up	7
Opportunity to work with people rather than things	8
None of these	9

(57)
SP

9

30. Listed below are six groups of occupations. The occupations within each group are similar to each other in many ways.

In Column A, circle the two types you would like best.

In Column B, circle the two types you would like least.

Consider the jobs as a group, not particular ones, and rate them only in terms of whether you would like that type of work regardless of whether such jobs are realistic career possibilities. Disregard considerations of salary, social standing, future advancement, etc.

Occupations	A. Two Best Liked Groups	B. Two Least Liked Groups
Construction inspector, electrician, engineer, radio operator, tool designer, weather observer	X	X
Physicist, anthropologist, astronomer, biologist, botanist, chemist	0	0
Social worker, clinical psychologist, employment interviewer, high school teacher, physical education teacher, public relations man	1	1
Bank teller, financial analyst, IBM equipment operator, office manager, statistician, tax expert	2	2
Business executive, buyer, hotel manager, radio program director, real estate salesman, sales engineer	3	3
Actor, commercial artist, musician, newspaper reporter, stage director, writer	4	4

(58) (59)
 y   y

31. Please circle all the statements which describe your feelings about these specific occupations. (Circle as many or as few as apply in each column.)

	(60) SP Research Physicist or Chemist	(61) SP College Professor	(62) SP High School Teacher	(63) SP Physician	(64) SP Engineer	(65) SP Business Executive
This sort of work would be very interesting	y	y	y	y	y	y
I don't have the ability to do this kind of work	X	X	X	X	X	X
I probably couldn't make as much money at this type of work as I'd like to make . .	0	0	0	0	0	0
One would have to devote too much time and energy to this work. I want to be able to spend more time with my family and friends	1	1	1	1	1	1
One would have to invest more time and money in preparing for this occupation than I feel I could afford	2	2	2	2	2	2
I know as a personal friend, or family friend, one or more people in this field. . .	3	3	3	3	3	3
My parents would disapprove of my going into this field . .	4	4	4	4	4	4
My personality isn't suitable for work in this field . . .	5	5	5	5	5	5
People with my religious, racial, or family background don't have much chance of success in this field . . .	6	6	6	6	6	6
Wouldn't be challenging enough for me	7	7	7	7	7	7
I wouldn't like the life I'd have to lead outside the job	8	8	8	8	8	8
This is my father's occupation	9	9	9	9	9	9

10

32. Please rate the following in terms of their effect on your career plans or decisions during college. (Circle one in each row.)

		Very Important	Fairly Important	Un-important	Never Received Any
a.	Vocational or similar psychological tests	5	6	7	8	(66) 9
b.	Discussions with my academic advisor . .	0	1	2	3	(67) 4
c.	Discussions with faculty members other than my advisor	5	6	7	8	(68) 9
d.	Advice from parents	0	1	2	3	(69) 4
e.	Interviews with a professional psychological or vocational counselor	5	6	7	8	(70) 9

33. a. What is your opinion about the recently established Peace Corps? (Circle one.)

$\qquad$ An excellent program about which I am enthusiastic . . . 2   (71) 9

$\qquad$ A good idea of which I am very much in favor 3

$\qquad$ A good idea but I am not enthusiastic 4

$\qquad$ Probably a good idea but I am not enthusiastic 5

$\qquad$ Probably not a good idea but I am not sure 6

$\qquad$ Definitely not a good idea 7

$\qquad$ Don't know enough about it to have an opinion 8

b. What are you personally likely to do about the Peace Corps? (Circle one.)

$\qquad$ Definitely not volunteer 0   (72) y

$\qquad$ Am thinking about volunteering but have not made up my mind yet 1

$\qquad$ Have thought about volunteering but probably would not. . 2

$\qquad$ Am probably going to volunteer 3

$\qquad$ Have already volunteered 4

$\qquad$ I am not sure what I will do 5

c. Have you filled out the Peace Corps Questionnaire? (Circle one.)

$\qquad$ Yes 6   (73) 9

$\qquad$ No, but I intend to do so 7

$\qquad$ Definitely No 8

d. Here are some reasons young people have given for their personal reactions to the Peace Corps. Designate reasons both for volunteering and for not volunteering if both kinds seem pertinent to you. (Circle any which apply in your own case.)

(1) Reasons for volunteering:

$\qquad$ To make a personal contribution to world peace 3   (74) 9

$\qquad$ The attraction of working closely with others 4

$\qquad$ The opportunity to learn about foreign cultures and languages . . . 5

$\qquad$ It would give me a chance to decide what kind of career I really want 6

$\qquad$ To help the poorer nations of the world improve their economic conditions 7

$\qquad$ It would further my career 8

(2) Reasons for not volunteering:

$\qquad$ Family and personal obligations 1   (75) 9

$\qquad$ Not eligible on physical grounds 2

$\qquad$ Opposed to the general idea of a Peace Corps 3

$\qquad$ It would interrupt my career 4

$\qquad$ Too long a period of service 5

$\qquad$ Low pay, undesirable working conditions, etc. 6

$\qquad$ I don't have skills which would be useful to the Peace Corps 7

$\qquad$ My personality isn't suitable for that type of service 8

11

BEGIN DECK II

III. College Experience

34. Did you do all of your college work at this school? (Circle one.)

Yes . . . . X (9)
No, transferred after freshman year 0   y
No, transferred after sophomore year. 1
No, transferred after junior year 2
No, started here, attended a year or more
    elsewhere, and then returned 3

35. Were you regularly employed during this academic year? (Circle any which apply.)

No 4 (10)
Yes--   9
    Full time job which is relevant to my anticipated career field 5
    Full time job which has nothing to do with my anticipated career field 6
    Part time job which is relevant to my anticipated career field 7
    Part time job which has nothing to do with my anticipated career field 8

36. In which of the following have you been an active participant at this school?
    (Circle any which apply.)

Editorial staff of campus publication 0 (11)
Musical or dramatic group 1   y
Business staff of campus publication or other campus group 2
Campus group concerned with national or world issues 3
Inter-collegiate (varsity) athletics 4
Fraternity, Sorority (or equivalent) 5
Special interest group (e.g., Psychology Club, Outing Club) 6
Student government 7
Other (Circle and specify:_____) . . 8
None 9

37. Please call to mind the students of your own sex who are your closest friends
    here. Where did you meet them? (Circle any which apply)

Knew them before I came here . . . . X (12)
Dormitory or rooming house 0   y
My Fraternity or Sorority (or equivalent) 1
Campus activities 2
Classes in my major field 3
Classes in other fields 4
Other (Circle and specify:_____) . 5
No close friends here 6

38. Of your close friends here, how many are going on next year for graduate or pro-
    fessional studies? (Circle one.)

All or almost all . . . . X (13)
More than half 0   y
Less than half 1
Few or none 2
No close friends here 3

39. Which of the following best describes where you lived this year? (Circle any
    which apply.)

Fraternity, Sorority (or equivalent) 5 (14)
Dormitory or other campus housing 6   9
Off-Campus room, apartment, house 7
With my parents 8

12

40. Listed below are some college courses which you might have taken. Please circle the number of any statements which describe your reactions. (Circle any which apply in each row. If none apply, leave the row blank.)

	(15) 9	(16) 9	(17) 9	(18) 9	(19) 9
	Course or Area				
	Physics, Chemistry	Mathematics	Biology, Zoology, Botany	Social Sciences	English
I took one or more courses in this field or area during college	X	X	X	X	X
I didn't take any courses in this field or area during college	0	0	0	0	0
I found this course content very interesting	1	1	1	1	1
I found this course content very dull . .	2	2	2	2	2
I have a flair for course work in this area	3	3	3	3	3
I found this area rough going academically	4	4	4	4	4
Teachers in this area encouraged me to go on in the field	5	5	5	5	5
I admire many of the teachers in this area as persons not just as professors.	6	6	6	6	6
By and large, the teachers in this area are not the kind of person I'd like to be	7	7	7	7	7
One or more of my close friends is majoring in this	8	8	8	8	8

41. Listed below are some purposes or results of college. Circle the one which is most important to you personally, and also circle the one which you think is most important to the typical student here. (Circle one in each column.)

	Most Important to me Personally	Most Important to the Typical Student here	
A basic general education and appreciation of ideas	0	5	(20)(21)
Having a good time while getting a degree	1	6	4 9
Career training	2	7	
Developing the ability to get along with different kinds of people	3	8	

42. Have you had any experience in original research (participating in collecting and analyzing raw data or conducting an experiment, not writing papers based on published sources or doing experiments from a laboratory manual) during your college studies? (Circle any which apply.)

        No, I have never participated in original research 2 (22)
                                                        9
        Yes, I have--

          a. Participated in research as part of a course 3

          b. Been employed by a faculty member as a research assistant 4

          c. Had an off-campus job (summer or during school year) working in research 5

          d. Participated in a summer research training program sponsored by the government or private foundation 6

          e. Conducted a research project on my own (e.g. senior thesis). 7

          f. Other (Circle and specify:_____) . 8

13

43. What is your current academic status? (Circle one.)

Registered Spring term and studying for a bachelor's degree to be
awarded at Spring commencement (May, June, July, but before Summer
session commencement) . . . . 0 <u>(23)</u>
                                                                              3
Registered Spring term and studying for a bachelor's degree to be
awarded at Summer session commencement 1

Other (Circle and briefly specify your academic status:_____

_____). 2

44. When you graduate, how much personal indebtedness will you have for your
education? (Count only money you owe for tuition or living costs during
school, not payments on car, appliances, clothes, etc.) (Circle one.)

                                    None . . . . 5 <u>(24)</u>
                                    Some, but less than $500 . . . 6   9
                                    $500 - $999 7
                                    $1,000 or more 8

45. What is your overall (cumulative) grade point average for undergraduate work at
your present college?

IMPORTANT: If your school uses letter grades (A,B,C, etc.) please circle the
code number which is closest to your letter grade average.

Warning: The number which you circle probably does not correspond to the number
equivalent at your school, e.g. at most schools "straight A" equals 4.0,
here it equals "0".

If your school does not use letter grades, there should be special instructions
accompanying your questionnaire. If, through clerical error, the instructions
are missing, write your average in the margin.

(Circle one.)   Letter Grade   Code Number
                                            A . . . . 0 <u>(25)</u>
                                            A- 1   y
                                            B+ 2
                                            B 3
                                            B- 4
                                            C+ 5
                                            C 6
                                            C- 7
                                            D+ 8
                                            D or lower 9

46. Listed below are a number of awards and honors. Which of these have you received
during college or which are you fairly sure you will receive by the time you
graduate? (Circle any which apply.)

Dean's List . . . . y <u>(26)</u>
                                                                                SP
Phi Beta Kappa x

Other honor society based on academic achievement 0

Graduation with honors (cum) (Magna) (Summa) 1

National Merit Scholarship holder, Finalist, or Semi-Finalist 2

Other scholarship awarded on basis of academic ability 3

Participation in "honors program" at this school 4

Prize or award for scholarship or research work (e.g. "Smith prize for
best biology experiment") 5

Prize or award for literary, musical or artistic work 6

Took one or more graduate level courses as an undergraduate 7

Other award or honor 8

No special honors 9

· 14

47. As best you know, how do you stand among the other people graduating in the same major field at your school? (Circle one.)

Top ten per cent . . . . 4 <u>(27)</u>
Top quarter, but not top ten per cent. . 5 9
Second quarter 6
Third quarter 7
Lowest quarter 8

48. What is your emotional feeling about your college or university? (Circle one.)

I have a very strong attachment to it . . . . X <u>(28)</u>
I like it, but my feelings are not strong . . . . . . 0 y
Mixed feelings 1
I don't like it much, but my feelings are not strong 2
I thoroughly dislike it 3

IV. Personal Characteristics

49. Your age at your last birthday? (Circle one.)

19 or younger . . . . . 0 <u>(29)</u>
20 . . . . 1 y
21 2
22 3
23-24 4
25-29 5
30 or older 6

50. Sex. (Circle one.)

Male . . . . 7 <u>(30)</u>
Female 8 9

51. Marital Status. (Circle one.)

Single, don't expect to be married before Fall, 1961 . . . . . 4 <u>(31)</u>
*Single, expect to be married before Fall, 1961 . . . . 5 9
*Married, one or more children or expecting a child . . . *. . . 6
*Married, no children 7
Widowed, Divorced, Separated 8

*IF "MARRIED" OR "EXPECTING TO BE MARRIED BEFORE FALL, 1961": What will your spouse or future spouse most likely be doing next year? (Circle any which apply.)

Working full time . . . . 3 <u>(32)</u>
Working part time 4 9
Housewife, Mother 5
Going to School 6
Military Service 7

15

52. Religion:
 a. In which you were reared. (Circle one.)

    Protestant (Circle and Specify)_____ X   <u>(33)</u>

    Roman Catholic 0   y

    Jewish 1

    Other (Circle and specify:_____). 2

    None 3

 b. Your present preference. (Circle one.)

    Protestant (Circle and specify:_____). 5   <u>(34)</u>

    Roman Catholic 6   4

    Jewish 7

    Other (Circle and specify:_____). 8

    None 9

53. Your racial background. (Circle one.)

    White X   <u>(35)</u>

    Negro 0   y

    Oriental 1

    Other (Circle and specify:_____). 2

54. How many--
 a. <u>Older</u> brothers or sisters do you have? (Circle one.)

    None 0   <u>(36)</u>

    One 1   4

    Two 2

    Three or more 3

 b. <u>Younger</u> brothers or sisters do you have? (Circle one.)

    None 5   <u>(37)</u>

    One 6   9

    Two 7

    Three or more 8

55. Are you a U.S. citizen? (Circle one.)

    Yes, U.S. born X   <u>(38)</u>

    Yes, Naturalized 0   y

    No, but I expect to stay in the U.S. 1

    No, and I do not expect to stay in the U.S. 2

56. Please indicate your parents' (or step-parent's if parent is dead) highest educational attainment. (Circle one in each column.)

	Father	Mother	
8th grade or less	3	3	(39) (40)
Part High School	4	4	9 9
High School graduate	5	5	
Part College	6	6	
College graduate	7	7	
Graduate or professional degree beyond the bachelor's	8	8	

16

57. **a.** Which of the following categories best describes the usual occupation of the head of the household in your parental family? (Circle one.)

           Professional 1   (41)

           Proprietor or Manager 2   y

           Sales (Other than Sales Manager or Administrator) 3

           Clerical 4

           Skilled worker 5

           Semi-Skilled worker 6

           Service worker 7

           Unskilled worker 8

           Farmer or farm worker 9

    b. If the head of the household is a woman, also circle here 0

    c. If the head of the household is retired, also circle here X

---

58. Which of the following is the appropriate income category for your parental family? Consider annual income from all sources before taxes. (Circle one.)

           Less than $5,000 per year 2   (42)

           $5,000 - $7,499 3   9

           $7,500 - $9,999 4

           $10,000 - $14,999 5

           $15,000 - $19,999 6

           $20,000 and over 7

           I have no idea 8

---

59. Which of the following best describes the community which you think of as your home town during high school days? (Circle one.)

           Farm or open country X   (43)

           Suburb in a metropolitan area of--   y

                more than 2 million population 0

                500,000 to 2 million 1

                100,000 to 499,999 2

                less than 100,000 3

           Central city in a metropolitan area or city of--

                more than 2 million population 4

                500,000 to 2 million 5

                100,000 to 499,999 6

                50,000 to 99,999 7

                10,000 to 49,999 8

                less than 10,000 9

---

60. Which of the following best describes the distance between your home town (when you were in high school) and your current college? (Circle one.)

           In the same city or within commuting distance X   (44)

           Within four hours automobile drive or less 0   y

           More than four hours drive, but in the same state 1

           More than four hours drive, but in a different state 2

61. Please rate yourself on the following dimensions as you really think you are. (Circle one in each row.)

		Very	Fairly	Neither	Fairly	Very		
a.	Unfavorable toward modern art	y	X	0	1	2	Favorable toward modern art	(45) 3
b.	Politically liberal	4	5	6	7	8	Politically conservative	(46) 9
c.	Conventional in opinions and values	y	X	0	1	2	Unconventional in opinions and values	(47) 3
d.	Religious	4	5	6	7	8	Non—religious	(48) 9

62. Listed below are some adejectives, some of which are "favorable," some of which are "unfavorable," some of which are neither.

Please circle the ones which best describe you. Consider only those which are most characteristic of you as a person. (Most people choose five or six, but you may choose more or fewer if you want to.)

(49) SP	(50) SP	(51) SP
Ambitious X	Good Looking X	Moody X
Athletic 0	Happy 0	Obliging 0
Calm 1	Hard Driving 1	Outgoing 1
Cautious 2	High Strung 2	Poised 2
Cooperative . . . 3	Idealistic 3	Quiet 3
Cultured 4	Impetuous 4	Rebellious . . . 4
Dominant 5	Intellectual 5	Reserved 5
Easy Going . . . 6	Lazy 6	Shy 6
Energetic 7	Low Brow 7	Sophisticated . . 7
Forceful 8	Methodical 8	Talkative 8
Fun Loving . . . 9	Middle Brow 9	Witty 9

APPENDIX VII

SURVEY QUESTIONNAIRE (1962)

BACKGROUND INFORMATION

1. **What are you doing this Spring?** *(Circle any which apply)*

Working full-time............................ 4   11/3
Working part-time............................ 5
Military service (full-time active duty)... 6
Housewife, mother............................ 7
Going to school.............................. 8
Other *(Circle and Specify).*_____ 9

2. **What is your current marital status?** *(Circle one)*

Single, no definite plans to be married at present................ X   12/y
Single, have definite plans to be married before Sept. 1, 1962.... 0
Single, have definite plans to be married, after Sept. 1, 1962.... 1
Widowed, Divorced, Separated *(answer A only)*..................... 2
Married *(answer A and B)*.. 3

IF WIDOWED, DIVORCED, SEPARATED, ANSWER A ONLY:
IF MARRIED, ANSWER A AND B:

A. How many children do you have now (count a current pregnancy as one child)? *(Circle one)*

None.................................... 5   13/R
One..................................... 6
Two..................................... 7
Three................................... 8
Four or more............................ 9

B. What is your spouse doing this Spring? *(Circle any which apply)*

Working full-time............................ X   14/R
Working part-time............................ 0
Military service (full-time active duty)... 1
Housewife, mother............................ 2
Going to school.............................. 3
Other *(Circle and Specify)*_____

_____ 4

3. **What is your sex?**

Female............................ 1   15/0
Male.............................. 2

A. IF FEMALE:

In the long run which one of the following do you really prefer and which one do you realistically expect?

	Really Prefer *(Circle one)*	Realistically Expect *(Circle one)*
Housewife only.	5	5
Housewife with occasional employment...	6	6
Housewife now, employment later........	7	7
Combining housewife with employment.........	8	8
Employment only.	9	9
	16/R	17/R

B. IF MALE:

1) Are you now on full-time active duty in the armed services? *(Circle one)*

Yes *(Skip to C below)* 0   18/R
No................................ 1

2) *IF NO:* Have you ever been on full-time active duty in the armed services for a period of at least six months? *(Circle one)*

Yes *(Skip to C below)*....... 3   19/R
No........ 4

3) *IF NO:* Do you expect to be on active duty in the armed forces for a period of at least six months during the next five or six years? *(Circle one)*

Definitely yes...................... 6   20/R
Probably yes........................ 7
Probably no......................... 8
Definitely no....................... 9

C. How has your military status affected your plans for further education? *(Circle as many as apply)*

Not at all............................... 5   21/R
An influence toward:
postponing entry into my graduate studies............................... 6
beginning my graduate studies sooner... 7
interrupting my graduate studies....... 8
not hurrying through my graduate studies............................... 9

2

4. A. Where are you living now? *(Circle one)*

   <u>Farm</u> or open country...X 22/y

   Suburb in a metropolitan area of--

       more than 2 million population... 0

       500,000 to 2 million... 1

       100,000 to 499,999.. 2

       less than 100,000... 3

   Central City in a metropolitan area of (or <u>non-suburban city</u> of)--

       more than 2 million population... 4

       500,000 to 2 million... 5

       100,000 to 499,999.. 6

       50,000 to 99,999.. 7

       10,000 to 49,999.. 8

       less than 10,000.. 9

   B. Is the community in which you are now living the one which was your home town when you were in high school? *(Circle one)*

                                           Yes.............................. X 23/y

                                           No............................... 0

5. Where were you living when you were in high school and where do you live now? *(Circle one in each column)*

		Home Town During High School *(Circle one)*	Now Living *(Circle one)*
NEW ENGLAND:	Conn., Maine, Mass., N.H., R.I., Vt.	X	X
MIDDLE ATLANTIC:	Del., D.C., Md., N.J., N.Y., Pa.	0	0
EAST NORTH CENTRAL:	Ill., Ind., Mich., Ohio, Wis.	1	1
WEST NORTH CENTRAL:	Iowa, Kans., Minn., Mo., Nebr., N.D., S.D.	2	2
SOUTH:	Ala., Fla., Ga., Ky., Miss., N.C., S.C., Tenn., Va., W. Va.	3	3
SOUTH CENTRAL:	Ark., La., Okla., Texas	4	4
MOUNTAIN:	Ariz., Colo., Idaho, Mont., Nev. N. Mex., Utah, Wyo.	5	5
WEST:	Calif., Oregon, Wash.	6	6
ALASKA OR HAWAII:		7	7
CANADA:		8	8
OTHER NON-U.S. *(Specify)*		9	9
		24/y	25/y

6. Please indicate:

	The highest degree you now hold *(Circle one)*	The next degree you expect to receive *(Circle one)*	The highest degree you expect to gain eventually *(Circle one)*
None or no further degree..................	5	X	5
Bachelor's (undergraduate) e.g., B.A., B.S., B.E., B.Phar., etc........................	6	0	6
POST BACHELORS — Professional e.g., LL.B., MSW, M.D., J.D., M.Ed., etc.	7	1	7
POST BACHELORS — Arts and Science Master's e.g., M.A., M.S., etc	8	2	8
POST BACHELORS — Doctorate e.g., Ph.D., Ed.D., J.S.D., etc.	9	3	9
	26/4	27/y	28/4

7. When did you receive your bachelor's degree? *(Circle one)*

           I do not yet have a bachelor's degree.................... X 29/y

           Spring commencement, 1961................................ 0

           Summer session commencement, 1961........................ 1

           Other *(Specify)*_____ 2

3

| EMPLOYMENT |

8. Are you employed now? (Include active military service but not reserve programs.)   No..................... 7   30/6
   (Circle one)   Yes, full-time........ 8
       Yes, part-time........ 9

9. Have you worked at any full-time job since last June which you <u>no longer hold</u>? *(Circle one)*
       Yes, Summer only.............. 2   31/1
       Yes, other.................... 3
       No............................ 4

10. How difficult was it to get a desirable civilian job? *(Circle as many as apply)*
        I don't know because I didn't actually try to get a civilian job.................................... X   32/y
        I continued with job I held before graduation... 0
        I got the kind of employment I wanted with very little effort.. 1
        I had to look around quite a bit, but I finally got the kind of job I wanted...................... 2
        I couldn't find the kind of job I wanted but I didn't look very hard............................... 3
        I couldn't find the kind of job I wanted even though I looked very hard............................ 4

IF YOU ARE EMPLOYED NOW, FULL-TIME OR PART-TIME, ON A CIVILIAN OR MILITARY JOB, ANSWER QUESTIONS 11 THROUGH 17 IN TERMS OF THIS JOB.

IF YOU ARE NOT EMPLOYED NOW, ANSWER QUESTIONS 11 THROUGH 17 IN TERMS OF YOUR MOST RECENT FULL-TIME OR PART-TIME CIVILIAN OR MILITARY JOB.

IF YOU HAVE NOT BEEN EMPLOYED AT ALL SINCE JUNE, 1961 SKIP TO QUESTION 18.

11. What field best describes your job? (Inside the letter enclosed with the questionnaire
    is a list of fields of employment and study. *Enter the code number that best describes*
    your job.)   33-34/XX

12. Which of the following best describes your employer? *(Circle any that apply)*
        I am self-employed, or in business owned by my family.. y   35/R
        Private company with 100 or more employees.. X
        Private company with fewer than 100 employees... 0
        Professional partnership.. 1
        Research organization or institute.. 2
        College or University or Junior College... 3
        Elementary or Secondary School or School System... 4
        Hospital or Clinic.. 5
        Church, Welfare, or other non-profit organization... 6
        Federal Government (U.S.).. 7
        State or Local Government.. 8

        Other *(Circle and Specify)* _____ 9

13. Please describe:

    A. What kind of work do you do (e.g., high school physics teacher, assistant sales engineer, wheat farmer,
       clothing buyer for department store)? _____

    B   The two major duties: (1) _____

          (2) _____

4

14. Whether or not they are important to you, personally, please rate your job in terms of... (rate each opportunity as either Excellent, Average, or Poor).

	Chances for this in my job			
	Excellent	Average	Poor	
Making a lot of money *(Circle one)*..	X	0	1	36/y
Being original and creative *(Circle one)*..	3	4	5	37/2
Being help to others or useful to society *(Circle one)*	7	8	9	38/6
Avoiding a high pressure job which takes too much out of you *(Circle one)*......	X	0	1	39/y
Living and working in the world of ideas *(Circle one)*...........................	3	4	5	40/2
Freedom from supervision in my work *(Circle one)*................................	7	8	9	41/6
Opportunities for moderate but steady progress rather than the chance of extreme success or failure *(Circle one)*	X	0	1	42/y
A chance to exercise leadership *(Circle one)*	3	4	5	43/2
Working with people rather than things *(Circle one)*	7	8	9	44/6
Opportunities for advancement *(Circle one)*	X	0	1	45/y

15. Which of the following describes your employer's policy regarding graduate or professional study for people in your type of job? *(Circle any which apply)*

There is no reason for graduate or professional study for people in my type of job, so there is no policy... X   46/y

In-service training provides the equivalent of graduate study.. 0

Advanced study is officially or unofficially discouraged... 1

Advanced graduate or professional training is useful, but my employer neither encourages nor discourages it.. 2

Employer encourages advanced study, but does not offer financial aid................................... 3

Employer would pay (is paying) tuition costs or part of them... 4

Employer would pay (is paying) part salary during advanced study....................................... 5

Employer would pay (is paying) full salary and tuition during advanced graduate or professional training 6

16. How do you feel about your job?

	Extremely Satisfied	Somewhat Satisfied	Neutral	Somewhat Dissatisfied	Extremely Dissatisfied	
Type of work *(Circle one)*	5	6	7	8	9	47/4
Salary *(Circle one)*	5	6	7	8	9	48/4
Employer or firm *(Circle one)*....	5	6	7	8	9	49/4

17. Thinking ahead one year from now, which job situation would you prefer and which job situation do you realistically expect? *(Circle one in each column)*

	I Would Prefer *(Circle one)*	I Realistically Expect *(Circle one)*
Same field of work, same employer...............	X	5
Same field, different employer..................	0	6
Different field of work, same employer.........	1	7
Different field of work, different employer.....	2	8
Not working full time...........................	3	9
	50/y	51/4

5

| CAREER PLANS |

EVERYONE PLEASE ANSWER:

18. Which field from the list in cover letter best describes your anticipated long-run career field? Please give what you expect to be your long-run career and ignore any stop-gap job or temporary military service which might precede it.

> *IF YOU ARE A WOMAN:* *If you plan to combine marriage and work, code the field of employment, not housewife. Use the code number for "Housewife"* only *if you do not expect to work at all.*

> *In addition to writing the code in the boxes, please describe your anticipated career in a few words here*

52-53/XX

19. If you were free to choose any field from the list, ignoring obstacles such as finances, time for training, admission requirements, etc., would you still choose the field just listed?

Yes, I would prefer the same field *(Write "yy" in the boxes)*

No, another field would be preferred *(Please indicate the field)*

54-55/XX

20. Which of these characteristics would be very important to you in picking a job or career? *(Circle as many as apply)*

Making a lot of money.. X   56/y
Opportunities to be original and creative... 0
Opportunities to be helpful to others or useful to society.. 1
Avoiding a high pressure job which takes too much out of you...................................... 2
Living and working in the world of ideas.. 3
Freedom from supervision in my work... 4
Opportunities for moderate but steady progress rather than the chance of extreme success or failure.. 5
A chance to exercise leadership... 6
Opportunity to work with people rather than things.. 7
None of the above... 8

21. Which of the following do you expect as your long-run future employer? *(If you have a definite expectation, circle one; if not, circle the most likely possibilities)*

I plan to be self-employed, or in business owned by my family...................................... y   57/R
Private company with 100 or more employees... X
Private company with fewer than 100 employees.. 0
Professional partnership... 1
Research organization or institute... 2
College or University or Junior College.. 3
Elementary or Secondary School or School System.. 4
Hospital or Clinic... 5
Church, Welfare, or other non-profit organization.. 6
Federal Government (U.S.).. 7
State or Local Government.. 8
Other *(Circle and Specify)* _____ 9
Do not expect employment... R

22. The following activities cut across a number of specific jobs. Which ones do you anticipate will be an important part of your long-run career work? *(Circle any which apply)*

Teaching........................... X   58/y
Research........................... 0
Administration..................... 1
Service to patients or clients..... 2
None of these...................... 3

6

23. Please indicate your parents' (or step-parent's, if parent is dead) highest educational attainment. *(Circle one in each column)*

	Father	Mother
8th grade or less	4	4
Part High School	5	5
High School graduate	6	6
Part College	7	7
College graduate	8	8
Graduate or professional degree beyond the bachelor's	9	9
	59/3	60/3

24. What kind of work did your father do when **you** were age 16? *(If deceased or retired, give his major occupation when he was working)*

Occupation: _____

Duties: _____

25. Have any of your relatives ever worked in the following occupations? *(Report occupation even if the relative is retired or no longer living. Circle one or more answers in each column.)*

	⇓ 61/R	⇓ 63/R	⇓ 65/R	⇓ 67/R
	Parents *(Circle one or more numbers in this column)*	Brothers, Sisters *(Circle one or more numbers in this column)*	Grandparents, Great Grand-parents *(Circle one or more numbers in this column)*	Uncles, Aunts, Cousins *(Circle one or more numbers in this column)*
NO ONE IN THIS RELATIONSHIP TO ME OR DON'T KNOW THEIR OCCUPATIONS	X	X	X	X
Civil Service Employee	0	0	0	0
Elected or appointed public official	1	1	1	1
Foreign Service Officer	2	2	2	2
Career Military. Officer	3	3	3	3
High School or Grade School Teacher	4	4	4	4
College Professor	5	5	5	5
Scientist (Other than college professor)	6	6	6	6
Engineer	7	7	7	7
Writer, Artist, Musician	8	8	8	8
Farmer	9	9	9	9
Blue Collar Worker	X	X	X	X
Small Business Proprietor	0	0	0	0
Executive in a large business	1	1	1	1
Certified Public Accountant	2	2	2	2
Lawyer	3	3	3	3
Clergyman	4	4	4	4
Physician	5	5	5	5
Other Health Profession (dentist, pharmacist, nurse, etc.)	6	6	6	6
Social Worker	7	7	7	7
Architect	8	8	8	8
NONE OF THESE OCCUPATIONS	9	9	9	9
	62/R	64/R	66/R	68/P

BEGIN DECK 2

26. Have you enrolled for one or more co·· in a program leading to a degree since you were graduated from college? *(Circle one)*

Yes *(Answer the questions in the green section)* X   11/y

No *(Skip to Q. 44. Do not answer questions on the green pages)* 0

7

NOTE: *FILL OUT THE GREEN PAGES IF YOU HAVE ENROLLED THIS ACADEMIC YEAR (1961-62) FOR COURSES APPLICABLE TO A DEGREE*

27. Please indicate the terms in which you were enrolled for courses applicable to a degree. *(Circle as many as apply)*

Summer, 1961.............................. X	12/y
Fall Semester or Quarter, 1961............. 0	
Winter Quarter, 1961-62................... 1	
Spring Semester or Quarter, 1962.......... 2	

28. IF YOU ARE NOT CURRENTLY ENROLLED THIS SPRING TERM, which of the following best explains why you are not enrolled now? *(Circle any which apply)*

Have already received my post-graduate degree... y	13/R
Completed the course work for the degree.. x	
Academic difficulties or fear of academic difficulties................................. 0	
Lost interest.. 1	
Required too much time... 2	
Decided to switch fields... 3	
Health, Called up for Military Service, or other unforeseen personal obstacle........ 4	
Financial costs.. 5	
Moved from the city.. 6	
Family responsibilities.. 7	
Am doing independent research, completing thesis, etc. 8	
Other *(Circle and Specify)* _____ 9	

29. Which of the following best describes your current (most recent) study program? *(Circle one)*

Studying in a program in which full-time study is possible
and carrying--

full-time load or greater.. 5	14/4
more than half, but less than full load.................................. 6	
half a course load or less.. 7	

Studying in a night school, or similar program in which ''full-time study'' is impossible 8

Taking a Correspondence course... 9

30. *Write the code number from the cover page which best describes:*

A. Your current (most recent) field of study................................. [ ][ ] 15-16/XX

B. Did you apply for graduate or professional (post-bachelor) studies in any
other field prior to beginning study in your current (most recent) field?

No *(Write "yy" in the boxes)*
Yes *(Indicate field)*........ [ ][ ] 17-18/XX

C. Do you plan to get a degree in any field other than the one in which you have been studying?

No *(Write "yy" in the boxes)*
Yes *(Indicate field)* ...... [ ][ ] 19-20/XX

IF YES: What are your reasons for changing? _____

---

31. Please write the name of the school which you are now attending or have most recently attended since receiving your bachelor's degree.

School	City	State (Country If Non-U.S.)

8

FILL OUT THE GREEN PAGES IF,YOU HAVE ENROLLED THIS ACADEMIC YEAR (1961-62) FOR COURSES APPLICABLE TO A DEGREE

32. Compared with the school where you completed your undergraduate work, is your current (last) school--*(Circle one)*

The same institution... X 21/y
A different institution--
  in the same city or within commuting distance.......................... 0
  within four hours' automobile drive or less............................ 1
  more than four hours' drive.. 2

33. Which of the following reasons played a part in your decision to attend this school rather than some other? *(Circle any which apply)*

Couldn't be admitted to one or more schools which I would have preferred........ y 22/R
Cheaper tuition... X
Offered more (some) financial aid by this school............................... 0
Course work appeared easier.. 1
Reputation and quality of University as a whole................................ 2
Reputation and quality of my department or professional school................. 3

Allowed part-time or evening courses... 4
Within commuting distance of my home or job.................................... 5
Course offerings more suited to my needs....................................... 6
Job opportunities for myself (or spouse) while in school....................... 7
Attracted to community or area in which school is situated..................... 8
Sent here by my employer... 9

Other *(Circle and Specify)* _____ R

34. What is your grade point average so far in your post-bachelor's studies?

IF LETTER GRADES ARE NOT GIVEN, translate into letter grades as best you can:

(Circle one).   A 0 23/y
                                              A- 1
                                              B+ 2
                                              B 3
                                              B- 4
                                              C+ 5
                                              C 6
                                              C- 7
                                              Less than C- 8
                                              No grades received yet...... X

35. For each of the following three aspects of your post bachelor's studies please indicate both the expectations you had before you began studying at this level and your experiences since you have been studying at this level. *(Circle one number on each line)*

I EXPECTED TO FIND..		Very	Fairly	Neither	Fairly	Very		
course work......	HARD	X	0	1	2	3	EASY	24/y
work load taking.	LARGE SHARE OF MY TIME	X	0	1	2	3	LITTLE TIME	25/y
course content...	FASCINATING	X	0	1	2	3	DULL	26/y
I ACTUALLY FOUND...								
course work......	HARD	5	6	7	8	9	EASY	27/4
work load taking.........	LARGE SHARE OF MY TIME	5	6	7	8	9	LITTLE TIME	28/4
course content...	FASCINATING	5	6	7	8	9	DULL	29/4

9

FILL OUT THE GREEN PAGES IF YOU HAVE ENROLLED THIS ACADEMIC YEAR (1961-62) FOR COURSES APPLICABLE TO A DEGREE

36. How would you rate the following aspects of your studies this year? *(Circle one answer for each aspect)*

	Excellent	Good	Average	Poor	Don't know, Inapplicable	
Caliber of class room teaching.............................	X	0	1	2	3	30/y
Curriculum and course offerings............................	5	6	7	8	9	31/4
Facilities and opportunities for research (including library)	X	0	1	2	3	32/y
Student housing..	5	6	7	8	9	33/4
Caliber of the students....................................	X	0	1	2	3	34/y
Knowledge and professional standing of the faculty..........	5	6	7	8	9	35/4
Personal contacts with faculty.............................	X	0	1	2	3	36/y

37. During the time you have been studying this academic year (1961-1962), which of the following will have provided you with $200 or more in financial support? *(Circle any which apply)*

    Full-time job... X 37/y
    Subsidy from present or future employer......................... 0
    Income from spouse's employment................................ 1
    Parents or relatives.. 2
    Withdrawals from savings... 3
    National Defense Education Act loan............................ 4
    Other loan.. 5
    Part-time job other than a research or teaching assistantship.. 6
    None of the above.. 7

38. During the academic year, did you receive a stipend (scholarship, fellowship, research or teaching assistantship) or similar financial aid to students?

    EXCLUDE... loans and gifts from parents or relatives
    INCLUDE... reduction in fees even if you do not receive the money directly
    CONSIDER... work as a stipend if you are receiving income from teaching or research in your field of study and are paid by your school or an affiliated organization

    No *(Circle and skip to question 40)*...... X 38/y
    Yes *(Circle and see instructions)*......... 0

    IF YES: On the back of the cover letter is a set of code numbers that describe stipends by source and type. Use the code numbers to answer the following questions:

    A. Describe your stipend (if you have two or more, describe the one that has the highest value).

    39-40/XX

    B. Do you have a second stipend?

       IF YES: Describe it
       IF NO: Write "yy" in the boxes   41-42/XX

39. Please estimate the total value you received from all stipends during the academic year 1961-1962. Include in your estimate the value of a tuition scholarship, or tuition remission (even if you received no money), income from teaching or research in your field if you were paid by your school or affiliated organization. *(Circle one)*

    Less than $200............ 1 43/0
    $ 200 -   499......... 2
    $ 500 -   999......... 3
    $1,000 - 1,499......... 4
    $1,500 - 1,999 5
    $2,000 - 2,499 6
    $2,500 - 2,999 7
    $3,000 - 3,999 8
    $4,000 and over.......... 9

10

PLANS FOR NEXT YEAR--1962-1963

ON THE BACK OF THE COVER LETTER IS A SET OF CODE NUMBERS THAT DESCRIBE STIPENDS BY SOURCE AND TYPE.   USE THE CODE NUMBERS TO ANSWER THE FOLLOWING QUESTIONS.

40. A. Have you **accepted** any stipend **for the academic year 1962-63?**

    IF NO: Write "yy" in boxes and skip to B.

    IF YES: (1) *Describe your stipend. (If you have two or more,*   44-45/XX

                 describe the one that has the highest value.)

            (2) *Do you have a second stipend?*

                 IF YES: Describe it.   46-47/XX

                 IF NO: Write "yy" in the boxes.

    B. Did you **decline** any stipend that you were offered for the academic year 1962-1963?

        IF NO: Write "yy" in the boxes.

        IF YES: Describe the stipend you were offered. (If you were offered more   48-49/XX

        than one, describe the "best" one.)

    C. Did you apply for the academic year 1962-1963 for any stipend that is **still pending?**

        IF NO: Write "yy" in the boxes.

        IF YES: Describe the stipend.   (If more than one is pending, describe   50-51/XX

        the "best" one.)

    D. Did you apply for the academic year 1962-1963 for any stipend for which you were **rejected?**

        IF NO: Write "yy" in the boxes.

        IF YES: Describe the stipend. (If more than one rejection, describe   52-53/XX

        the stipend you would have preferred.)

41. Indicate your plans for the coming (1962-1963) academic year, by circling one of the following:

                Will continue studies in...

                       Same field, **same** school........................... 2   **54/1**

                      •Same field, but different school.................. 3

                      •Same school, but different field.................. 4

                      •Different field and different school.............. 5

                Will not be enrolled because...

                       Work for degree will be completed................. 6

                       Studying in absentia............................. 7

                      •Interrupting my studies temporarily............... 8

                      •Quitting my studies short of the degree........... 9

•Why are you making the change or changes indicated (•) above? _____

_____

42. If you plan to go to school in the coming year, 1962-1963, do you plan to go... *(Circle one)*

                                     Full-time................. X   **55/y**

                                     Part-time................. 0

43. Did getting (or not getting) a stipend influence your plans for next year?

                           No *(Circle and skip to Q. 49)*........ 3   **56/2**

                           •Yes......... 4

IF YES: What was the influence? _____

PLEASE SKIP TO QUESTION 49.

11

ANSWER THE FOLLOWING QUESTIONS IF YOU HAVE NOT BEEN ENROLLED SINCE JUNE, 1961 FOR COURSES APPLICABLE TO A DEGREE. (IF YOU HAVE BEEN ENROLLED FOR SUCH COURSES DURING THE SPECIFIED TIME PERIOD, SKIP TO Q. 49.)

BEGIN
DECK 3

44. A. Had you at any time considered enrolling during this current (1961-1962) school year for degree study (on campus or by correspondence)? *(Circle one)*

No.. X   11/y

*Considered it, but did not apply to any school..... 0
*Applied to one or more schools, was not accepted by any.. 1
*Applied to one or more schools, accepted by one or more.. 2

*B. IF YOU CONSIDERED OR APPLIED: *Write the code number from the cover page which best describes the field you considered.*   [ ][ ]   12-13/XX

45. Which of the following describes your reasons for not enrolling this past year? *(Circle as many as apply)*

No desire to do so.. y   14/R
Could get a desirable job without further schooling...................... X
I wanted to get practical experience first............................... 0
Finances.. 1
Fear of academic difficulties... 2
Problem of admission to the school (type of school) I wished to attend... 3
Military service, active duty or reserve program....................... 4
Health or other personal obstacles..................................... 5
Family responsibilities.. 6
Lack of time... 7
No school available where I was living................................. 8
Other *(Circle and Specify)* _____ 9

46. Have you considered enrolling next year (any time between June, 1962 and June, 1963) for courses applicable to a degree (on campus or by correspondence)?

No *(Circle and skip to Q. 48)*...................... 4   15/3
Yes *(Circle and continue with Q. 47)*............... 5

47. IF YOU CONSIDERED ENROLLING NEXT YEAR:

A. Have you applied for admission to any school for the coming year (1962-1963)? *(Circle one)*

No, and I'm not planning to apply this year *(Circle and skip to D)*....... 0   16/R
No, but I'm still planning to apply *(Circle and skip to B)*............... 1
*Yes, I applied to one school... 2
*Yes, I applied to two or three schools.................................. 3
*Yes, I applied to four or more schools.................................. 4

*IF YOU'VE APPLIED: (1) What is the current status of your applications? *(Circle one in each column)*

	Accepted by: *(Circle one)*	Rejected by: *(Circle one)*	Pending at: *(Circle one)*
No schools................	5	5	5
One school................	6	6	6
Two or three schools......	7	7	7
Four or more schools......	8	8	8
	17/R	18/R	19/R

ON THE BACK OF THE COVER LETTER IS A SET OF CODE NUMBERS THAT DESCRIBE STIPENDS BY SOURCE AND TYPE. USE THE CODE NUMBERS TO ANSWER THE FOLLOWING QUESTIONS.

B. (1) Have you accepted any stipend (scholarship, fellowship, research or teaching assistantship) or similar financial aid to students, for the academic year 1962-1963?

EXCLUDE...loans and gifts from parents or relatives

INCLUDE...reduction in fees, even if you do not receive the money directly

CONSIDER..work as a stipend, if you are receiving income from teaching or research in your field of study and are paid by your school or an affiliated organization.

IF NO: *Write "yy" in the boxes and skip to (2).*

IF YES: (a) *Describe your stipend. (If you have two or more, describe the one that has the highest value.)*   [ ][ ]   20-21/RR

(b) *Do you have a second stipend?*

IF YES: *Describe it.*
IF NO: *Write "yy" in the boxes.*   [ ][ ]   22-23/RR

12

47. Continued

B. (2) Did you decline any stipend that you were offered for the academic year 1962-1963?

    IF NO: Write "yy" in the boxes.
    IF YES: Describe the stipend you declined. (If you declined more than one, describe the "best" one.)

    24-25/RR

(3) Did you apply for any stipend for the academic year 1962-1963, that is still pending?

    IF NO: Write "yy" in the boxes.
    IF YES: Describe the stipend. (If more than one is pending, describe the "best" one.)

    26-27/RR

(4) Did you apply for any stipend for the academic year 1962-1963, for which you were rejected?

    IF NO: Write "yy" in the boxes.
    IF YES: Describe the stipend. (If more than one rejection, describe the stipend you would have preferred.)

    28-29/RR

C. Did getting (or not getting) a stipend influence your plans for next year?

    No............. 0   30/R
    Yes............ 1

D. Do you expect to **enroll** for further degree study during the coming academic year (1962-1963) either on campus or by correspondence?

    No *(Circle and answer Question 48)*.......... 6   31/R
    *Yes, on campus full-time................... 7
    *Yes, on campus part-time................... 8
    *Yes, correspondence....................... 9

*What are you planning to study? (Indicate the field by copying the code numbers from list inside the cover letter.)

    32-33/RR

    SKIP TO Q. 49

48. FOR THOSE NOT PLANNING TO BE ENROLLED DURING THE COMING ACADEMIC YEAR (1962-1963)...

A. Do you expect to go on for further degree study (on campus or by correspondence) in the future? *(Circle one)*

    No *(Circle and skip to Q. 49)*............... 0   34/R
    Probably not *(Circle and skip to Q. 49)*..... 1
    *Probably yes............................... 2
    *Yes....................................... 3

*IF YES OR PROBABLY YES:

(1) When do you expect to begin? Make your single best prediction. *(Circle one)*

    Academic Year:
    '63-'64...................... 5   35/R
    '64-'65...................... 6
    '65-'66...................... 7
    '66-'67...................... 8
    No specific date in mind.................... 9

(2) Refer to the field list and write the code number which best describes the field in which you expect to study.

    36-37/RR

(3) Which of the following best explains why you are postponing your further studies? *(Circle any which apply)*

    I want to get practical experience first.......... 2   38/R
    Finances... 3
    Military service, active duty or reserve program... 4
    Problem of getting admitted....................... 5
    Health or other personal obstacle................. 6
    Family responsibilities........................... 7
    No school available where I am now living.......... 8
    Other *(Circle and Specify)*_____ 9

13

| ATTITUDES AND OPINIONS |

EVERYBODY PLEASE ANSWER:

49. How would you rate the following aspects of your *undergraduate* college or university? *(Circle one answer for each aspect)*

	Excellent	Good	Average	Poor	Don't Know or Inapplicable	
Caliber of class room teaching..	X	0	1	2	3	39/y
Curriculum and course offerings............................	5	6	7	8	9	40/4
Facilities and opportunities for research (including library)	X	0	1	2	3	41/y
Student housing..............................	5	6	7	8	9	42/4
Caliber of the students.....................................	X	0	1	2	3	43/y
Knowledge and professional standing of the faculty.........	5	6	7	8	9	44/4

50. During the year since you graduated, have any of the following been a source of worry or concern for you? *(Circle as many as apply)*

My children's health and development.......... 1   45/0
Ability to make friends........................ 2
Physical health................................ 3
Finances....................................... 4
Loneliness..................................... 5
Dating, relations with opposite sex........... 6
Goals in life.................................. 7
Relations with spouse......................... 8

Career plans....................................... 1   46/0
School studies this year........................... 2
Emotional state.................................... 3
Relations with my parents.......................... 4
World conditions................................... 5
Relations with in-laws............................. 6
My job... 7
Other problems *(Circle and Specify)*_____
                                                    8
None, no worries................................... 9

51. Which of the following do you expect to give you the most satisfaction in your life?

	Most Satisfaction *(Circle one)*	Next Most Satisfaction *(Circle one)*
Your career or occupation...........	X	X
Family relationships...	0	0
Leisure-time recreational activities..	1	1
Religious beliefs or activities...	2	2
Participation as a citizen in the affairs of your community....................	3	3
Participation in activities directed toward national or international betterment....	4	4
	47/y	48/y

52. Listed below are some adjectives, some of which are ''favorable,'' some of which are ''unfavorable,'' some of which are neither. *(Please circle the ones which best describe you.)* Consider only those which are most characteristic of you as a person. *(Most people choose five or six, but you may choose more or fewer if you want to.)*

Ambitious.............. 0	Energetic............. 0	Methodical............. 0	Quiet.................. 0
Athletic............... 1	Fun Loving.............1	Middle Brow............ 1	Rebellious............. 1
Calm................... 2	Good Looking.......... 2	Moody.................. 2	Religious.............. 2
Cautious............... 3	Happy.................. 3	Nervous................ 3	Reserved............... 3
Conventional........... 4	Hard Driving.......... 4	Non-religious.......... 4	Shy.................... 4
Cooperative............ 5	High Strung........... 5	Obliging............... 5	Sophisticated.......... 5
Cultured............... 6	Idealistic............ 6	Outgoing............... 6	Talkative.............. 6
Dominant............... 7	Impetuous............. 7	Poised................. 7	Tense.................. 7
Easy Going............. 8	Intellectual.......... 8	Politically Liberal.... 8	Unconventional......... 8
Efficient.............. 9	Lazy.................. 9	Politically Conservative 9	Witty................. 9
49/R	50/R	51/R	52/R

53. How would you feel about working overseas for a few years, in your regular occupation, for each of the following types of organization? *(Circle one for each kind of organization)*

	Private Business *(Circle one)*	Non-Profit Organization *(Circle one)*	Federal Government Agency *(Circle one)*	U.N. or Other International Agencies *(Circle one)*
Definitely would like to.................	X	3	7	X
Would like to under certain conditions...	0	4	8	0
Definitely would not like to.............	1	5	9	1
	53/y	54/2	55/6	56/y

14

54. A. Since you began college, have you seriously considered employment in any of the following Federal Governmental departments or agencies or in the Peace Corps? *(Circle any which apply)*

IF NO: *(Circle and skip to Q. 55)*........ X   57/y

IF YES: *Indicate which agency(ies)*

State Department.................. 0	Agriculture....................................... X 58/R	
United States Information Agency.. 1	Commerce (includes Census) 0	
Central Intelligence Agency....... 2	Federal Reserve Board............................ 1	
Agency for International Development (formerly I.C.A.)... 3	Health, Education, and Welfare................... 2	
Peace Corps....................... 4	Interior... 3	
Other in international affairs *(Circle and Specify)*	Justice (includes FBI)........................... 4	
	Labor (includes BLS)............................. 5	
_____ 5	Defense (includes career military service)....... 6	
	Post Office...................................... 7	
	Treasury (includes internal revenue)............. 8	
	Other in domestic fields *(Circle and Specify)*	
	_____ 9	

B. Have you taken any of the following Federal Governmental examinations? *(Circle one or more of the alternatives for each of the examinations)*

	Peace Corps (PC) *(Circle one or more)*	Federal Service Entrance (FSEE) *(Circle one or more)*	Management Interne (MI) *(Circle one or more)*	Foreign Service Officers (FSO) *(Circle one or more)*	United States Information Agency (USIA) *(Circle one or more)*
I have taken it.............................	0	0	0	0	0
I took it and plan to take it again.........	1	1	1	1	1
I haven't taken it but plan to do so........	2	2	2	2	2
I never heard of the exam	3	3	3	3	3
I've heard of it but have decided not to take it because:					
...I don't think I could pass the exam....	4	4	4	4	4
...Even if I passed the exam I probably wouldn't be selected.................	5	5	5	5	5
...I wouldn't like to be subjected to the investigation involved...............	6	6	6	6	6
...It takes too long to find out whether you're selected......................	7	7	7	7	7
...I'm not interested in the types of governmental positions filled through this exam...........................	8	8	8	8	8
...Other *(Circle and Specify)* _____					
	9	9	9	9	9
	59/R	60/R	61/R	62/R	63/R

FINANCES

55. Considering money borrowed for education (tuition, living expenses while in school, books, etc.)... how much money...

	None	Less than $500	$500 to $999	$1,000 or more	
A. do you personally owe now for undergraduate training? *(Circle one)*	6	7	8	9	64/5
B. have you borrowed for post-graduate studies? *(Circle one)*	6	7	8	9	65/5
C. do you expect to borrow for post-graduate studies next year (Academic year 1962-1963)? *(Circle one)*	6	7	8	9	66/5

15

56. How much do you have in the form of savings and securities (or other assets which could be converted into cash in an emergency) and how much are you currently in debt (excluding mortgages, bills paid within the month, etc.)?

	Assets (Circle one)	Debts and Liabilities (Circle one)
Nothing.....................	X	X
Less than $199..............	0	0
$100 - 499................	1	1
$500 - 999................	2	2
$1,000 - 4,999..............	3	3
$5,000 or more.............	4	4
	67/y	68/y

57. Please estimate your current average monthly income before taxes and deductions. Do not include any income you may have from scholarships, assistantships, or other stipends awarded to students. *(Circle one in each column)*

	From Your Own Employment (Circle one)	Total Monthly Income (Including spouse's and other income) (Circle one)			What do you regard as an adequate monthly income for a person in your circumstances? (Circle one)
None..........	2	2	None............		2
$1 - 199.	3	3	$1 - 199.		3
$200 - 299.	4	4	$200 - 299.		4
$300 - 399.	5	5	$300 - 399.		5
$400 - 599.	6	6	$400 - 599.		6
$600 - 799.	7	7	$600 - 799.		7
$800 - 999.	8	8	$800 - 999.		8
$1,000 or more.	9	9	$1,000 or more...		9
	69/1	70/1			71/1

58. How many of your grandparents were born in the United States? *(Circle one)*

None.......... 0	72/X
One........... 1	
Two........... 2	
Three......... 3	
Four.......... 4	

59. What is your predominant national background?

	Mother's side of family (Circle one)	Father's side of family (Circle one)
English, Scotch, Welsh, English Canadian, Australian, New Zealand..............	X	X
Irish..	0	0
German, Austrian, Swiss..	1	1
Scandinavian...	2	2
Italian..	3	3
French, French Canadian, Belgian...	4	4
Polish...	5	5
Russian and other Eastern European...	6	6
American Negro...	7	7
Spanish, Portuguese and Latin American (Mexican, Puerto Rican, Central and South American)...	8	8
Other *(Circle and Specify)* _____	9	9
	73/y	74/y

60. How frequently do you attend religious services? *(Circle the closest number)*

Weekly, almost without exception.... 4	75/3
Several times a month............... 5	
Once a month........................ 6	
Two or three times a year........... 7	
Once a year......................... 8	
Never............................... 9